IMMIGRATION
AND THE DECLINE OF INTERNATIONALISM
IN THE AMERICAN WORKING CLASS
1864–1919

Charles R. Leinenweber

P.O. Box 626
Alameda, CA 94501
http://csh.gn.apc.org
csh@gn.apc.org

Editor's Note

The first part of this book is based on Charles Leinenweber's 1968 University of California doctoral dissertation. The Appendix consists of three articles written in the next few years which also dealt with the evolution of the American socialist movement in the early years of the twentieth century.

In his dissertation Charles Leinenweber used the phrase "native American" to describe citizens who were born in the U.S. as opposed to immigrants who had acquired citizenship. We have changed the phrase to "native-born American" to avoid confusion,

The dissertation also used the term "Negro" which was acceptable at the time. We have replaced it with "African American" except in quotes from original sources.

E. Haberkern

Acknowledgments:

I would like to thank the members of my committee — Professors Nathan Glazer, Jan Dizard and Hyman Berman — for their prompt help and guidance, and for enabling me to finish within a relatively short time. I would also like to thank my friends — including Martha Sonnenberg, and Wayne Collins, Sam Farber, John Hippolyte, Harry Hobbs, Sam Kushner and David Rynan — for helping to keep my spirits high during the course of this study. The hours of sociability that I spent with them at home, on the Terrace and in the Albatross, were as important as the hours I spent in the library.

At the University of California, Berkeley, a list of acknowledgements would not be complete without mentioning the Administration. In the four-and-a-half years that I have spent here, the University Administration has been responsible for the arrest and jailing of some nine hundred students, campus employees and community people. It has expelled or suspended student political leaders on a regular basis. On two occasions the Administration summoned armies of more than five hundred police to occupy the campus. It has augmented the University's own police force with persons whose sole responsibility is to spy and keep tabs on political movements. Under these conditions, students at the University must finish in spite of the Administration.

To Huey P. Newton

and all men and women who

fight for liberation

Table of Contents

INTRODUCTION

The close of the American Civil War marked the beginning of a new epoch in the history of mass immigration to the United States.[1] The expansion of American industrial capitalism, the introduction of the trans-Atlantic steamship, severe economic and political crises in Europe — these and other factors combined to bring ever-increasing numbers of immigrants to America's shores. The dimensions of the influx were monumental: Between 1860 and 1890, some ten million immigrants landed; between 1890 and 1914, fifteen million more.

These two periods, 1860–1890, and 1890–1914, correspond roughly to two major "waves" of immigration. The first was composed predominately of immigrants from Northern and Western Europe — Germany, Ireland, Great Britain, Scandinavia, Switzerland and the Netherlands. The second was composed predominately of immigrants from Southern and Eastern Europe — Italy, Austria-Hungary, Russia, Greece, Rumania and Turkey. For various reasons, the two waves are commonly referred to as the "old" and the "new" immigration, respectively.

In 1882, the peak year of the "old" immigration — and the year of greatest influx prior to 1903 — seven hundred and eighty-eighty thousand immigrants landed. 87 percent came from Northern and Western Europe, while 13 percent came from Southern and Eastern Europe. By 1907, the peak year of all immigration, the proportions had been reversed: 19.3 percent "old" immigrant, 80.7 percent "new." That year one million, two hundred and eighty-five thousand Europeans entered the country.

Most immigrants were integrated into American society by becoming workers and experiencing the range of influences — from work, residence, politics — that affected the working class. During both major periods of immigration, immigrants comprised a majority of the unskilled working class. In 1909, the U.S. Immigration Commission made a study of wage workers in twenty principal mining and manufacturing industries. They found that 60 percent of the men and 47 percent of the women were immigrants. The percentages were only slightly less in sixteen minor industries.

Because the impact of immigration was felt most directly by the working class, it was inevitable that the working class movement[2] itself developed perspectives on immigration that took into account the sectional interests of American workers. In broad outlines, the perspectives that emerged closely paralleled the level of trade union development: During the early years of the "old" immigration, the trade union movement was characterized by the predominance of pre-industrial craft unions. These unions — represented by the National Labor Union and later, by the Knights of Labor — considered only one aspect of immigration, imported contract labor, to be a problem. They neither felt threatened by nor opposed free immigration, and their perspective was internationalist.

Shortly after the peak year of "old" immigration, 1882, the unions experienced a gradual transformation. A new craft unionism emerged in the form of the American Federation of Labor, and industrial unionism began to take hold among the coal miners affiliated with the Knights of Labor. Coincidental with the rise of "new" immigration in the 1890s, the AFL matured into a mass-based, stable organization. At the same time the coal miners, with their industrial unionism, entered the AFL.

The rise of the AFL represented not only the victory of new craft unionism over pre-industrial forms, but also the victory of a narrow, gradualistic wage-consciousness over a broader, reformist political consciousness. Both the National Labor Union and the Knights of Labor emphasized cooperative and educational goals for the working class movement. The AFL, on the other hand, emphasized adaptation to American industrial capitalism through the elevation of the workers' standard of living. In contrast to its predecessors, the AFL had come into existence in a mood of pessimism. The frontier was closed, there were restrictions on mobility and, as Selig Perlman has pointed out, the working class now seemed permanently locked into the wage system.

In this context, the AFL's perspective on immigration departed markedly from previous ones. Pressured by increasing mechanization and rapid expansion of the unskilled labor force through immigration, the AFL adopted the perspective of an aristocracy of labor. It abandoned the internationalism of the earlier working class movement, and took up a position in favor of restricting free immigration. Implementing restrictions became a major goal of the AFL. Ultimately, their effort took on a nativist tinge, against the "new" immigration.

The AFL's departure did not come easily, for there were ideal counter-pressures in the situation; the working class movement was affected by these, as much as by material conditions. The most important of these ideal counter pressures was the long-standing tradition of working class internationalism. During the immediate post-Civil War period, inter-nationalism received its major impetus from the First International, which attempted to unify the perspectives of trade unionism and revolutionary Marxism. Following the International's decline, the idea of internationalism was carried forward both within the mainstream of the working class movement — the founders of the AFL, for example, had been active in the International — and its Left wing. The Left wing was, however, the primary contributor to the movement's internationalist tendencies.

Eventually, the Left wing itself began to abandon internationalism. In part, the Left's turn can be traced to the lengthy process of "Americanization," which started with the American branch of the First International. Until 1900, the most obvious weakness of the Left was that it remained immigrant-based. Before it could become viable, the Left had to attract more native-born Americans. The Americanization effort had a strange impact on some immigrant socialists. They became caricatures of Americans, hypersensitive to the irrational currents of nativism surfacing in the working class movement. They literally adopted the slogan, "America for the Americans," when they themselves were immigrants.

More important than the Americanization effort was the Left's relationship to the mainstream of the working class movement. As the AFL matured in the late 1890s, it became more conservative. Accusing the leadership of following a policy of collaboration with the capitalist class, many socialists withdrew to pursue revolutionary dual unionism. For the first time, the Left counterposed itself to the mainstream of the working class movement. Although this first major attempt of dual unionism failed, subsequent attempts met with greater success. The revolutionary dual unionists maintained their internationalist perspective without difficulty.

In the meantime, other elements on the Left attempted to re-enter the AFL. Predominant among them was the reformist wing of the newly-formed Socialist Party, the first socialist organization with a native-born American base. Although repulsed by the leadership, Socialist reformists continued to orient themselves toward the AFL. Like the German Social Democrats, they believed the trade union movement to be one of "twin pillars of socialism." In a few areas, the reformists were successful in developing an AFL organizational base for their party. Feeling an identity of interests with their trade union base, they gradually abandoned internationalism and, like the AFL, advocated restrictions on free immigration. This signalled the downfall of a solidly internationalist Left, and the end of the Left's contributions to internationalist tendencies in the working class movement as a whole. Moreover, the reformists' abandonment of internationalism helped prepare the way for the rapid disintegration and decline of the Socialist movement, after World War I.

Approach and Methodology

This is a study in the sociology of knowledge. As such, it does not focus so much on the object of perception — in this case, the immigrant — as on the perceivers themselves, activists in the American working class movement. It is a study of how these men developed and shaped class-based perspectives on immigration, containing both rational and irrational elements, out of the interaction of limited, concrete experience with generalized, abstract thought. The methodology is historical and analytical, dealing with the genesis and resolution of contradictions in the theory and practice of the working class movement.

Concretely, it is a study of the sources of failure of working class internationalism in America — the attempt by revolutionaries and trade unionists to generate a spirit of solidarity that would transcend national and ethnic boundaries. It focusses on one major aspect of internationalism, the attitude of the working class movement of a recipient nation toward immigrant workers from other nations. The study assumes an internationalist perspective on immigration to be one that at all times reflects a fundamental spirit of solidarity with immigrant workers. It further assumes that the content or program of this perspective may change, depending on the historical situation but the spirit does not. The study takes as its point of departure the "model" perspective on immigration developed by Karl Marx and the First International, as part of the idea of international working class solidarity. It was the spirit — not necessarily the content — of this perspective that socialists and other elements of the working class movement tried to maintain. It was the spirit, too, that proved to be so elusive

Part I:

The Mainstream of the Working Class Movement and Immigration.

Chapter 1
The First International and Immigration: The Failure of Synthesis

1. Introduction

The idea of international working class solidarity found one of its earliest, and perhaps best, exponents in the First International. It was through the efforts of this organization in general, and its revolutionary elements in particular, that working class movements in Europe and America began to develop a self-conscious internationalism.

In its formative years, a major aspect of the International's work concerned immigration. British trade unionists were concerned with the importation of foreign strikebreakers. Revolutionaries joined with them to formulate a perspective on immigration that would be in harmony with the broad goals of working class internationalism. The ultimate result was a perspective that reflected the highest ethical values of the working class movement. Fundamentally, it was a statement of solidarity with immigrant and foreign workers.

The International's perspective on immigration served as a model for working class movements both during the organization's existence and — through socialists — long after its decline. However, the applicability of this perspective, in its concrete form, was limited. It fit best the historical situation of pre-industrial craft unions, whose members came into direct conflict with immigrant workers brought in under contract. Morcover, for the International's revolutionary elements, the organization's concern with immigration proved to be a source of frustration during periods of revolutionary upheaval.

2. Trade Unionists and Revolutionaries in the First International

The First International was not founded as a revolutionary organization, nor did it have its roots in revolutionary upheaval. Rather, originally it was conceived as an internationally-oriented association of trade unions. Its roots lay in the general revival of trade unionism throughout Europe in the late 1850s and early 1860s. The First International's predecessors, the Fraternal Democrats and the International Association, had been failures. Cosmopolitan rather than truly international, they had appeared at times when the working class movement was either too weak, or too unprepared for an entrance into politics. The stage for a successful International had been set by a series of strikes in the London building trades, over the years 1850–1862. The strikes awakened the political senses of London workers, increased agitation for a shorter working day, and resulted in the setting up of a central Trades Council and the establishment of a working class press. Moreover, as news of the strike spread abroad, building workers made first contact with foreign trade unionists, particularly in France.[1]

If the International was not a revolutionary organization, it was at least working class, both in its social and political bases. This fact was sufficient to arouse the interest of revolutionary figures, most notably Karl Marx. Marx had remained aloof from previous attempts at international movement, believing that socially and politically they had no future. The International differed not only in its trade union support, but in that it represented the estrangement of the British working class movement from middle class reform politics. A succession of international events had driven a political wedge between the working and middle classes; Marx sought to drive it deeper. From the Italian *Risorgimento* and the writings of Mazzini, had come the idea that workers could make a distinctive contribution to foreign policy. George Odger, leader of the building trades and the first and only President of the International, was deeply impressed by the notion that workers alone could develop a foreign policy based on morality and justice. The American Civil War highlighted this belief, as the Whig and Tory establishments supported the South. Finally, the Polish insurrection, widely denounced in the Liberal press and refused support by middle class reformists, inspired a combined effort by British and French trade unionists to help the Polish cause. From this point, it had been only a short step to the founding of the International.[2]

Marx was a passive figure at the International's founding meeting. Representatives from the building trades, including Odger and, later on, Robert Applegarth of the Carpenters, dominated the General Council, its officiating body. Marx was pressed into service soon, however, to draft the organization's Inaugural Address. From then on, Marx became the International's intellectual guide and the key figure on the General Council.[3]

From its inception, the International was rife with political con- tradictions. Throughout its earliest and strongest years, the major differences lay between the Marxists, or revolutionaries, and the relatively conservative British trade unionists. But until Europe became caught in the throes of revolutionary upheaval, Marx was willing to subordinate these differences to the necessity for building a broad and viable International. All the while, he remained keenly sensitive to the fact that Odger, Applegarth and their colleagues were among the foremost leaders of the English working class, and reflected their level of development. In matters concerning British trade unions, Marx trusted their judgment.[4]

Nothing demonstrated Marx's flexibility better than his Inaugural Address. At best, it was only implicitly socialist. The Address dealt primarily with concrete data on the condition of the working class, and echoed Odger's concern with a moral foreign policy. Marx explained to Engels, "It will take some time before the reawakening movement allows the old boldness of speech."[5]

In its conclusion alone — "to conquer political power has therefore become the great duty of the working classes" — did the Address go beyond the aspirations of the British trade unionists. Marx hoped that eventually they would accept this idea. They did not, and in time the inherent contradictions between revolutionary Marxism and conservative trade unionism surfaced.

3. Perspectives on Immigration

The question of immigration played a vital role in revealing and accentuating fundamental differences between the revolutionaries and trade unionists. It was around this that the International developed its organization approach to British trade unions. Yet to each tendency, agitation on the immigration question meant something different. For the Marxists, it was supposed to provide a bridge between various national working classes, a means by which collective, international action became possible. With this as a practical starting point, they hoped to achieve a revolutionary synthesis of diverse working classes. In intellectual terms, the Marxists wanted to see emerge a self-conscious international working class, co-operating on a rational basis. Control over immigration, a commonly-desired matter, was merely the first glimmering of international working class co-operation.

For the British trade unionists, on the other hand, control over immigration soon became the end-point and major reason for the International's existence. As revolution broke on the Continent, it became clear that they were less interested in advancing working class consciousness than in defending their own short-term gains. Once the International's usefulness in restricting immigration had been exhausted, they began to drift away.

The International turned to the question of immigration in haphazard fashion. During the first year of its existence, when it experienced only grudging and sporadic success, the International ignored immigration. Then, in February, 1866, twenty-eight British members of the General Council published an appeal for trade union support of the International's projected Geneva Conference. The appeal made scant mention of the International's social program. Instead, it emphasized the need to "bring about a common understanding between the peoples of all countries, so that in the struggles of labor with unprincipled capitalists they may not be able to execute the threat which they so often indulge in, of using the workingmen of one country to defeat the just demands of the workmen in another."[6]

This proved to be the key to success, as it marked the turning point in the International's fortunes. In March 1866, fifteen thousand London tailors went on strike under threat of an industry-wide lockout. The General Council learned that employers planned to break the strike by importing European tailors. Robert Shaw, a signatory to the February appeal, suggested that the International could help by contacting its European secretaries, "with a view to keeping Continental workmen away from London during the struggle now pending."[7] The London tailors won their strike. Grateful for the resolute support of the International, the Tailors' Association voted to affiliate immediately. A member of the Executive Committee of the Tailors' Association told the General Council that it was "through the influence and agency of the International Association that the master tailors had failed to procure men on the Continent."[8]

Within a month, the International encountered another opportunity to play a major role in a British strike. This time, the London wire-workers went out. Once again, the General Council instructed its European secretaries to appeal against emigration, and once again the British workers were grateful. The wire-workers thanked the Council for their efforts, and, like the tailors, promised to join.[9]

By now, the pattern for success had been established. The International was rapidly gaining esteem among British trade unions, and within a few months some twenty more affiliated or were negotiating with the General Council. The biggest prize to date came with the affiliation of the Excavators, the only unskilled laborers' union ever to be represented on the General Council. British excavators had been replaced by Belgians, lured over by promises of high pay. Fighting broke out, but the International resolved the dispute by convincing the Belgians to return home, or join the union.[10]

The model spirit of the International's effort against the importation of strikebreakers was set by Marx himself in May 1866. Word reached the General Council that the master tailors of Edinburgh planned to break a strike by bringing in tailors from Germany. Marx offered to draft an appeal to German workers, urging them to stay home. Entitled "A Warning," it was eminently successful.[11]

Marx's statement combined elements of international working class solidarity and struggle, with an appeal to the self-interest of both parties of workers. He emphasized not only the damage inflicted upon the English workers, but the miserable existence awaiting the arrival of immigrant strikebreakers. His approach became a model for the International's appeals to European workers during strikes in England.

Marx began by sketching the history of the dispute, pointing out that having been defeated in England, the master tailors had chosen Scotland to open a new campaign against the workers. Concentrating their efforts at strikebreaking in Edinburgh, they hoped victory would enable them to carry the fight back to London with renewed energy. Their tactic was to take advantage of the national divisions among the working class; their ultimate goal, the "*perpetuation of slavery*." Marx wrote,

> If the Edinburgh masters succeeded, through the import
> of German labor, in nullifying the concessions they have
> already made, it would inevitably have repercussions in
> England. *No one would suffer more than the German
> workers themselves*, who constitute in Great Britain a
> larger number than the workers of all the other
> Continental nations. And the newly-imported workers,
> being completely helpless in a strange land, would soon
> sink to the position of pariahs.[12]

He went on to challenge the German tailors to prove their worth as members of the international working class. The workers of France, Belgium and Switzerland had heeded previous appeals of the International. It was a "point of honor" that the German workers likewise show they will not "*become obedient mercenaries of capital* in its struggle against labor." Finally, Marx suggested that German tailors should contact the German branch of the London Tailors' Association, to find out more about the true conditions in Britain.[13]

By the time of its Geneva Congress in September 1866, preventing the importation of strikebreakers had become a major task of the International. It occupied a prominent place on the agenda at Geneva, yet had not even been considered at the London conference one year earlier. The General Council's instructions, drafted by Marx for the delegates to the Congress, stated,

> To counteract the intrigues of capitalists always ready, in
> cases of strikes and lockouts, to misuse the foreign
> workman as a tool against the native workman, is one of
> the particular functions which our Society has performed
> with success. It is one of the great purposes of the
> Association to make workmen of different countries not
> only *feel* but *act* as brethren and comrades in the army of
> emancipation.[14]

In several important instances, the policy of the International with respect to immigration worked as Marx had hoped. In October 1866, London basket makers asked the General Council for help in preventing the importation of Belgians.[15] The Council wrote to Belgium, warned that an agent to recruit strikebreakers would arrive soon, and stated that "Belgian workers should do their duty and reject this agent's offer, thereby making it possible for their British brothers to advocate their just demands. That will be a small victory in awaiting the great triumph."[16] The basket-makers affiliated with the International but a dozen Belgian strikebreakers arrived nonetheless. The basket-makers' delegation returned to the General Council, complaining that the company had isolated the Belgians so that they could not be contacted. Two members of the General Council went shortly to the workshop where strikebreakers were employed, passing themselves off as relatives of Belgians who wanted jobs. Once inside, one man engaged the master in conversation, while the other "was pointing out to the Belgians the injury they were inflicting on the English basket-makers ... " In the end, the Belgians were so impressed of the wrong that they were doing to the English, that they resolved to go back to the shops, [and] pack up their tools ... " Moreover, they promised to spread the word of the strike in Belgium. London basket-makers bought passage back for the men and saw them off with fraternal feelings.[17]

The international bonds that developed among tailors were especially strong. London tailors, frequently out on strike, began to appeal to European and American tailors for funds. Eventually, they used the International as their liaison. At the same time, Paris tailors were also often engaged in strikes, and London tailors sent them money, along with the assurance that "no London house would be allowed to execute work for Paris houses." As a result, there developed among tailors a strong sentiment for a union "extending throughout the world."[18]

But such cases were exceptional. Even the London tailors, the most internationally-minded of all British trade unionists, inclined toward a narrow interpretation of the International's role. When Matthew Lawrence, president of the London Operative Tailors, returned from the Geneva Congress, his report to the union dealt almost exclusively with the question of imported strikebreakers. Lawrence had addressed a mass meeting of Geneva tailors while attending the Congress, and used the opportunity to advise them not to accept jobs in London during a strike.[19] Similarly, in April 1867, Hermann Jung told a mass meeting of London tailors that "if the I.W.A. could, last year, prevent the tailors of Paris from supplanting the men of London, it could do the same thing with the men of Belgium and Germany this year. Consequently, the master tailors would only be wasting money by sending to those countries for men."[20]

Despite Marx's hope that the International's appeal would promote bonds of solidarity, its effort was clearly one-sided. From the point of view of the British trade unionists who comprised the bulk of its membership, the International was merely protecting them from European immigration. With only one side of the equation complete, the Marxists' attempts to achieve a revolutionary synthesis of national working classes, through a British-based International, failed. The feeble quality of the British unionists' internationalism was further dramatized by the fact that they themselves engaged in emigration schemes, over the opposition of American unions.

4. The Nature of the International's Trade Union Base

The clue to how the revolutionaries' approach to immigration failed as a starting point, lies not only in the conservatism of British trade unionists in general, but in the specific nature of the trade unions that supported the International. It is important to note that most of the British trade unions that joined the International represented either dying crafts that were being undermined by the advance of mechanization, or traditional crafts that had remained untouched by the Industrial Revolution. Tailoring and cordwaining were indicative of trades suffering from mechanization. Shortly after the International disappeared from the scene, a sizable fraction of cordwainers gave in to mechanization, and seceded, from their union, to form the National Union of Boot and Shoe Operatives. Cabinet-making and book-binding were indicative of trades that mechanization had by-passed.[21]

These trades alone were threatened by European strikebreakers. The rest of the organized British working class — who best approximated the Marxists' model of an advanced working class-were protected from European strikebreakers by the immense superiority of British technology. Thus, the very conditions that helped make the English working class the most highly organized in the world, militated against their developing a need for the International so long as it remained fixated on immigration.[22]

The revolutionaries were at least faintly aware of these deficiencies at the International's base, but made no effort to correct the situation. First of all, as noted above, Marx entrusted British trade union affairs to their own representatives on the General Council. But secondly, although he was willing to go this far, he was reluctant to pass control over the British sector completely into their hands. The guiding factor in his decision was the conservatism of the British working class movement as a whole. Marx believed the British working class to be an indispensable element for European revolution. Yet it was conservative, so conservative that in his estimation the General Council was forced to act as a counter-balance. The revolutionaries believed that unless the trade union leaders were compelled to act through the General Council, they would drift out of their sphere of influence and down the paths of liberal reformism and trade union economism. Several years too late, Marx stated his case in a confidential circular to the General Council. He wrote:

> Although the revolutionary initiative will probably come from France, England alone can serve as the lever of a serious economic revolution. . . . If this country is the classic seat of landlordism and capitalism, by virtue of that fact it is also here that the material conditions of their destruction are most highly developed. The General Council being at present placed in the happy position of having its hand directly on this great lever of the proletarian revolution, it would be sheer folly, we would almost say it would be an outright crime, to allow that hold to fall into purely English hands!

He continued,

> The English have all the material requisites necessary for the social revolution. What they lack is the spirit of generalized and revolutionary ardour. It is only the

> General Council which can supply this deficiency, which
> can thus accelerate the truly revolutionary movement in
> this country and consequently everywhere.[23]

Because of the English workers' conservatism, Marx consistently opposed any decentralization of the General Council's authority in England. He argued successfully against the setting up of a separate English branch, distinct from the General Council. His decision not to decentralize had two immediate damaging effects on the International. First, it meant that the organization was permanently cut off from centers of heavy industry. The General Council was located in London, a commercial, not manufacturing center. Second, it meant that the social base of the International remained, not the "great lever of the proletarian revolution," but remnants from the past.

By 1867, the International reached the limits of its expansion in England. The organization had failed to penetrate heavy industries such as coal, textiles and engineering, or with the exception of the excavators, to attract unskilled labor. It could claim only one representative of heavy industry, the ironworkers, and it is likely that they were influenced to join not by contacts in England, but in America. The engineers, or machinists, showed occasional interest, but unafraid of European strike-breakers, they never joined.[24] Marx had hoped to attract unions in heavy industry indirectly, through the affiliation of the London Trades Council.[25] His hopes were crushed when the Trades Council failed to show any sustained interest. Still, he refused to agree to a separate British section.

As the International reached its limits in England, the conservative nature of its base became self-evident. While the revolutionaries more and more aimed toward seizure of state power by an internationally-oriented working class the trade unionists found satisfaction in the ongoing liberalization of the English political climate. So long as their unions were secured from domestic opposition, they asked little more of the International than it protect them from foreign strikebreakers. As events quickened in Europe and the International developed another base there, long-submerged antagonisms between the revolutionaries and trade unionists finally erupted. At this time, the revolutionaries cast aside the question of immigration, as their patience with the trade unionists wore thin.

5. The International Looks Toward Europe

Just as the London tailors' strike in March 1866 marked the turning point for the International in England, the Paris bronze-workers' strike one year later established it on the Continent. Fifteen hundred workers, locked out, appealed to British trade unions for help. Through the General council, they were able to make direct contact with numerous unions, which responded generously. On the Continent itself, branches of the International were equally as successful in raising gifts and loans. Thrown into panic by the sudden entrance of the International, the employers ended their lock-out. The victory of the bronze-workers "acted as a tonic throughout the French labor movement."[26]

From this point on the General council became more and more concerned with Europe. The International's success with the Paris bronze-workers was repeated regularly, the most notable instance connected with a lockout of building workers in Geneva in early 1868.[27] By 1869, the International was rightly given credit for providing the major impetus for the trade union movement in Germany.[28]

At the same time as the General council became more concerned with Europe, it became less concerned with England. Only three British trade unions affiliated during the period 1867–69, while British attendance at General Council meetings dropped considerably.[29] In August 1867, John Hales of the Elastic Web Weavers suggested that the General Council abandon its reliance on British trade unions, and undertake political work. James Carter of the Hairdressers agreed, stating that "with the exception of our interference in strikes we had done nothing and neglected everything regarding the practical application of the great principles of the Association." Marx stated that he was against "turning our Association into a debating club," although not against "discussing great questions." He agreed that, with few exceptions, the British trade union delegates were showing little enthusiasm. But he found consolation in the fact that "we had made considerable progress abroad and had obtained good standing in France."[30]

The annual report of the General Council, for the year 1867 emphasized activities in England as much as had previous reports. Yet there were strong hints that stagnation had set in. The report noted that only three British unions contributed to the fund to cover expenses for the Lausanne Congress, while contributions had been generous the previous year. Moreover, twelve out of thirty affiliated unions failed to make any contribution at all to the organization's general fund, while the rest contributed much less than the previous year.[31] The General Council pointed out that 1867 was an especially hard year for the unions, but it might also have noted that so had been 1866.

As British trade unionists drifted away from the General Council, and as its attention shifted to Europe, the question of immigration came up less frequently. Preventing the importation of strikebreakers was of little importance to the European unions in their current phase of struggle. Only one European trade union, the Paris book-binders, ever indicated to the General Council that this determined their interest in the International.[32]

While the General Council's report of September 1867 emphasized the International's role in keeping out strikebreakers — a role which, actually, it had played irregularly although successfully during the year — their report of September 1868 made no mention of it.[33] By then, in line with events in Europe, the International had broken from the limits imposed by Marx's Inaugural Address, and had come out openly for class struggle.

England as a whole deserved only one brief paragraph in the General Council's 1868 report, devoted mainly to another explanation for inactivity. This time, instead of depression, the blame was placed on the demands of reform politics.[34] Again, in the September 1869 report, England received only scanty notice, and preventing the importation, of strike-breakers went unmentioned.[35] Finally, the question of immigration did not appear on the agendas of any of the International's Congresses, after the Geneva Congress of 1866. For the Lausanne

Congress of 1867, Marx had urged instead that the first order of business be a discussion of the working class's "complete emancipation from the domination of capital."[36] The British trade unionists, who continued to articulate the dangers of immigration — and free trade — had been left far behind.[37]

6. Division and Decline

By late 1869, the lines of division between the revolutionaries and the British trade unionists were clearly drawn. The British press, including much of the trade union press, had become openly hostile toward the International after its Basle Congress, in September. Shortly after, in November, the Irish question was debated heatedly by the General Council, with Odger opposing Marx. Applegarth sided with Marx, but half-heartedly. In substance, he agreed with Odger.[38]

During the debate, Marx introduced a resolution condemning Gladstone for his Irish policy, linking it to his support for the Confederacy during the American Civil War.[39] Marx's intent was to reopen the schism between British trade unionists and middle-class liberals, which had called the International into existence. In this he failed, although his resolution gained a clear majority on the Council. Despite hints of sympathy for the Fenians, Odger refused to desert Gladstone. Marx was disappointed, for he was convinced that the English working class,

> . . . can never do anything decisive . . . until it separates its policy with regard to Ireland in the most definitive way from the policy of the ruling class, until it not only makes common causes with the Irish, but actually takes the initiative in dissolving the Union established in 1801 and replacing it by a free federal relationship. . . . If not, [Marx warned] the English people will remain tied to the leading strings of the ruling classes, because it must join with them in a common front with Ireland.[40]

Marx added that the overthrow of the British landed aristocracy would be much easier in Ireland than in England, because "it is not merely a simple economic question, but at the same time a *national* question."[41] Finally, the "great blow against official England" must be struck in Ireland because the "artificially encouraged division between Irish and English workers is the real secret of the maintenance of their power."[42]

The Curriers' Society disagreed and subsequently withdrew, announcing that it "felt bound to sever its connections, not having any faith in workingmen's societies that meddled with politics."[43] No others followed, however, and even into the year 1870, the British sector showed a few signs of life. But their primary interest remained, how to keep out strikebreakers. In November 1869, as the amnesty movement for the Fenians broke, the cigar-makers threatened to withdraw from the International "because it did not stop foreigners from coming to London." Jung, who long before had become an errand-boy for British trade unions on this question, volunteered to look into the matter. The rest of the Council showed little interest.[44]

The decisive break came shortly after the Paris Commune. Odger, along with Benjamin Lucraft, resigned angrily from the International with the appearance of Marx's *Civil War in France*. Their exodus marked the loss of two of the General Council's most important trade unionists. Applegarth did not resign, probably because of his long-standing friendship with Marx. But he had been just as reluctant to have his name associated with Marx's address, and it did not appear.[45]

Marx and his followers were embittered by the apathy that British workers had shown throughout the Franco–Prussian war, and the Paris Commune. Their posture of non-involvement had dashed all hopes that British workers would play a decisive role in European revolution. Much to the dismay of its revolutionaries, the International's narrow appeal to British workers had not prepared them to support revolution in Europe.

In August 1871, the engineers sent a delegation to the General Council, requesting its aid in preventing the importation of strikebreakers. They implied that if aid were forthcoming, they would join. Marx agreed that the General Council should help, but added sharply, "It always did that in every labor struggle that was brought under its notice. The misfortune was that the trade unions and labor organizations held aloof from the International until they were in trouble, and then only did they come for assistance."[46] After the delegation left, Engels revealed the extent of the revolutionaries' disgust with British workers. He charged that during the Commune uprising:

> . . . the working class of England had behaved in a disgraceful manner: though the men of Paris had risked their lives, the working men of England had made no effort either to sympathize with them or assist them. There was no political life in them.[47]

By the end of 1871, the International was in a state of precipitous decline. Outlawed and broken in most of Europe, and deprived of its working class base in England, it tended more and more toward irrelevance and internal fighting. Its last true congress, held in The Hague, in 1872, was swamped by wrangling over credentials, and the final resolution of the conflict between Marx and Bakunin.[48]

After the Hague Congress, the General council was removed to New York, where at last, it died. When Engels heard of its demise, he wrote

> That is well. It belonged to the period of the Second Empire, when the oppression throughout Europe prescribed unity and abstention from all internal controversy for the labor movement, then just reawakening. It was the moment when the common, cosmopolitan interests of the proletariat would come to the fore. . . .

Engels concluded,

> The International dominated ten years of one side of European history — the side on which the future lies —

and can look back upon its work with pride. But in its old form it has outlived itself. In order to produce a new International like the old one — an alliance of the proletarian parties of all countries — a general suppression of the labor movement like that which prevailed from 1849 to 1864 would be necessary. For this the proletarian world has become too big, too extensive. I think the next international — after Marx's writings have been at work for some years — will be directly Communist and will openly proclaim our principles ... [49]

The first great success of the young working class movement, Engels believed, was bound to explode the "naive conjunction" of diverse elements which the International represented. With the Paris Commune had come that success. [50]

7. Conclusion

The first International was founded as a broad-based, working class organization with limited, reform aspirations. Once infused with the spirit of revolutionary Marxists, its aspirations soared. Yet neither the International's work nor its political appeal kept pace. In developing a base for support in England, the organization relied on working class elements least likely to favor revolutionary developments. Far from being a model industrial working class, most of these elements were either fighting a losing battle against mechanization, or had been bypassed by it. They had a great deal to fear from the importation of strikebreakers from Europe, and sought the International's aid in preventing it. In response, the International sought to approach all British workers on its ability to prevent strikebreaking.

At first, this approach was successful. But it stopped short of the factory gates. The International was unable to arouse the enthusiasm of unionists in heavy industry, who because of England's technological superiority were not threatened by European immigration. Furthermore, the Marxists' refusal to set up an independent British section increased the General Council's isolation from skilled and unskilled workers in heavy industry.

The Marxists intended control over immigration to be the starting point for rational, working class cooperation on an international scale. But for the British workers who feared European strikebreakers, it was merely a defensive posture. Instead of an organization to promote world-wide solidarity, the International for them became an instrument of protection from foreign competition. With upheaval in Europe, the contradictions between revolutionary Marxism and conservative British trade unionism became clear, and the International's original base split and eroded.

Despite its rather short history, the International, through Marx's contributions, left a rich heritage for working class movements. Its distinctive contributions included the idea of international working class solidarity, and, for socialists, the necessity for workers to form their own economic organizations. The International's position on immigration was framed within the perspective of solidarity.

In the United States, the International's perspectives had a lasting, although selective, effect. The working class movement there was in the peculiar position of being internationally-constituted from the start. Moreover, it was the recipient of a continuous and at time increasing influx of immigration from Europe. It constituted, then, a testing-ground for international solidarity. Throughout its early years, the perspective of the American working class movement on immigration bore a close resemblance to the International's. The National Labor Union and the Knights of Labor both emphasized solidarity with the immigrant worker. This reflected not only the influence of the International, but certain similarities between the International's English base, and American trade unions. American trade unions as a whole were still pre-industrial craft unions.

Yet conditions in America differed importantly from those in England. The working class was the recipient of large numbers of free immigrants, who were integrated into American society through it. The International's concern was limited to imported strikebreakers and contract laborers. As long as American trade unionists felt threatened only by these, this marked the limits of their concern, too. But as the unions gradually changed and adapted to industrialization, their concern broadened. Moreover, as the racial and ethnic character of immigration changed, their concern intensified. During these critical periods, the United States became a severe testing-ground for working class internationalism.

Chapter 2.
The National Labor Union:
Origins and Limitations of Early Working Class
Opposition to Immigration

1. Introduction

Paralleling the rise and decline of the International in Europe, was the first major attempt to organize American trade unions into a national federation, the National Labor Union. The impulse toward national federation came in part from agitation for an eight-hour work-week, led by Ira Steward, a Boston machinist. Steward began in 1864 to organize eight-hour leagues, to combat the conservative doctrines of restricting the labor force to keep wages up — a theory prevalent among British craft unions — and providing make-work for the unemployed.[1] However, the limited success of the National Labor Union ultimately depended on the efforts of its foremost founder, William Sylvis, president of the Iron Molders' Union and eventually the NLU itself.

Throughout its existence, the NLU reflected the mixed character of the early working class movement. Ideologically it was conservative and individualistic in the American tradition, although at times it became imbued with a strong *sense* of class-consciousness. The NLU's major emphasis was on cooperative and educational programs, in which Sylvis played a leading role. It made occasional forays into working-class politics, but without much success. In its decline, the NLU became little more than a monetary reform sect.

At their first National Labor Congress, in August 1866, the leaders of the NLU were hesitant to deal with economic problems of trade unionism. They feared that this would threaten the autonomy of individual unions, and a general exodus would result. Since the basis for unity had been the necessity to win an eight-hour day by concerted political action, a solution was evident: The NLU would be concerned with political, not economic action.[2]

Among the craft unions affiliated with the NLU, one widely-shared problem that suggested a political solution was the importation of strike-breakers from Europe. Increasingly, they had been threatened with destruction by this tactic. In this respect, NLU members shared the concern of British trade unions that had gone to the International for help. As with the British trade unions, the General Council was quick to seize the opportunity for a major American affiliate, using control over immigration as the key attraction. Unlike Great Britain, however, conditions in American industry enabled NLU craft unions to develop and maintain a fairly consistent, although temperate, internationalism, without serious challenge. Toward the end, this internationalism was restricted by anti-Chinese sentiment and weakened by confrontation in the mining industry, but remained basically unchanged.

2. NLU Perspectives on Immigration

Both Ira Steward and William Sylvis were deeply interested in the question of immigration. Steward, the more internationally minded of the two, saw immigration through a broad, world-historical perspective that suggested no immediate solution. Sylvis, on the other hand, developed his attitudes within the narrower perspective of fighting against strike-breaking. It was this perspective, not Steward's, that prevailed in the National Labor Union.

Steward's views are of interest because they foretold the pressures that mass immigration would exert on the modern labor movement.

Steward believed that gains workers made in any industrially advanced nation such as the United States, would soon be undercut by cheap competition from less advanced nations. The development of a world market by capitalism made possible the "power of the cheaper," and also created mass immigration from poorer to richer nations. Immigration was a natural process, redressing the imbalance between these nations. Thus, no amount of legislation against even the importation of contract labor could stop the flow for long. "The misery and the terrors that the Chinamen have already inflicted upon western America," Steward wrote, "are the moral judgement that has already begun to fall upon the world's highest civilization as a retribution and punishment for forgetting the brotherhood of the entire human race."[3] The task for the worker, Steward felt, was to look beyond the individual capitalist when his wages fell, and to recognize the need for worldwide solidarity and world-wide remedies.[4] In line with his beliefs, Steward was active in various international reform groups until his death.

In contrast to Steward, Sylvis was relatively unconcerned with either the causes or the long-range effects of free immigration. He recognized that national resources would eventually be taxed by population increases, but failed to consider the direct and powerful impact this would have on the working class. While Steward anticipated a nativist response, Sylvis assumed that population increases through immigration would sharpen antagonisms between the capitalist and working classes, not within the working class.[5] Through his experiences as leader of the Iron Molders, Sylvis limited his concern to only one aspect of immigration, contract labor. For the time being, this was true for the majority of the organized working class, the skilled craftsmen.

3. The Iron Molders and Immigration

The experiences of the Iron Molders with immigrants, and their attitudes toward them, were typical of the skilled craft unions of the early working class movement. Iron molding was a highly skilled-although extremely heavy trade. At the time, it was not threatened with extinction by technological advances, and the union, founded in 1859, was strong. Like most others, the iron industry expanded rapidly after the Civil War, and the demand for skilled labor far exceeded the output of the apprenticeship programs. Thus the Iron Molders felt no economic compulsion to oppose free immigration, but like most other unions, welcomed it.[6]

Shortly after the close of the Civil War, however, the question of imported contract labor became important. Immigration had slowed to a trickle, and under pressure from manufacturers the federal government passed an Act to Encourage Emigration. The Act had an immediate effect on skilled craft unions. It made provisions for an office of Commissioner of Immigration, and legitimated labor contracts registered with the Commissioner.[7] Under this shield several corporations for importing contract laborers were revitalized, the most notable being the American Emigrant Company. The search for strikebreakers from Europe became their major business.

In the summer of 1865, the American Emigrant Company shipped Scottish iron molders to Chicago, to break a strike at the Eagle Iron works. Sylvis was outraged, and his fury became even greater when Scottish unions refused to cooperate in the Iron Molders' attempt to stop the importation. Previously, in 1864, the Missouri Board of Immigration had been instrumental in importing twenty-five molders from Berlin to break a strike in St. Louis. The St. Louis molders had won concessions from every foundry operator but one, Giles Filley. The German molders' contract obligated them "not to join any clubs or associations, of which in any way harm or disadvantage could arise to Mr. Filley, but to make the entrance of such workmen or similar associations always dependent upon the permission of Mr. Filley." Moreover, it limited their wages to two dollars a day, while workers at other foundries were paid three.[8]

Fortunately for the Iron Molders they were able to contact the German workers, persuade them to break their contract and join the union. There were many similar instances of the failure of contract labor to break strikes, but it remained enough of a threat to arouse Sylvis' undying hostility.

At first, Sylvis sought help from the British trade unions in combating importation of labor. On the whole, his efforts were rebuked. During the 1865 strike against the Eagle Iron works in Chicago, Scottish trade union leaders refused to accept the Iron Molders' warnings, and instead urged their members to take advantage of the offers of the American Emigrant Company.[9] At this time, many British unions were promoting emigration schemes in the belief that it would keep wages high. Marx had noted the fallacy of such schemes in his Inaugural Address, but even the International occasionally dabbled in them.[10] In January 1867, Peter Fox, British journalist acting as American secretary for the General Council, received authorization to "correspond with the American protectionist journals and statesmen" to promote the emigration of unemployed Lyons silkweavers."[11]

4. The NLU and the International

While Sylvis failed to make headway against the British trade unions' emigration schemes, they in turn were using the International as a means to restrict importing strikebreakers to Britain. The irony, of the situation was not lost on Sylvis. He trusted neither the British union leaders nor the International. When A.C. Cameron called the NLU's attention to the International's Lausanne Congress in 1867, Sylvis stated that "he did not think a man would gather half as much knowledge from attending the congress as by looking around among the workmen." He explained that "he had not been able in the past of succeeding in letting the people there know of the existence of strikes in this country, as the secretary of the union in England had been in league with the emigration agent, and shared the head money with him."[12] Sylvis believed that rank-and-file British trade unionists, unlike their leaders, would respond favorably to an appeal against emigration.

Prior to the NLU's 1867 convention, Sylvis had also been reluctant to deal with the International. Fox, the General Council's American secretary, sent the proceedings of the Geneva Congress to Sylvis in April 1867, but received no acknowledgment.[13] In June, Fox again contacted Sylvis, requesting donations for the striking London tailors and expressing the General Council's interest in establishing contact with the NLU. Sylvis turned down the request for funds, explaining that his union's treasury had been exhausted by strikes, and that thousands of molders were out of work.[14] He gave the name of William Jessup, vice-president of the NLU, as the person whom the General Council should contact in America. Sylvis could not have made a better choice for the International. Jessup held a variety of key trade union positions. Besides being vice-president of the NLU, he was secretary of the New York Ship Joiners, president of the New York State Working Men's Assembly, and corresponding secretary of the New York Working Men's Union.[15] Fox wrote to him in July, and received an enthusiastic reply. Jessup apologized for the incompetence of his colleagues and stated, "I have long desired to open correspondence with the working men of England, and have written two or three letters with that end in view." He felt that the NLU convention would be held too late to send a delegate to the International's Lausanne Congress, but promised to inform the delegates of it. Jessup also expressed an interest in maintaining contact with the General Council, and offered to "furnish any information in my power that you may desire, or exchange papers or documents of interest."[16]

Shortly after Jessup wrote to the General Council, a French Internationalist living in New York sent a letter stating that he had met many influential men, "but none were serious about the International except Mr. Jessup. Writing letters to the others was labor in vain."[17] Besides Jessup, one other important ally the International had in the American trade union movement was A.C. Cameron, editor of the Workingman's Advocate. Cameron exchanged columns with the International Courier, of London, and published exerpts from the proceedings of the International's Geneva Congress of 1866. He became the first official NLU representative to the International in 1869.

At their 1867 Congress, the NLU decided to follow Sylvis' suggestion to set up their own agency in Europe to prevent the importation of strikebreakers. Two delegates from the glass blowers of Pittsburgh pointed out the urgency of the situation. One said that the masters had contacted the American consul in Prussia, "who, for $40,000, agreed to send 1,000 men over here and did send about 800."[18] In later years, the glass blowers were instrumental in the drive for ending imported contract labor. Another delegate mentioned the Emigrant Aid Society, a "perfect pack of swindlers" set up by capitalists. He agreed with Sylvis that American capitalists had found allies among the European working class leaders, pointing out that, "the men who have been at the head of the trades organization in Europe have too often accepted bribes from employers here to send men over to the states like a pack of cattle, while it is well known that there are hundreds of thousands here out of employment."[19] The Congress passed a resolution condemning the collusion of American consuls in Europe with American capitalists, and expressed sympathy with the struggles of European workers.[20] However, no provision was made to set up an anti-immigration agency, and none ever materialized.

Shortly after their 1867 Congress, the Times of London attacked the National Labor Union as a nativist organization. Immediately, the International sprang to their defense. Richard Hinton, the International's American representative at the time, wrote in the *Bee-Hive* that neither immigrant nor native-born American workers were opposed to further immigration. He assured them that "there was room for all who were willing to work for their living. What they objected to," Hinton explained, "was that European working men should come at the bidding of American capitalists to be used against the resident workmen of America."[21] He felt, and the General Council agreed, that a closer relationship was necessary between not only the trade unions of England and the United States, but the "leading social and political spirits of the two countries ..."[22]

The basis on which the "leading social and political spirits" were to develop a close relationship, remained, however, narrow. In 1868, the NLU once again turned down a request by the International to send a delegate.[23] In 1869, they accepted. By then, the International had gained considerable prestige among the NLU for their support of a conductors' strike in New York, and for their efforts against impending war between Great Britain and the United States.[24]

Under the threat of war, shortly before his death, Sylvis himself had developed a deep admiration for the International. Nevertheless, the NLU's decision to send a delegate was based on the International's effectiveness in preventing the importation of contract labor. The General Council had already proven its abilities by keeping potential strikebreakers in Europe during a paper stainers' strike in New York.[25]

The International's appeal to the 1869 National Labor Congress was particularly narrow. It did not reflect the General Council's work against war led by Marx. Drafted by the immigrant tailor and close friend of Marx, Georg Eccarius, it instead reflected the International's conservative trade unionist tendencies. Eccarius wrote,

> "There is a particular reason *why* you should strain a point to send a delegate, — the emmigration mania. Once a year during *our* congress week all the scribes of Europe are busy with our doings. A sketch of what things are in the New World, given by an American, would not only find its way into all the papers, but would greatly tend to disabuse many of their illusions of the happiness in store for them if they could only manage to cross the big lake."[26]

Eccarius concluded with the observation that immigration as a whole, not simply that of contract labor, tended to "perpetuate the existing villainy" on both sides of the Atlantic.[27]

Eccarius' appeal found a sympathetic audience among some elements of the National Labor Union. The question of immigration as a whole was just coming into focus, with a resurgence of anti-Chinese racial nativism. Prior to 1869, anti-Chinese sentiment within the NLU had been limited to contract, or "coolie" labor. Similarly, the question of European immigration had been discussed solely within the context of the importation of strikebreakers. Although Chinese and European immigration were considered to be separate questions, there can be little doubt that the attitudes developed toward Chinese conditioned those toward Europeans. With the marked shift in the NLU's Chinese immigration policy — which is discussed in detail below — came a less marked but still perceptible shift in its European policy. Sylvis' concern with contract labor was broadened, after his death, into the first glimmerings of a concern with all immigration.

A.C. Cameron, the NLU's delegate to the 1869 Basle Congress of the International, represented the dominant, conservative strain in the American labor movement. His newspaper, the *Workingman's Advocate*, espoused the values of thrift, industry and individualism. By contrast Sylvis, who died shortly before the Basle Congress, occasionally leaned toward a revolutionary viewpoint on working-class politics. Cameron did not share his more radical inclinations, but did agree on the need to regulate immigration. It was on this point that he dwelt during his trip to Europe.

Cameron addressed the General Council shortly after his arrival, limiting his remarks almost exclusively to problems of immigration.[28] His reports of the Basle Congress, printed in the Workingman's Advocate, included sketches of events and conditions in Europe, but stated that while the Congress's resolutions fitted those, they "would be somewhat out of place in an American assembly."[29] It should be noted that Cameron's statement also held true for the British trade unionists. It was at this time that contradictions between the conservative orientation of the British movement and the revolutionary orientation of the European, were beginning to appear. Cameron developed a close affinity for the British trade unionists such as Applegarth, who "steer clear of the more ultra views. . . ."[30]

For the working class movement in the United States, Cameron felt that the only role for the International concerned immigration. He urged that the organization set up an emigration bureau, "through which a supervision shall be jointly exercised by the American and European associations, over the emigration, which is constantly flowing to this country."[31] Cameron promised his American readers that "under proper management, branches of the emigration bureau can be established in every city in Europe where the authority or influence of the 'International' is recognized, and our own people placed in direct communication with its officials."[32]

At Basle, Cameron went beyond Sylvis's concern with contract labor. He stated that the NLU did not desire "to interfere with what is known as legitimate immigration," and noted that "the truest friend the emigrant finds in his new home is his fellow-craftsman." "But," he continued, "there is as much difference between the advent of an emigrant who comes to strengthen our hands, and the importation of a class of men who are brought to thwart the legitimate claims of our mechanics, to pauperize labor and flood the market, as there is between and angel of darkness and angel of light. . . ."[33] Here, Cameron indicated that the NLU was groping toward a consideration of broader problems of immigration, most notably, the building up of a labor surplus by capitalists. Importantly, Cameron chose the example of the anthracite coal fields of Pennsylvania to illustrate his point. In this instance, the operators brought in Scottish and English miners to build up a labor surplus and destroy the union.[34] In the future, they would bring in Irish, then Polish, Italian and Hungarian miners, as conditions in mining played a crucial role in the development of working class attitudes toward immigration.

At the 1870 National Labor Congress, president Richard Travellick dealt exclusively with the question of immigration. In his report on the International he mentioned with concern the proposed emigration bureau and mechanisms to inform European workers about strikes in the

United States.[35] At the same Congress, Frederich Sorge put forward a resolution stating that the National Labor Union "declares its adhesion to the principles of the International Workingmen's Association, and expects at no distant date to affiliate with it."[36] The resolution was passed, but the NLU implemented neither it nor any of its schemes to control immigration. Claiming more than 600 thousand members just one year before, the NLU, like the International, went into precipitous decline and never recovered.

5. The Chinese Question

Anti-Chinese sentiments played an important role in the long-term development of the working class movement's attitudes toward European immigration. In the American Federation of Labor and later on, in the Socialist party, anti-Chinese agitation conditioned responses to the "new" immigrants from Southern and Eastern Europe, who were commonly considered racially inferior. For the National Labor Union, as for the later movement, anti-Chinese racial nativism contradicted internationalist sentiments. It automatically raised the question of whether immigration as a whole was desirable, and provided at least a partial answer. Logically, anti-Chinese sentiment laid the basis for immigration restrictions by race and nationality. In practice, however, the connections between Chinese and European restrictions developed slowly and unevenly.

The 1869 National Labor Congress was the first to see indications of anti-Chinese racism. In his presidential address, C.H. Lucker, who had succeeded Sylvis, referred to the Chinese as "a people so base that in California where they are known, all parties by common consent have in their political platforms condemned them as totally unworthy of being made citizens of the United States."[37] The Congress did not endorse an exclusionist proposal, however. Instead, it endorsed a more traditional resolution drafted by A.C. Cameron, which opposed coolie labor but affirmed that "voluntary Chinese emigrants ought to enjoy the protection of the laws like other citizens."[38]

Between the 1869 and 1870 Congresses, anti-Chinese agitation increased considerably. The U.S. government had just signed the Burlingame treaty, an agreement that allowed some Chinese citizens to immigrate in exchange for American commercial exploitation of Chinese cities.

Cameron's paper, the *Workingman's Advocate* began to run anti-Chinese articles. One which appeared shortly before the 1870 Congress warned, "The Chinese are still coming by the thousands to dig our gold and to overrun the country with cheap labor. . . . " Written by a San Franciscan, it presented an unbelievable picture of the Chinese immigrants' ability to live off practically nothing and under crowded conditions. "Twenty-five hundred of them in this city live in one house" the article claimed, "while that number of other people would occupy at least two hundred houses."[39]

At first, the protest against coolie labor was characterized by moral outrage at the conditions of work Chinese immigrants faced. Gradually, this emphasis gave way to the simple fear that Chinese workers would destroy the gains of American workers. Instead of organizing Chinese workers into the unions, as was attempted with African Americans, the decision was to drive them out of the country. Thus, the element of solidarity was overcome by one of hatred. The new emphasis was exemplified in an article which appeared in the *Workingman's Advocate*, in 1870. It stated

> We do not oppose them [the Chinese] merely because they are the slaves of those who employ them, but because 'bond or free,' they are a curse to our country.[40]

At the 1870 Congress, the National Labor Union reversed this position on voluntary Chinese immigration. In his presidential address to the Congress, Richard Travellick repeated the sense of the 1869 resolution, stating that "we are ever ready to welcome the oppressed peoples of all nations" but are opposed to the importation of coolie labor. Despite the fact that he added that China was a "bigoted and superstitious nation," the committee on the presidential address refused to accept "that portion which extends a welcome to Chinese immigration."[41]

In the course of the debate on Chinese immigration, Travellick drifted toward the exclusionist position. At subsequent Congresses, however, he returned to supporting voluntary Chinese immigration. Travellick maintained this position as long as he was president, even when the NLU had dwindled to a handful of members.

Two resolutions on Chinese immigration were introduced at the 1870 Congress. The first, written by Charles McLean of Boston, stated that "we welcome every man, every race, and every creed," and that "every immigrant should be naturalized" and given the vote. It also denied "the right of capital to import human freight" to lower wages and degrade labor.[42] The second resolution was written by Albert Redstone, from Vallejo, California. It demanded the abrogation of the Burlingame treaty, and made no mention of voluntary immigration. This resolution was adopted by the committee on coolie labor — chaired by another Californian, W.W. Delaney of San Francisco — and by the Congress. The Congress also added a plank on Chinese labor to its program. It stated that the presence of large numbers of Chinese labor is "an evil entailing want and its consequent train of misery and crime on all other classes of the American people, and should be prevented by legislation ..."[43]

Clearly, the majority of delegates to the 1870 Congress favored Chinese exclusion. Few trade unionists outside California had come into contact with Chinese workers, although some Eastern shoemakers had, and feared that "American labor is to be reduced to the Chinese standards of rice and rats."[44] Most delegates were influenced by the California labor movement, which was organized on an anti-Chinese basis. California was, of course, the center of anti-Oriental racism, and it nourished the mainstream of racist sentiment throughout the nation, just as did the South. Anti-Oriental racism continued to play a role in the labor movement even after the Chinese Exclusion Act of 1882, and eventually became mixed in with Socialist nativism.

It was by no means inevitable that the American labor movement take a racist turn. Coexisting with the racist sentiments that emerged at the 1870 National Labor Congress, were anti-racist ones. Although only two delegates — neither from the International — defended Chinese workers, the vast majority were in favor of bringing African American workers into the NLU, on an equal basis. This seems odd, if it is assumed that hostility toward the Chinese was based on their potential threat to the gains of white American workers. African American workers posed much more of a threat — but in their case, were invited into the NLU because of it. Undoubtedly, the fact that trade unionists had been outspoken opponents *of* chattel slavery, and that the era immediately following the Civil War was one of supposed good will toward African Americans, help explain the NLU's anti-racist sentiment. It should be noted, too, that within the NLU there still existed a great deal of anti-African American prejudice that could not properly be called racism. Sylvis himself was the best example of a prejudiced labor leader willing to organize African American workers. But the important fact is that anti-racism did exist, that it was a well-developed tendency in the labor movement, and that the movement took a conscious step in the opposite direction when it declared against the Chinese. During the time of the AFL, a wave of anti-African American prejudice coincided with anti-Chinese racial nativism, and had a strong impact on their European immigration policy.

6. Conclusion

The resurgence of trade union activity in the 1870s completely bypassed the National Labor Union, By then, the NLU had became totally absorbed in monetary reform, and had lost its working class support. Nevertheless, the NLU left its mark on the American working class movement. Although their ideologies for the most part did not out-last the Knights of Labor, their concern with immigration foreshadowed decades of further work.

The NLU's heritage was mixed. The major impulse for their immigration policy came from skilled craft unions, such as the Iron Molders, which were threatened by European contract labor. At the same time, because the expansion of industry in the post-Civil War period outstripped apprenticeship programs, these unions had a large immigrant membership and welcomed more. Consequently, on the one hand they rejected capitalist-induced immigration intended to break strikes, while on the other they accepted free immigration. Thus, the craft unions developed an internationalism narrow in some respects but broad in others.

Their contacts with the International and European trade unions were limited strictly to controlling immigration. In part, this was due to the desire of the International's conservative elements to contact American unions on that level alone, thereby strengthening their own position against the revolutionaries. More important, however, was the fact that the American unions shared many of the characteristics of their British counterparts, including their conservatism. The American unions differed in that they were in a more optimistic position. Neither threatened with the extinction of their crafts by mechanization, nor severely pressured by free immigration, they were willing to leave the gates open to persons emigrating for political and economic reasons.

Two other sources contributed to the NLU's immigration policy, besides the craft unions. First, anti-Chinese elements arose, weakening internationalist tendencies and broadening the focus of immigration problems. Second, isolated segments of the organized working class made first contact with intensive, free immigrant competition under conditions of low or uncertain employment. In both the Knights of Labor and the AFL, these segments — most notably, the miners — contributed heavily to anti-immigrant sentiment.

These two sources developed too late to change the National Labor Union's position on European immigration markedly. The NLU did, after Sylvis's death, transcend its limited concern with contract labor. However, it did not change its perspective qualitatively. The NLU limited itself to acting within the international channels developed by the working class movement; it did not seek allies from either the government or other social classes. During the reign of the Knights of Labor, while anti-Chinese sentiment remained subdued, conflict with free immigrant labor intensified. Then, the first serious challenge was posed to the early labor movement's internationalist posture toward Europeans.

Chapter 3.
The Knights of Labor: Old and New Sources of
Working Class Opposition to Immigration

1. Introduction

Following the decline of the National Labor Union, no working class organization of national prominence appeared until the Knights of Labor.[1] Ideologically, the Knights were rooted in the earlier movement. Like Sylvis before them, their leaders emphasized the cooperative and educational values of organization. In contrast to Samuel Gompers and other modern working class leaders who followed, they can be characterized primarily as social reformers.

Organizationally, the Knights differed in several important respects from their predecessors. Although founded as a tight-knit, secret organization — a common feature of trade unions during the '60s — they gradually abandoned this form. After some ten years the Knights had become a broad, comprehensive organization with diverse trade unions and heterogeneous district assemblies grouped under their banner. The Knights' most distinctive feature was their willingness to organize unskilled workers who had previously remained outside the trade unions. They were not, however, an industrial union. Also in contrast to their predecessors, the Knights' leadership attempted to exert centralized control over the activities of their affiliates. In this effort, they met more with failure than with success.

Programatically, the Knights differed little from the National Labor Union with respect to immigration. The bulk of the members were immigrants — although the organization was largely run by native-born Americans — who upheld the traditions of internationalism.[2] However, the Knights' major activities were concentrated in the period of heaviest immigration during the 19th century. In organizing the unskilled, they felt the pressures of immigration more acutely than any previous organization. Moreover, the Knights witnessed the first influx of "new" immigrants, from Southern and Eastern Europe. This combination of factors meant that the Knights were to reflect both the past and the future of the working class movement, an amalgamation of old programs for immigrants with new attitudes. The Knights were also concerned with Chinese immigration, but neither their activities nor their ideas represented a departure from the racism of the earlier labor movement.[3]

2. The Early Years

Founded in 1869, the Knights experienced little success during their first years of existence. Then, in 1872, the organization began to develop staying power in the Philadelphia area. From there it expanded westward. The organization's growth was steady, despite a high rate of turnover. By 1878 the Knights claimed nearly 10 thousand members. Within one year the figure had doubled, and by 1883 there were more than 50 thousand members.[4] Secrecy had been abandoned by the entire organization in 1881. At the same time, the Knights' leadership began to assert its hegemony, and to intensify organizational efforts.

Until the mid-1880s, the Knights drew their support primarily from local trade unions without national affiliation, and from revived national unions such as the Knights of St. Crispin.[5] The Knights were organized into district assemblies largely of heterogeneous composition. However, in a few areas of work, district assemblies were organized purely along trade lines, as trade unions. The most important of these were coal mining and window-glass working. The trade element predominated in coal-mining because in mining districts, almost all workers were engaged in that occupation. The window-glass workers, on the other hand were more widely dispersed but their already-powerful trade union forced the Knights' leadership to give in to the demand for separate organization. Significantly, it was in these areas, coal mining and window-glass working, that the Knights first developed their attitudes on immigration.

3. Coal Miners and Immigrant Strikebreakers

When the Knights first entered the coal fields in 1875, the prospects for organization were dismal.[6] The miners' union in the anthracite fields of Pennsylvania had been obliterated after a six-month strike, and the Molly Maguires, following a brief but explosive revival, were proceeding rapidly to their doom. The miners' union in the bituminous fields was also in a state of disintegration.

Throughout the Eastern states most miners were immigrants. Among the anthracite miners, Irish immigrants made up the largest single ethnic group. Next came the Welsh, followed by English and Scottish miners. In some areas

Germans also formed a significant fraction. A similar ethnic distribution prevailed in the bituminous fields. In all mining districts, among the immigrants the Welsh and English held a near-monopoly on skilled work.[7]

The Welsh and English elements had been instrumental in forming the Workingmen's Benevolent Association in the anthracite fields, shortly after the Civil War. After a series of impressive victories in Pennsylvania, the union was suddenly confronted with a new, more powerful enemy, the railroad trust. The railroads had taken over independently-operated mines in an effort to regulate production and fix transportation rates.[8] They saw the destruction of the union as one of their first tasks, and as their major weapon chose to build up labor reserves. In doing so, the operators relied upon the labor exchanges of New York and Philadelphia to supply them with unskilled Irish laborers. It was the existence of this labor surplus that assured the union's defeat in 1875.[9]

The story was much the same in the bituminous fields. Unions in the bituminous fields of six states were brought into the Miners National Association in 1873. Faced with an organization that united miners throughout the bituminous fields of the East and Midwest, operators decided to import immigrant, strikebreakers from the labor exchanges. Charlotte Erickson reports that prior to the miners' formation of a national organization, there was only one instance of the use of immigrant strikebreakers, over a six-year period. After the Association was formed, however, there were fourteen such instances, over a three-year period.[10]

The immigrants used as strikebreakers were of diverse nationalities. In the bituminous fields of Pennsylvania, Swedish immigrants were used to break five strikes, Germans three and Italians three.[11] The immigrant strikebreakers were kept in compounds under armed guard, in order to isolate them from the striking miners. In the rare instances where strikes succeeded, persuasion of the strikebreakers to support the union played a major role.

With the revival of trade unionism in the coal regions in the early 1880s, the Knights of Labor began to take hold. Once again, the operators in the bituminous fields resorted to importing immigrant strikebreakers from the labor exchanges. This time, however, in contrast to previous efforts, the strikebreakers brought in were Southern and Eastern Europeans. In March 1882, Knights of Labor miners in the Cumberland region of western Maryland struck in response to a wage-reduction. Two months later, the operators began to erect barracks-style housing sufficient to hold one thousand strikebreakers. In late May and again in June and July, shipments of strikebreakers arrived. Predominant among them were Hungarians.[12] Thus were drawn the lines of division between "old" and "new" immigrants, that remained unbreachable for nearly two decades.

In the anthracite fields, the railroad trust operators once again began building a labor surplus. This time, however, instead of Irish laborers, they brought in Hungarians, Italians, and Poles.[13] Once again, surplus labor was instrumental in defeating the union, in the Knights of Labor strike of 1887. A decade was to pass before miners' unions could renew their challenge to the anthracite operators.

Although numerous nationalities were represented among strikebreakers and the surplus labor force, Hungarians, Italians and Poles predominated. The hostility with which they were greeted by native-born American and old immigrant miners far surpassed the conflicts between previous groups. A letter written by Grand Master Workman Terence Powderly to the Scranton, Pennsylvania, *Truth*, and presented before the Knights' 1884 convention, reflected the depths of this hostility. Powderly wrote:

> The opposition to the Hungarians in the coke regions amounts to a hatred — a hatred which is liable at any time to burst forth in a blaze which may sweep them entirely out of that country. This antipathy is not confined to the workingmen alone, it is shared in by BUSINESS MEN AND WORKINGMEN ALIKE; and they all unite in cursing the advent of the Hungarian to the coke region. . . . They work for little or nothing, live on a fare which a Chinaman would not touch, and will submit to *any* and every indignity which may be imposed on them. In a word, they

are utterly devoid of that spirit necessary to make them good and patriotic American citizens.

Powderly continued,

> If it were possible to make good. and useful citizens of these men, I would never raise my voice against then, but that is . . . impossible. . . . He may be fit to work — so is a mule. . . . I believe that this country was intended for a race of freemen, and, believing that, I will always oppose the introduction of such men as are not capable of enjoying, appreciating, defending, and perpetrating the blessings of good government.[14]

In later years, Powderly became head of the Federal Division of Information, set up to assist immigrants in finding jobs upon arrival. Ironically, Powderly's most persistent opponents were the trade unions, which by then had almost universally adopted his earlier nativist stance.[15]

Throughout the coal fields, antagonisms between the old and new miners flared. Native-born Americans and old immigrants laid down their tools where new immigrants were hired. Fights erupted continuously. Finally, the union miners sent a delegation to Washington to protest and testify against immigration.

As it turned out, the miners' protest was restricted in focus. Mistakenly believing that new immigrant miners were contract laborers imported from Europe, they simply demanded that contract labor be prohibited.[16] On the surface, they went no further than the National Labor Union. Moreover, Powderly's own plan for alleviating the problems caused by immigration was consistent with that of the National Labor Union, and also the First International. Powderly proposed that the Knights extend their organization to Europe, to "teach the people of these lands that there is no truth in the representations of those who would lure them from their homes."

Like the miners, he believed that new immigrants were enticed to the United States under contract.[17]

4. The Window Glass Workers and Immigration

Of all the unions affiliated with the Knights, only one was seriously affected by imported contract labor. These were the Window Glass Workers, who comprised Local Assembly 300. Unlike skilled workers in many other trades, the Glass Workers faced no threat from mechanization. They did, however, face the continuous threat of contract labor imported from England and Belgium. Thus the Glass Workers were in much the same position as the British skilled workers who, untouched by technological innovations, affiliated with the International for protection from immigrant competition.

In 1881, two years after its formation, the union claimed to have enrolled every skilled window glass worker in the nation. Since a sizable number of immigrant glass workers had been imported by masters from the time the union was founded,[18] it can be assumed that the union experienced little difficulty in organizing them. In one case involving imported Belgian strikebreakers, the union convinced the immigrants to break their contracts and return home. Part of their passage was paid from the union treasury.[19] At the Knights' 1881 convention, the Glass Workers continued to display a friendly attitude toward immigrants, when they requested permission to organize foreign-language locals.[20]

In 1882 and again in 1883, the masters engaged in region-wide lockouts to break the union and reduce wages. In both instances strikebreakers were imported from Europe under contract. The masters' efforts failed, however, because the union was able to organize the immigrants without difficulty.[21]

In contrast the coal miners, the Glass Workers were able to maintain friendly relations with fellow-tradesmen from other countries, despite their competition. Hostility was rare, and occurred only when glass workers who were learning a more skilled aspect of their trade felt that the presence of highly-skilled immigrants would deprive them of the opportunity for advancement. In large part, friendly relations prevailed because in the window glass industry, there existed no labor surplus and no possibility of one. The industry was expanding rapidly, as it had been since before the Civil War, and skilled labor was in short supply. It is interesting to note in this connection that the craft-oriented AFL, in proposing general immigration restrictions in later years, did not oppose the free immigration of skilled labor.

On the national level, the response of the Window Glass Workers to the importation of contract labor was two-fold: First, they worked through the Knights and the federal government for its prohibition. Second, they made contact with glassworkers' unions in Europe, and attempted to set up an international federation. After sending delegations to Europe, the Glass Workers organized a Universal Federation in July 1865. Among the agreements reached was that:

> Each National branch shall have control of its members, and no member shall be allowed to go from one country to another without first having notified the National Secretary of his desire to change. In such cases the National Secretary to which *such* member desires to emigrate shall be appraised to the fact, and after submitting the matter to the National Council, they shall determine whether the condition of trade and labor in their country warrant such change, and their decision shall be final.[22]

The efforts of the Window Glass Workers to control immigration in no way departed from those of previous unions, such as the National Labor Union. In fact, their demands were basically the same as those made through the NLU by the Window Glass Blowers of Pittsburgh, in 1867.[23] The Glass Workers were a highly skilled trade, and their indifference toward unskilled labor reflected the attitudes of an "aristocracy of labor." Yet it was only in later years, when unskilled threatened skilled labor, that the aristocracy's indifference became translated into open hostility toward new immigrants. For the time being, the privileged position of highly skilled workers insulated them from such hostility, and from nativism.

5. Conclusion

The Window Glass Workers were able to pressure the Knights' leadership into working strenuously for anti-contract labor legislation. Their efforts were important in securing the passage of the Foran Act of 1885, which prohibited the importation of contract labor, and for which the Knights took credit. The testimony of the Glass Workers was limited to contract labor. However, the bulk of the Knights' evidence for the bill was supplied by the coal miners. Although the miners were ostensibly concerned with contract labor only, their testimony ranged over the food, dress and habits of Hungarian and Italian immigrants.[24] Thus, the Foran Act was passed on a wave of chauvinism and nativism, alien to the spirit of the earlier working class movement, but not that which was to follow.

The Glass Workers, it may be said, were representative of earlier trade unions. The coal miners, on the other hand, were representative of a peculiar type of industrial unionism that later developed in the AFL, an industrial unionism that grew out of sheer necessity while retaining a strong craft-orientation. If the Knights as a whole did not programmatically abandon the limited internationalism shown toward Europeans by the earlier working class movement, indications of what was to happen in the later movement were beginning to appear. The rise of anti-new immigrant nativism was, of course, the most important sign. Occasionally, nativism took an anti-radical form, as it later did in the AFL. Shortly after the Haymarket affair in 1886, a Chicago delegate warned the Knights' convention that new immigrants were,

> . . . a class of men who, bred under iron rule of monarchical forms of government, have developed into apostles and teachers of anarchism and socialism, and coming here with no care for our free institutions, and a bitter hatred of *all forms* of established government, they are spreading among our people the ethics of destruction . . . They are the enemies of all, both employers and employed, and should be given a wide berth by organized workmen, as they are by all organized governments.[25]

With respect to immigration, then, the Knights' contribution to the modern labor movement was a set of contradictions. In terms of concrete proposals, they did not go beyond their predecessors. In terms of ideologies, they both did and did not. The ideology of the Glass Workers, an archaic craft union, was akin to the moderate internationalism of the NLU. The ideology of the miners' unions, organized on an industrial-trades basis, was akin to that developed by the AFL near the turn of the century. Both the Glass Workers and the miners contributed to the Knights' position on immigration, but the result was a legislative proposal that completely by-passed the problems of the miners.[26] The miners' difficulties remained until they were absorbed into the AFL, where once again their attitudes were an important force in shaping a position on immigration. In the meantime, the AFL developed its "new unionism," simpler and more exclusive than the Knights', although theoretically far more profound. It was the AFL position on immigration that finally decided the question

Chapter 4.
The American Federation of Labor:
New Craft Unionism and opposition to Immigration

1. Decline of the Knights and Rise of the AFL

By the mid-1880s, the Knights of Labor had become the most important force in the American working class movement.[1] Within one year, 1886, the Knights' membership had grown from 150 thousand to more than 700 thousand. Most of this gain came from the ranks of unskilled and semi-skilled workers.

At the same time as the Knights grew, however, cracks began to appear in its structure and a new organization — the American Federation of Labor — arose to challenge its hegemony. In line with their goals of social reform, the leadership of the Knights had chosen to organize workers into mixed assemblies — heterogeneous groups geared more toward political rather than economic action. This brought them into conflict with the trade union element of their constituency, who demanded organization along homogeneous craft lines and less attention to social reform.

The AFL very accurately reflected the interests of these trade union elements. Much smaller than the Knights, but more compact and single-minded, the organization represented a profound departure from its predecessors. While the Knights and the National Labor Union represented the struggles of pre-industrial craftsmen against the conditions of industrial capitalism, the AFL represented a gradual adaptation to them. The Knights' and the NLU's program of cooperation and education was not resurrected by the AFL. In its place stood a highly-developed wage-consciousness, which included tight economic organization and a propensity to strike.

As the Knights swelled their ranks with unskilled workers, the conflict with trade union elements intensified. The Knights leadership, recognizing that sheer numbers were not enough, attempted to gain control over the strategic occupations of skilled workers. Calling for the solidarity of the entire Working class, they had as their aim the sub-ordination of the struggle of skilled workers to that of the unskilled. The trade union element, much of it close to or already affiliated with the AFL, refused to subordinate itself. Not only was the conflict one of political reformism versus trade unionism, then, but it was also one between different segments of the working class.

Selig Perlman writes:

> From the viewpoint of a struggle between principles, this was indeed a clash between the principle of solidarity of labor and that of trade separatism, but, in reality, each of the principles reflected only the special interest of a certain portion of the working class.[2]

It was "fundamentally a struggle between the unskilled and the skilled portions of the wage-earning class."[3] Thus, the AFL's new craft unionism appeared not only as a rejection of aspirations of political reform but as the organizational manifestation of the aristocracy of labor.

The Knights of Labor faded as rapidly as it had grown; following 1887 the clashes between it and the AFL were, with few exceptions, relatively minor disputes. After the threat from the Knights subsided, the AFL felt no need to wage a struggle against unskilled workers as a class. But within a few years, the unskilled immigrant loomed on the horizon as a new, even more deadly threat to organized skilled labor. Once again, the AFL reacted as an aristocracy of labor, but this time the struggle was much more prolonged, its consequences far more severe and lasting.

2. The AFL Favors Immigration Restrictions

Up to and shortly beyond the period of its clash With the Knights of Labor, the AFL was only routinely concerned. with the question of immigration. Restriction was rarely mentioned, and then only as a collective, international effort by trade unions. F.J. McGuire wrote in 1882, of the need for the American labor movement to establish ties with European unions to check immigration. He suggested:

> . . . we may expect international trade union congresses annually to meet and determine, among other questions,

on means of preventing the importation and immigration of labor from one country to another in case of trade troubles . . . as well as the dangers of unrestricted immigration, in flooding a country at the behest of cheap labor capitalists.[4]

McGuire's proposal was in keeping with the policy on immigration established nearly two decades earlier by the National Labor Union. When the AFL finally adopted a restrictionist program, however, it turned to the U.S. government, not European trade unions, to implement it. Generally, the AFL at this time considered only two aspects of immigration as problems — the importation of European contract labor, and Chinese immigration. The AFL's interest in contract labor was a holdover from the earlier labor movement. Concern over Chinese immigration was mainly a product of West Coast agitation, that had permeated the entire labor movement — including the Knights and the NLU — over a period of nearly twenty years. Gompers had a keen personal interest in Chinese immigration, because his trade once had been threatened by competition from Chinese cigar-makers. The AFL kept the question of Chinese immigration distinct from European, but there can be little doubt that its attitude toward Chinese conditioned its attitude toward European immigrants. Especially, the AFL's evolution of racial nativism with respect to Chinese weakened its internationalist tendencies, and helped pave the way for anti-European nativism.

The first convention of the Federation of Organized Trades and Labor Unions, the embryonic AFL, passed a resolution calling for the exclusion of Chinese from the U.S. but did not discuss European immigration. Its anti-Chinese resolution was harsh, but not racist. A sole delegate, Sherman Cummin of Boston, opposed it. Cummin felt that the Chinese "represented a civilization that has endured much longer than ours," and that "they should have the same rights as other foreigners."[5] His was the only statement ever made at an AFL convention favorable to the Chinese. In 1882, the U.S. government passed the Chinese Exclusion Act, and for the next ten *years* the AFL was content simply to ask for more rigid enforcement of it.

The first resolution on European contract labor, in support of stricter regulations, appeared at the 1884 convention.[6] But it was not until five years later, in 1889, that the AFL convention received the first of just a handful of reports of the actual use of European contract labor. The Granite Cutters' union complained that workers were imported from Scotland to Austin, Texas to cut convict-quarried stone after union members refused.[7]

The 1889 convention also saw the first resolution to stop all immigration, because of widespread unemployment. At this time, the AFL was just beginning to feel the pressures of immigration, and was not yet ready to oppose it forthright. Consequently, the resolution was referred to the Executive Council, where it lay forgotten.[8] Enjoying steady growth and feeling complacent, the AFL continued to look to contract labor as the only problem with European immigration. Within two years the situation changed profoundly. Financial panic struck in 1890, signalling a chain of disastrous economic setbacks that culminated in the depression of 1893–97. The immigrant now seemed a real threat to prosperity, and restrictionist sentiment built up throughout the nation. The AFL moved rapidly but unsteadily from its limited concern with imported contract labor to a broader concern with all immigration.

At the 1891 convention, Samuel Gompers for the first time spoke in favor of restricting European immigration. He told the convention that the situation with regard to immigration was "appalling." In the past there had been plenty of room for immigrants, because the nation's resources were undeveloped. Now, however, "there is not an industry which is not overcrowded with working people who vainly plead for an opportunity to work." Gompers demanded relief from immigration, but suggested that the problem could be remedied "without bigotry, narrowness and a spirit of 'Know-nothingism' ... " He also said that he viewed immigration restrictions "not from the mere selfish standpoint of our own protection," but from the standpoint of strengthening the institutions of European workers.[9]

Gompers set up a special committee to study *European* immigration, but nothing much came of it. Although the first step had been taken, restrictionist tendencies remained subdued. There was no overt sign of nativism as existed in the nation as a whole; Gompers' remarks were a conscious effort in the opposite direction. Moreover, there was not yet any clear sign of racism with respect to Chinese.

At the 1892 convention, Gompers again came out for restricting immigration. This time he attacked "supposed philanthropists" who gather "hordes of people, pack them in vessels worse than cattle," and then force them to work in the mines, railroads and sweatshops of the nation. Gompers said, "We do not wish to join in the general cry of completely shutting out all,"[10] but that some restriction was necessary. The garment workers persuaded the convention to condemn the "misdirected philanthropy" of the United Hebrew Charities, who were "importing large numbers of poor, persecuted and deceived working people of Europe" to work in the sweatshops.[11] Clearly, the AFL now perceived free immigration as a major source of trouble.

During the next two years, 1893 and 1894, contradictions developed in the AFL's attitude. On the one hand, anti-Chinese racial nativism emerged for the first time as a major force. On the other, the AFL reaffirmed internationalism as its 1894 convention endorsed unrestricted free immigration from Europe. As it turned out, racial nativism became a permanent feature of AFL policies. Support for unrestricted immigration was temporary, and unenthusiastic.

In his presidential address to the 1893 convention, Gompers brought up the question of Chinese exclusion, which had lain dormant for several years. His remarks were brief and, as usual, confined to pointing out violations of the Chinese Exclusion Act.[12] Then, in a move that took Gompers and his fellow officers by surprise, John Green of the Woodworkers introduced an outspokenly racist, anti-Chinese resolution. The resolution stated that the Chinese "are a degraded people, and bring with them nothing but filth, vice and disease, and all efforts to elevate *them* to a higher *standard* have proven futile." If Americans knew how much the Chinese had degraded people on the West coast, they would "sweep them off the face of the earth."[13]

Green's resolution was so out-of-keeping with the traditional, non-racist policy of the AFL, that the Committee on Resolutions refused to consider it. In its place, the Committee simply called for stricter enforcement of the Chinese Exclusion Act — the same position Gompers had taken. However, convention delegates rejected the Committee substitute — despite an attempt by

Gompers to toughen it — and adopted Green's.[14] From this point on, whenever the question of Chinese immigration came up, it was within the context of racial nativism.

Gompers himself took halting steps toward a racist perspective at the 1894 convention. Uncomfortable with the racial nativist turn of his organization, he stated that American workers have no antipathy toward the Chinese "because of their nationality." Then, Gompers tried to bridge the distance between that sentiment and the new currents. He added that since the Chinese "have allowed civilization to pass them by untouched," they "menace the progress . . . of the workers of other countries, and cannot be fraternized with."[15]

As years passed, Gompers moved more and more toward the camp of anti-Chinese racial nativism, until he ended up squarely inside it.

At the same time as anti-Chinese sentiments hardened, pro-European sentiments made a surprisingly emphatic appearance. The 1894 convention declared without debate that "further restriction of immigration is un-necessary"; this policy remained in effect for the next year, while John McBride was president.[16] Since no previous convention found it necessary to make such a statement it is reasonable to ask, why did this one? It did not represent a complete rejection of Gompers' warnings about European immigration, because the same convention set up a committee to carry out "the recommendations of President Gompers for the amendment of the Immigration laws."[17] For most delegates it probably represented an attempt to formulate some of the broad, internationalist sentiments of the working class movement, in the face of nationalism in the dominant society — and their own equivocation. To a large extent, they wanted to register their sympathy with immigrant workers at the same time as they were losing it.

Two years later, this expedient was no longer possible. The debate broke into the open in 1896, and carried over to the next year. Gompers warned the 1896 convention that "We cannot remain neutral" while the question of restricting immigration "is so widely discussed and seeking adjustment."[18] He appointed a special Committee on Immigration to draw up concrete proposals for restriction. In presenting them, the Committee insisted, "we do not share in the old Knownothing sentiment which uses the immigration question as a pretext to gloss over social wrongs." It further suggested that the nation could support a much larger population if "the greedy interests of speculators and monopolists would not consign so many willing workers to idleness."[19] However, some delegates saw the Committee's proposals — including a literacy test — as betraying these internationalist sentiments. They asked, if the capitalist class is responsible for unemployment, then why fight the immigrants? After considerable debate, the whole question was referred to the incoming Executive Council.[20]

Prior to the 1897 convention, the Executive Council conducted a referendum on immigration restriction. All AFL affiliates were asked to participate, and to instruct their convention delegates according to the results. At the convention itself, three resolutions were introduced favoring restrictions against one which reiterated the "no further restrictions" position.

When the time for debate arrived, it soon became clear that the forces favoring restriction were in control. The Executive Council reported that the majority of unions participating in the referendum favored restrictions,[21] and the convention vote bore that out. The delegates who opposed restrictions pointed out the contradictions in the AFL's attitude. Phil Hofher, of St. Louis, said, "We have been talking about international unions and consolidation of the brotherhood of man, and now we turn around and want to debar the brother from the other side."[22] A few implied that the AFL was tail-ending a capitalist movement.[23] Those who favored restrictions argued that it was an economic necessity. Charles Myers, of Baltimore, warned that "cheap foreign labor is taking the work that rightfully belongs to the American laborer."[24] After debate closed, a resolution favoring restrictions by literacy passed by a five-to-one margin.[25] On the heels of depression, anti-immigrant sentiment in the AFL had finally broken clear of opposition.

3. Why Restrictions?

The AFL rarely mentioned strikebreaking as a reason for opposing immigration, except with regard to skilled contract labor. All evidence indicates that this was not seen as a major problem, and certainly was not a motivating force. In 1896, the year restrictionist sentiment came into dominance, the Secretary reported that for AFL affiliates, "in cases of strike or lockout scabs were secured from no particular locality, but generally where the trouble occurred, or in neighboring states." Of some twenty unions reporting trouble with scabs, only one indicated they were immigrants.[26] Interestingly, the period during which the AFL policy emerged was one of unparalleled success in the field of industrial war. During 1897, the year AFL affiliates voted overwhelmingly for restrictions, the Secretary reported 189 out of 276 strikes won, with thirty-one compromised and thirty-three relatively minor ones lost. All told, more than 165 thousand workers benefitted, while just 940 did not.[27] In the 1896–97 debate on restrictions, no delegate mentioned strikebreaking except for one, who favored unrestricted immigration. P.H. Clifford of the socialist Western Federation of Miners stated that "the first scabbing done in Pennsylvania was by natives; not one foreign-born scab was now at Leadville; all were natives and a despicable set." His remarks went unchallenged. The leadership of the United Mine Workers, a predominantly industrial rather than craft union, and one which included many new immigrants in its ranks, favored restrictions but did not list strikebreaking as a reason.[28]

If the point of conflict between immigrant workers and the AFL did not lie in strikebreaking, neither did it lie in the root causes of depression. Although the AFL's restrictionism surfaced during depression, the organization refused to single out immigration as its cause. The leadership demonstrated that in fact immigration slowed down during depression, but warned that it would increase during periods of prosperity. The depression was important in that it laid bare the mechanisms of the labor market of industrial capitalism; it is in this area that the point of conflict lay.

In 1896, Gompers told an Italian labor leader that the AFL would soon abandon its 'no further' restrictions policy. He explained.

> ... we have a hard and bitter struggle to maintain or to make any progress in our standard of life, and ... with the inventions and introduction of machinery, and the application of new forces to industry, on the one hand, and the wholesale immigration of low-paid workers from other countries, on the other hand, we have a conflict that increases in intensity and bitterness with each recurring day.[29]

Clearly, the AFL's restrictionist policy was a product of its mode of adaptation to American industrial capitalism. Pinned between increasing mechanization on the one hand and expansion of the unskilled labor force on the other, AFL leaders attempted to gain breathing space by stabilizing the labor market. They sought to strike a balance between skilled and unskilled labor, in which the proportion of unskilled labor would not rise drastically. From the AFL's point of view, a fraternal relationship with unskilled labor depended on a stable labor market. Here the question of immigration assumed great importance. The *AFL never opposed the free immigration of skilled labor.* But the vast flood of unskilled immigrants threatened to disrupt the proper balance between skilled and unskilled labor, and along with it ruin the existing institutions of the working class movement. Skilled wages would be pulled downward by the increase in unskilled labor, and the ignorance and isolation of the immigrants would make them insensitive to the needs and demands of skilled labor. In January 1911, Gompers published an essay that traced the development of restrictionist sentiment in the AFL. It is one of his clearest statements and worth quoting at length. He wrote:

> At last the great body of the American industrial wage-work-ers have come to see one fact above others, which is that the immigrants are assimilated through the wage-working class. This means that the American-born wage-earners and the foreign wage-earners who have been here long enough to aspire to American standards are subjected to the ruinous competition of an unending stream of men freshly arriving from foreign lands who are accustomed to so low a grade of living that they can underbid the wage-earners established in this country and still save money. ...
> Entire industries have seen the percentages of newly arrived laborers rising, until in certain regions few American men can at present be found among the unskilled. ... This remarkable change in America, it must be kept in mind, is almost wholly in the wage-working class.[30]

Gompers went on to say that "the advocacy of exclusion, is not prompted by any assumption of superior virtue over our foreign brothers," but explained, "It is simply a case of the self-preservation of the American working classes."[31]

The AFL faced this choice if it wanted to stay alive: either transform itself into an organization broad enough to encompass the new immigrants, or oppose unskilled immigration altogether. It experimented briefly with industrial unionism — a mode of inclusion — but chose the course of exclusion.[32] Unwilling to transform itself, the AFL instead consolidated as an aristocracy of labor, and opened a struggle against immigration that soon became one against unskilled labor as a class.

4. Conservatization and the Rise of Nativism in the AFL

After 1897, all that remained was for the AFL's restrictionist policy to become nativist. The first glimmering of nativism came in an article that appeared in the *American Federationist*, shortly before the 1897 convention. It complained of the "replacing of the independent and intelligent Welsh and English coal miners of Pennsylvania by Huns and Slavs," and told of an ominous trend in the ethnic composition of immigration.[33] But the article was a few years ahead of its time. It was not until the AFL had passed through a period of conservatization that nativism took a firm hold. Against a backdrop of increasingly accommodating attitudes toward the capitalist class, three major issues arose which conditioned the AFL's attitude toward new immigrants. These were first, American expansionism, second, Chinese exclusion, and third, domestic racial segregation.

(i) The Spanish–American War and Chinese Exclusion

Following the Spanish–American war, the AFL swept aside any nationalistic prejudices. Gompers, especially, reached new highs in his inspired attacks on imperialism. He told the 1899 convention that the war had been designed "to ruthlessly trample under foot every principle upon which our Republic was founded. . . ." He compared U.S. military rule over Cuba with the crushing by militia of the Coeur d' Alène Idaho, miners' strike, and warned that American militarists and imperialists "hope to crush out the memory of, and the aspiration for, true liberty and freedom for all our people."[34] The previous convention had adopted a strong anti-war resolution, which stated:

> As a result of the war with Spain, a new and far-reaching policy, commonly known as 'imperialism' or 'expansion,' is now receiving the attention of the National Government, and if ratified by the United States Senate will seriously, burden the wage-workers of our country, thrust upon us a large standing army, an aristocratic navy, and seriously threaten the perpetuity of our Republic.[35]

There was, however, a flaw in the vigorous internationalism of the AFL that proved fatal.

The question of Chinese exclusion, now developed wholly within a racist perspective, became mixed in with the anti-imperialist politics of the AFL. Gradually, racist sentiment came to play a predominant role in the AFL's anti-imperialism, until it became jingoism. This remarkable transformation was made possible by the fact that the AFL reconciled itself to U.S. territorial gains. Samuel Gompers, in his address to the 1898 convention, touched briefly on the fact that if the U.S. were to annex the Philippines — an act he opposed — it would have to "open the gates" once more to the Chinese.[36] By 1901, the year before Chinese exclusion was scheduled for reconsideration in Congress, Gompers was demanding that it be applied to all American possessions. He introduced one of seven resolutions on Chinese exclusion at the 1901 convention, calling for "an act excluding Chinese from our country and wherever our flag floats."[37] At the 1902 convention, Gompers criticized Exclusion bills pending in Congress because "they took no cognizance of the changed conditions consequent upon the possession of Hawaii, Puerto Rico and the Philippine Islands." He wanted to insure that the "people of these possessions might have an opportunity of development as well as protection from Chinese."[38] The committee on the President's Report agreed, adding that to permit any Mongolian immigration "is treason to our civilization and to our race."[39] The next year, Gompers stated that there were too many "half-breed Chinamen" in the Philippines, and also demanded Japanese exclusion from Hawaii, where they "have invaded every industry and calling."[40] Gompers told the 1905 convention that the strategic position of Hawaii meant it must become the barrier of protection for American civilization. He noted that Americans and Europeans formed only a small proportion of its population, and complained that "No serious honest effort has thus far been made to Caucasianize, to Americanize, Hawaii."[41]

Nothing demonstrates the AFL's turn from anti-imperialism better than an incident at its 1903 convention. Andrew Furuseth of the Seaman's Union introduced a resolution condemning the U.S. plans to build a canal in Panama. The resolution stated that U.S. "greed for sovereignty" over the canal would inevitably lead to interference with "sister republics," and even their annexation. But the convention adopted instead, by a two-to-one margin, a committee substitute that both endorsed the canal and demanded that "none but citizens of the United States" be employed in its construction. It further suggested that the government employ "Italian and other southern races adapted in every way to the class of work to be undertaken at Panama," to relieve a congested labor market.[42]

It should be noted that this did not mark the total extinction of anti-imperialist sentiment in the AFL. Throughout this period and beyond, the AFL expressed strong sympathy for Puerto Rican workers and made persistent efforts to help organize them. Later on, the AFL forthrightly opposed U.S. intervention in Mexico. However, it remained silent on most aspects of the "dollar diplomacy" of the Roosevelt and Taft administrations.[43] There were also strong pacifist sentiments in the AFL — most notably those of Gompers himself — but these were brushed aside when the U.S. entered the war in Europe.

(ii) Racial Segregation

At the same time as the AFL began to accommodate itself to U.S. expansion, it also began to recognize racial segregation as a durable and tolerable institution. The rapid decline of pro-African American sentiment in the AFL can best be seen in two opposite reactions to attacks by Booker T. Washington. In 1897, Washington stated that trade unions impede the material advancement of the African American worker by failing to organize him. The AFL replied with its traditional declaration that it:

> ... welcomes to its ranks all labor, without regard to creed color, sex, race, or nationality, and that its best efforts *have* been, and will continue to be, to encourage the organization of those most needing its protection, whether, they be in the North or the south, the East or the West, white or black.[44]

The AFL often gave this policy substance — the previous year it had denied affiliation to the Brotherhood of Locomotive Firemen because of its refusal to admit African Americans.[45] Nevertheless, many AFL affiliates at this time did bar African Americans from membership, and within three years the organization as a whole supported pure Jim Crow unionism.[46] Thus, Gompers asked the 1900 convention to affiliate African American locals in the south directly to the AFL, instead of local central labor councils.[47] By 1901, when the AFL again *came under* fire from Washington, it replied not so much with a traditional anti-racist declaration, as with an apology for discrimination. Gompers wrote in the *American Federationist*:

> When a white man desires to become a member of an organization he is proposed for membership and is required to submit to rules which experience has demonstrated to be necessary. Certainly, no greater privilege can be conferred upon a negro simply because of the color of his skin.[48]

The rules to which both whites and African Americanes submitted equally were ones that excluded African Americans from membership.

(iii) Nativism

Shortly after the turn of the century, racist and jingoist sentiments reached their apex in the AFL. The same period found the AFL moving steadily in a conservative direction, with respect to the capitalist class. With the return of prosperity in the late 1890s, the organization had embarked on a mission of cooperation with the capitalist class, through the trade agreement.[49] The culmination of this effort came when the AFL joined the National Civic Federation, in 1901. It was also a period of remarkable growth, as the AFL grew from less than 500 thousand members in 1897 to more than one million in 1901, and two million in 1904.

It was at this juncture of conservatizing issues — each directly or indirectly antagonistic to internationalism — plus accord with the capitalist class and organizational stability, that the AFL's opposition to European immigration took a nativist turn. By then, nativism had become common ideological currency in American society as a whole. The AFL adapted it to its own purposes.

The first official sign of a nativist immigration policy for the AFL came in the form of an address to the 1901 convention by the Assistant Commissioner of Immigration, Edward McSweeny. Invited by Gompers to speak, McSweeny informed the delegates of a "marked change in the character of the incoming races." From 1850 to 1880, he said, German, Irish and Scandinavian immigrants "came here in families to settle down ... and subdue the forces of nature." After 1880, "Instead of the hardy, religious, and agricultural Northern Europe, the more Southern and Eastern races of Europe began to be in evidence." McSweeny described these *new* immigrants nation-by-nation, characterizing them as "people associated with a low degree of civilization. ... " He added that "The character of immigration has been growing steadily worse for years, not only racially, but individually." McSweeny proposed no basic changes in the law, however, but simply urged that its enforcers be given more support.[50]

Gompers accepted McSweeny's nativist attitude but not his political program. He continued to work for a literacy test, and told the 1902 convention that he had played "no small part" in getting such a bill through Congress the previous year. Concerning its effectiveness, Gompers promised,

> This regulation will exclude hardly any of the natives of Great Britain, Ireland, Germany, France or Scandinavia. It will

exclude only a small proportion, of our immigrants from North Italy. It will shut out a considerable number of south Italians and Slavs and others equally or more undesirable and injurious."[51]

In 1903, he reminded the AFL of McSweeny's address, and warned that conditions had by now deteriorated even more. He said that American workers should not be made to compete with "the worst elements that can be gathered from every corner, and the worst corners at that, of the whole world."[52]

The AFL's nativism was a watered-down version of mainstream American sentiment — a convenient form in which to express the restrictionist sentiments developed over the years. Its importance for the AFL lay in the fact that it was highly adaptable to the formation of an aristocracy of labor — although in this it played no determining role. Nativism reinforced the lines of division between skilled and unskilled labor, as the ethnic composition of the unskilled labor force shifted to new immigrant, while skilled labor became native-born American and old immigrant. Furthermore, nativism took some of the pressure off the consciences of old immigrants in the AFL, who had been reluctant to forget their own pasts. If the new immigrants were really a new breed, there was no reason to associate them with one's own self.

Within a few years after the turn of the century, AFL immigration policy was completely set. In years to come, the only changes were in the form of addition — head tax, means test, and similar restrictive measures. There were still expressions of sympathy for the plight of the immigrant, but these had a false ring. The AFL demanded legislation to relieve crowded conditions on steamships because it meant fifty percent more ships would be needed to bring as many immigrants.[53] In 1906, the year it entered mainstream politics once and for all, the AFL presented its famous "Labor's bill of Grievances" to President Theodore Roosevelt and leaders of the House and Senate. A key demand — and one of the few Roosevelt sympathized with — called for "relief from the constantly growing evil of induced and undesirable immigration."[54] For a brief period, the AFL advocated a five-year suspension of immigration, but ultimately settled for the quota system.

5. Conclusion

Throughout its formative years, one of the major problems the American Federation of Labor faced was what to do about immigration. Samuel Gompers — himself an immigrant Jew — revealed the depths of his organization's concern when he wrote, in 1911, "The local, and then the international unions, and finally the annual conventions of the American Federation of Labor itself, have had immigration up for consideration as one of the principal labor topics on literally thousands of occasions." After many years of discussion and debate, the AFL position finally evolved.

> The membership as a whole, [Gompers continued], from upholding the sentiments the great majority once entertained: namely, that this country could go on indefinitely absorbing the entire possible stream of immigration, have reluctantly, in view of the facts, passed over to the sway of the sentiment that their own good heartedness toward the immigrants and the laborers of the Old World was being exploited by large employers for the purpose of reducing wages as well as by the steamship combine and its myriad of parasites for the sake of their own profits.[55]

The AFL decided — in 1897 — that immigration must be cut drastically, and launched an aggressive, prolonged and successful campaign to see that it happened.

From the standpoint of a purely materialistic analysis, this decision was "natural" — a product of the inherent tendency of trade unionism to devote its energies to the workers' sectional and temporary advantages. To a large extent, the AFL itself accepted this point of view by arguing that it had no choice — that its decision to oppose immigration was dictated by sheer economic necessity, in the interest of the organized American working class. Yet there is considerable evidence to indicate that this wasn't the case, the economic necessity was not the sole or major determinant in the AFL's opposition to immigration. It is a mistake to assume that the AFL's attitude on any important question was merely a reflection of material conditions. For example, what

Selig Perlman describes as "pure wage consciousness" was a product not only of the "locking in" of American workers by the wage system, but also of self-conscious intellectual activity. It was as "natural" for socialists to choose the abolition of the wage system as it was for AFL leaders to accept it. Similarly, it was as "natural" for Left-wing elements in the working class movement to favor unrestricted immigration as it was for AFL leaders to oppose it. Both experienced the same material conditions; each shaped its reaction within a different theoretical framework.

Socialist labor economist Isaac Hourwich challenged the AFL's argument of economic necessity in an exhaustively documented study of immigration and labor, published in 1912. Immigrants, he said, were attracted by expanding industries that needed labor far beyond the resources of the domestic labor market. They did not drive out the old work force; either "they supplemented it or it moved upward, out of the ranks of the unskilled." Despite the rapid influx of new immigrants, the proportion of surplus labor available to capitalists remained the same. Generally, Hourwich said, the new immigrants were paid more than the native-born and old immigrant workers preceding them, and more than native-born workers in similar jobs, in regions where there were no immigrants. Thus, they posed no economic threat to the organized American working class.[56]

We do not have to assume — as Hourwich concluded — that the AFL's argument was entirely specious, in order to dismiss sheer economic necessity as the major determinant in its opposition to immigration. There can be no question that the AFL's claims were grossly exaggerated. On the other hand, there can be no question that a large proportion of its membership believed them. More important for our purposes is the fact that the argument of economic necessity was simply one aspect of a much more inclusive theoretical orientation that shaped the AFL's opposition to immigration. As part of a working class movement with distinctive traditions, the AFL inherited a commitment to internationalism that demanded solidarity with foreign workers. This tradition was especially strong in the AFL because of its immigrant base — its members were reluctant to forget their own pasts. Before it could evolve a restrictionist policy, the AFL had to overcome this and related traditions, such as anti-racism. Ultimately, the AFL overcame its internationalism by adopting the theoretical orientation of an aristocracy of labor.

The AFL's posture as an aristocracy of labor was closely linked to its strategy of new craft unionism — highly pragmatic, wage-conscious, and adaptable to industrial conditions. The AFL's new unionism represented a complete break with the traditions of its predecessors, the Knights and the NLU. While they had chosen to resist the advance of industrial capitalism, the AFL rode with the tide. All the while, however, the position of the AFL — and the skilled worker — was precarious. Threatened by mechanization and the rapid influx of unskilled immigrant workers, the AFL sought to maintain itself and its constituency by stabilizing the unskilled labor market through immigration restrictions.

This choice meant the final defeat of an internationalist perspective on immigration within the mainstream of the American working class movement. The moderate internationalism of pre-industrial craft unions was no longer viable. The pressures of industrialization and mass, unskilled immigration were too severe for the old traditions to hold up. Moreover, once the AFL had consolidated as an aristocracy of labor, internationalism retained little ideological force. This contradiction — between material interests and internationalist ideology — is discussed at length in the concluding chapter.

Chapter 5.
The American Federation of Labor:
Industrial Unionism and Opposition to Immigration

1. Introduction

As the AFL's new craft unions ascended to the position of an aristocracy of labor, they acted as the mainspring of restrictionist sentiment in the working class movement. Yet there was still another major source — the industrial union of the Mine Workers.[1] By far the largest and most important industrial union in the nation, the Mine Workers stood in the forefront of the fight for restrictions. At the same time, they were the first union to organize new immigrants on a massive scale. In the years prior to World War I, the Mine Workers' union was overwhelmingly new immigrant at its base.

These facts seem to contradict a major assumption of the previous chapter — that industrial unionism represented an alternative to the aristocracy of labor, and as such counteracted the tendency toward restrictionist sentiments among the working class. How is it that the Mine Workers were both an industrial union and advocated restrictions? Moreover, how could they do this with an immigrant base?

The answers to these questions can be found in the peculiar development of the Mine Workers. First of all, although the Mine Workers were structurally an industrial union, ideologically they were a craft union. Not only was the leadership deeply influenced by Gompers, but the rank and file thought of themselves as craftsmen working a distinctive, skilled trade. Certain work conditions in the mining industry — the blurring of lines of skill — lent themselves to industrial unionism, however. But at the same time, intense ethnic conflict precluded this form of organization. Hostility toward new immigrants was overcome only to the extent necessary for the union to maintain a strong, industrial form in order to match the power of the coal operators. Thus, not only was the Mine Workers' industrial unionism a product of sheer necessity, but so was its inclusion of new immigrant miners. The fact that the Mine Workers became an industrial union did not change its craft-orientation. Nor did the fact that new immigrants were brought into the union change its immigration policy. Once inside, new immigrants were relegated to second-class status, and had little voice in union affairs.

2. Work Conditions and Industrial Unionism

There were a number of conditions in mine work that made industrial unionization a more natural form than craft. Paradoxically, one of the most important followed from the fact that the miner typically looked upon himself as a craftsman, or skilled worker.[2] In the mines, the major distinction was between miner and laborer. Yet the laborer was not permanently fixed in an unskilled position: he was also an apprentice miner. The flow from laborer to miner was continuous, and often unregulated. As miners exhausted seams of coal, they turned over the remainder to their helpers, who then became miners themselves. Moreover, when the demand for coal was high, it was not unusual for green workers to skip over preliminary stages. Where the union and state agencies demanded a formal period of apprenticeship, it was usually put at two years as a miner's helper, a relatively short period. Even this was often ignored.

As a result of this situation, lines of demarcation between levels of skill were blurred. The pride of craft that the miner developed had a broader and more inclusive focus than that of skilled workers in most other industries. During the great Mine Workers' strikes at the turn of the century, solidarity was threatened not by divisions between miners and laborers, but between both groups on the one hand, and the distinctive, highly-skilled workers such as engineers.

The career of the lifetime miner also helped blur, lines of skill. Typically he began as a breaker boy in childhood, then progressed through the ranks until, in maturity, he became a contract miner. As he grew older and weaker, he passed back down through the ranks until, in old age, he was once again a breaker boy. Consequently, the unskilled ranks were filled not only with apprentice miners, but with men who had once been skilled miners. Their presence among the unskilled, combined with the awareness of skilled miners that they would eventually join them, helped to bridge the gap between miner and laborer.

Besides weakness of lines of skill, the intensely cooperative nature of mine work also contributed to industrial unionization. Mine workers, to a degree unparalleled in any other industry, were bound together by the mutual threat of danger. Mine work was so dangerous that even the slightest bit of carelessness on the part of one worker could result in the deaths of scores. The worst mining disasters of the period, although prepared by the negligence of mine operators were touched off by a handful of miners ignorant of danger. In May 1900, in Schofield, Utah, 250 miners were killed when a single, improperly-packed charge released deadly afterdamp. In May 1901, at Coal Creek, Tennessee, 216 miners were killed when one miner penetrated a gas-infested, abandoned mine.[3]

Under such conditions, each worker had an immediate stake in what every other worker was doing. It was essential for self-preservation that the entire work force, regardless of differences in skill, come under systematic, centralized control. In the absence of interest on the part of mine operators, this task was left to the workers.

3. Ethnic Divisions and Industrial Unionism

If lines of skill were blurred by work conditions in mining, the lines that divided ethnic groups were not. Until 1900, miners were divided into two major, hostile camps: native-born Americans and old immigrants on the one hand, and new immigrants on the other. There were further subdivisions, but this remained the most important and the most threatening to the aspirations of the Mine Workers' union.[4] The union, therefore, faced a two-fold task: First, to convince native-born American and old immigrant miners of the necessity for bringing new immigrants into the organization; second, to convince new immigrants of the necessity for joining the union, and to educate them in the basic tenets of trade unionism.

The prejudices of native-born Americans and old immigrant miners against new immigrants were in part rooted in the belief that new immigrants represented a serious economic threat to their standard of living. In the chapter on the Knights of Labor, we saw how these beliefs were given credence in the operators' use of new immigrants for strikebreaking, and for the creation of surplus labor pools.

The bitterness felt by native-born American and old immigrant miners was manifested on a day-to-day basis in racial slurs, fighting and discrimination. New immigrants were kept out of better jobs by a variety of formal and informal mechanisms, including requirements that examinations be conducted in English.[5] When ethnic barriers were broken down, as occasionally happened, it was cause for special notice. In June 1900, the *United Mine Workers' Journal* reported an instance where mutual danger generated bonds that transcended ethnic divisions. Flower-laden school children led an integrated procession in Clinton, Indiana, in memory of some one hundred miners killed in accidents over previous years. The *Journal* noted:

> It is an event of the greatest significance when white and black, Italian, German, Polander, Frenchman, Englishman, Irishman, Scotchman, Welshman, Dane and Swede . . . can assemble in true fraternal spirit here on a common Sabbath, while little children lead them, and their hearts are touched and warmed by the memories of the life and tragic death of so many of their fellow men who went to their doom by blast and accident and falling stone or coal, or crushing beneath cars or in any of the many ways that death comes to them.[6]

Such events were rare, however. A much more common response to danger, for example, was to blame accidents on the immigrant miner. That new immigrant mine workers were oblivious to danger and hazardous to work with was probably the most frequent charge levied against them by other miners. The statistics on mining accidents gathered by the Immigration Commission do not bear out this charge.[7] Nevertheless, since most immigrants were inexperienced in mining, it can be assumed that they were less knowledgeable about their work than native-born Americans and old immigrants and, consequently, less careful. Accident statistics would not necessarily detect differences in the level of precaution taken in such jobs as timbering, especially since all miners fell victim to accidents caused by careless work. Native-born American and old immigrant miners were, however, keenly sensitive to such differences. Their beliefs about new immigrant miners were dramatically reinforced by such tragedies as the Johnstown, Pennsylvania mining disaster of July 1902. At Johnstown, 130 miners were killed when two Polish miners entered a known gaseous section wearing open lamps.[8]

4. Overcoming Ethnic Divisions

By 1900, the Mine Workers' leadership was in the midst of a strenuous campaign to overcome the prejudices of native-born American and old immigrant miners. Launched in 1898 with John Mitchell's ascension to the presidency, their campaign was more a product of necessity than a conscious rejection of nativism. It stopped short of full integration of new immigrants into the union, insisting only that they be organized.

The major factor forcing the organization of new immigrants was the nature of the operators' control over miners. As in other industries, native-born American and old immigrant miners were better-off than new immigrants, and comprised something of an aristocracy of labor. Nevertheless, not only was this aristocracy a shaky one, but it was one only in a minimal and relative sense. While native-born American and old immigrant miners held a near monopoly on highly skilled and above-ground labor, they lived and worked under the most oppressive institution of contemporary American capitalism — the company town. Regulated according to the mine operators' whims, the company town represented the consolidation of political and economic control in the hands of a small but powerful, and highly visible ruling class. The anthracite coal fields of Pennsylvania, the major focal point of union effort, were almost solely controlled by a trust of nine railroads. Prior to 1900, these operators had proved impervious to strikes.

These extreme conditions forced the Mine Workers to seek allies among new immigrant miners, who by the turn of the century made up the majority of the work force. They could not challenge the comprehensive power of the operators through a craft union, which the Mine Workers' were tending to become by a combination of circumstances. The circumstances were first the predominance of new immigrants in less skilled jobs and native-born Americans and old immigrants in more highly-skilled, accompanied by the subsequent reinforcement of craft lines by ethnic divisions and, second, the union's reluctance to organize new immigrants, thus making it an organization primarily for the skilled segment.

Although forging an alliance between native-born American and old immigrant miners on the one hand, and new immigrants on the other, was essential for building a strong union, there was considerable resistance to the idea among the rank-and-file. The Mine Workers' leadership saw overcoming this resistance as its first task in organizing the anthracite fields. John Mitchell took personal charge of the organizing drive, urging the union membership to take in new immigrants. The nature of his appeal revealed the elementary hostility shown new immigrants by English-speaking miners. In an interview with William F. Leiserson, Mitchell stated that "he appealed to the native-born workers to discard derisive names like 'Hunky' and 'Dago,' and if they could not pronounce the foreigners' surname to address them by their Christian names."[9]

The culmination of this effort came with the 1900 anthracite strike, which marked the first time new immigrants were taken into the union on a large scale. Still, the results were uneven. At the close of the strike a friendly observer felt obliged to remind the Mine Workers that "the foreign-speaking element is largely in the majority, and is composed of a proud and jealous people who resent a preference shown one nationality more than another in a greater degree than the English speaking peoples."[10] T.L. Lewis, vice-president of the Mine Workers and chief organizer, reported to the 1901 convention that there still existed "intense prejudices, jealousy and discord," and "bitter feelings" among miners in western Pennsylvania. He emphasized again the importance of recruiting new immigrants, stating that seventy percent of the miners were immigrants, "the large majority of whom desire to become members of our organization."[11] In 1902 he reported that prejudice against new immigrants had subsided in Pennsylvania, although not in West Virginia.[12]

5. Organizing New Immigrant Miners

Prior to the 1900 strike, the Mine Workers' leadership feared that new immigrants would not join the union. Several months before the strike began, Benjamin James warned that in Pennsylvania, "about 75 per cent of our men here are non-English speaking, lately increased by thousands from foreign shores, and they appear to be afraid to organize, lest a repetition of the Lattimer massacre should occur."[13] Once the strike call was issued, such fears were proved unfounded; immigrant miners joined almost to a man. With the end of the strike the *Mine Workers' Journal* stated that,

> A unique page has been added to the history of industrial warfare — a page that glows with credit to the strikers. With almost as great a number as ever participated in any former strike in the history of labor troubles, with the great majority of them on strike for the first time in their lives, in a field where almost all nations are represented . . . they endure six weeks with remarkable firmness, and conducted themselves in a most orderly, peaceful manner, finally achieving an honorable and merited victory.[14]

The operators attempted to break the solidarity of the strikers by resurrecting ethnic divisions. During the 1902 strike a leaflet was circulated urging immigrant miners to "go to your priest; let them tell the mine owners that you are ready to go to work. . . . " The leaflet continued, "Your forefathers never permitted the Irish to do as they do by you . . . you have fallen into the hands of bad men, the Irish leaders, who lied to you and who coaxed you from your work so that they may be called great men." Far from being great men, the Irish leaders were "loafers and drunkards."[15]

The operators' appeals met with total failure. The immigrants were not splitting from the union, but were becoming more strongly attached to it. Foreign-language organizations that acted as union auxiliaries abounded in the strike situation. One group that developed out of the 1900 strike, the Lithuanian–Polish club of Luzerne County, gained ten thousand members within a year of its founding, and had more than six hundred delegates at its first convention.[16]

The immigrant miners also developed an intense loyalty to John Mitchell. Whenever Mitchell appeared at a strike site he was thronged by appreciative immigrant miners and their families. At the conclusion of the 1902 strike a committee representing Polish, Lithuanian and Slavic miners presented him with an award symbolizing their loyalty. In receiving it, Mitchell reflected on the union's success among them. He stated,

> When I first came to the anthracite coal fields I found the mine workers disorganized and separated by race prejudices and religious animosities. There was no unity of action, and no effective power of resistance, but now they are united; they have grown to know one another better; they recognize the idea of their interests, and are prepared to move as one man in the advancement of their common cause.[17]

6. The Union's Accommodation of Ethnic Prejudices

The resistance to bringing new immigrants into the union was accommodated by relegating them to second-class status once they were in. Initiated out of sheer necessity, the union's organizational activity among new immigrants was designed to bring them into the ranks, but not to have them play a role in decision-making. Mechanisms for limiting the participation of new immigrants existed both on the national and local levels.

Following the anthracite strikes the overwhelming majority of Mine Workers were new immigrants. Yet none of the national officers or district leaders were drawn from their ranks. New immigrants were limited to a handfull of second-level district posts. However, a sizable proportion of field organizers were new immigrants, which points out the limits of the Mine Workers' interest.

The union used foreign-language field organizers and great quantities of foreign-language literature to attract new immigrants. But its official language was English, which automatically restricted the participation of new immigrants. At the 1902 convention, T.L. Lewis pointed out that election notices for the union's national officers were printed only in English. He proposed that they be sent out in other languages also, but his proposal was defeated.[18]

The effect of the use of English on participation was clearly de-monstrated during the 1902 anthracite strike. Although new immigrants made up the majority of the strike force, and foreign-language organizers were instrumental in making the strike successful, their representatives played a negligible role in directing it. At the convention called to ratify Mitchell's arbitration plan, proceedings were conducted entirely in English. Foreign-language delegates sat quietly through the convention. Only at its conclusion were the decisions finally translated.[19]

The Mine Workers published no regular foreign-language press, despite the fact that most of its members could not read English. Their official newspaper, the *Mine Workers' Journal*, ran a Slavonic supplement briefly but dropped it in 1901 because of high expense, low circulation and advertisers' complaints. At the time, the *Journal* had close to sixteen thousand English-language subscribers and less than one thousand foreign-language.[20] The miserable showing of its supplement was probably due not so much to the apathy of the immigrant members as to the fact that it was simply a digest of the English-language section. That the union was not serious about a foreign-language press was demonstrated when its 1904 convention turned down a request by the self-supporting Italian-American miners' paper, *Lavoratoria Italiana*, to be recognized as official.[21] Other efforts to start foreign-language newspapers met with similar lack of interest on the part of English-speaking unionists.

On the local level, too, the Mine Workers' attempted to enlist the support of new immigrants without enlisting their full participation. Organizational control remained firmly in the hands of native-born Americans and old immigrants. The reports of the Immigration Commission on the mining industry reveal this fact, even though the Commission was inclined toward the union.

In one union town in the bituminous coal fields of Pennsylvania, with a Mine Workers local of 1400 members, predominately new immigrant, the Commission reported, "The control of the organization is in the hands of the Americans and the older English, Irish, Scotch and Welsh immigrants. They instruct the recent immigrants in the tenets of the union and enforce obedience to its rules and policies. . . . The older members of the union look upon the recent immigrant as a necessary evil, and so long as he abides by the rules of the organization they treat him with indifference, but any infraction is met by a demand for conformity."[22]

In the Southwest, native-born American and old immigrant members followed similar lines of action. The Commission reported, "Although there is prejudice against immigrants from Italy, Austria-Hungary, and Russia on the part of the English-speaking races, still their attitude is not openly unfriendly as long as they can control the situation, but if any of the first-mentioned immigrants try to show their power in any measure, they are usually forced into submission."[23]

7. Trade Unionism vs. Primitive Rebellion

If the Mine Workers were reluctant to give new immigrants an equal voice in union affairs, they were not averse to educating them in the principles of conservative unionism. Some years after the great anthracite strikes, John Mitchell explained how and why this was done. He said,

> The immigrants were organized first in local unions of each nationality, and an interpreter was assigned to guide and foster each local. Not understanding trade union principles, the immigrants were impatient to strike as soon as they were organized, and a great deal of pains had to be taken to educate them to the importance of being businesslike, and the necessity of building up a strong union by paying dues regularly, so that their strikes and other efforts at improving conditions might prove successful.[24]

Prior to Mitchell's time, mine workers' unions had encountered similar problems with immigrants. The Immigration Commission reported that during a series of strikes in the 1880s, in the bituminous fields of Pennsylvania, "the American and Irish leaders induced many of the immigrants to join in the strikes, but they found difficulty in restraining them from violence during the strikes and in retaining their membership after the strikes were settled."[25]

During previous decades, the 1860s and 1870s, prior to the influx of new immigrants, violence and instability were also common. At that time, however, such phenomena were characteristic of Irish immigrants — most notably, the Molly Maguires.

Sporadic outbursts of violence and ill-prepared strikes of short duration were manifestations of primitive rebellion among immigrant miners. Clearly, the Molly Maguires were primitive rebels in the full sense of the term as E.J. Hobsbawm uses it.[26] Whether the same was true for new immigrants is not so clear because of a lack of evidence regarding the traditions of the various groups. Nevertheless, new immigrant miners did exhibit a strong tendency toward pre-political, pretrade union primitive rebellion.

The primitive rebellion of new immigrants stood in marked contrast to the Mine Workers conservative unionism. Although the Mine Workers were an industrial union, their official ideologies owed as much to Gompers' AFL as to their own experiences. The union conducted its pioneering anthracite strikes with extreme caution, emphasizing the minimal nature of the miners' demands, and appealing to the good will of such public figures as Mark Hanna and J.P. Morgan. During the 1902 strike, the leadership checked efforts to extend the strike into the bituminous fields.[27] Throughout these struggles, the *Mine Workers' Journal* ran a series of bibliographical sketches of the union leadership, never failing to emphasize each one's conservatism.

At the beginning of the 1900 strike, which lasted six weeks and involved 134 thousand striking miners, the leadership showed extreme anxiety about the conduct of immigrant strikers. Above all, they feared that the rebellious tendencies of the immigrants would gain an upper hand. In September, the *Mine Workers' Journal* warned:

> On Monday morning, under the guard of this army of state troops, they will attempt to open the mines. When this attempt is made serious trouble is expected to arise, as the foreign element among the strikers is likely to overrule the counsels of the English-speaking miners and to resort to violence.[28]

Elsewhere, the *Journal* reported:

> Armed guards have been imported into the anthracite region by hundreds and this is causing much ill feeling, especially among the foreign miners. Several hundred Lithuanians, in direct defiance of the orders of the strike leaders, created disturbances about Shenandoah. . . . It is needless to say that

President Mitchell and his lieutenants deplore and decry such actions.[29]

As it turned out, the rebellion that Mitchell feared did not materialize. For a strike of such magnitude, random acts of violence were kept to a minimum. There were occasional acts of sabotage and mob action, but on the whole the strikers created little disorder. Often, they showed remarkable self-discipline. For example, at one critical point during the strike, armed deputies cordoned off a road to halt a march. Although the deputies were notoriously trigger-happy, the marchers refused to panic, but passed through their ranks with arms raised. They repeated this gesture twice more.

During the 1902 strike, which lasted five months, immigrant miners show-ed even less inclination toward violence. Although the anthracite mining communities were polarized by a thorough-going boycott, there were vitually no instances of violence. Instrumental in keeping order throughout both strike periods were the union's efforts at discipline. The union leadership not only exhorted strikers to remain calm, but called off marches when threatened with police violence, and set up union guards to protect mining property.[30]

8. Conclusion

In the year 1897, the Mine Workers were a fairly small union, with barely a foothold in the mining industry. Their ten thousand members represented only a small fraction of the hundreds of thousands of workers engaged in mining. Within a few years, however, the union had taken a firm grip on major mining centers. It grew phenomenally, to almost 200 thousand members by 1901, and more than 250 thousand by 1904.[31] Two factors help account for the Mine Workers' success. First, the union's industrial form of organization proved the proper tool for defeating the mine operators. Second, and closely tied to the first, the union was able to arouse the support and loyalties of new immigrant miners. Unlike AFL craft unions, the Mine Workers organized new immigrants — but only out of necessity. Their attempts to organize miners on an industrial basis — the only way they could defeat the operators — had ground to a halt because of their exclusion of new immigrants. Once new immigrants were accepted, they were relegated to second-class status within the union. In this way, the nativist prejudices of American and old immigrant Mine Workers' were accommodated.

Compared with most AFL leaders, the Mine Workers' leadership developed a favorable public image among new immigrants. Mitchell was especially sensitive to their needs and desires, and became an immensely popular figure during the anthracite strikes. Yet once out of range the leadership's friendliness vanished. Mitchell was one of the major AFL spokesman for immigration restriction, basing his case on the Mine Workers experiences with them.[32] In part, the leadership's attitudes reflected those of the native-born American and old immigrant rank-and-filers who had built the union in its infancy. As miners these men had developed intense hostilities toward new immigrants, and as trade unionists they were willing to let them into their organization only so long as they themselves retained control.

The leadership's attitudes toward new immigrants also reflected their own iron-clad conservatism, and that of fellow AFL officers. Ideologically, Mitchell placed himself squarely in the camp of Gompers, even though he rejected craft organization as a strategy for the Mine Workers. Mitchell conducted strikes reluctantly and cautiously, utilizing the services of the Civic Federation with pioneering enthusiasm. The tendencies toward primitive rebellion among new immigrant miners threatened the leadership's conservative unionism.

No other industrial union shared the Mine Workers' hostility toward immigrants, or its restrictionist program. The Western Federation of Miners, who confronted immigrants in much the same way as the Mine Workers, remained steadfast opponents of restrictions. The same was true for the Brewery Workers, at least until the First World War. Finally, the needle trades unions — both inside and outside the AFL — which had an immigrant base, opposed restrictions.[33] The major differences between these industrial unions and the Mine Workers were political. While the Mine Workers can with few qualifications be characterized as a conservative union, the others were socialist. By the turn of the century, socialists had become a distinct — and often separate — segment of the American working class movement. They alone carried the banner of working class internationalism, and they alone opposed immigration restrictions. The following section deals with the difficulties American socialists encountered in attempting to relate to the mainstream of the working class movement, while at the same time retaining their internationalism.

Part II.
Labor Radicals, Americanization and Immigration.

INTRODUCTION TO PART II

Until the collapse of the Knights of Labor and the rise of the AFL, Left wing elements in the American working class movement operated primarily within the movement's mainstream. Prior to that time, their relationship with the establishment trade unions had been for the most part a close and friendly one. Considering its relatively limited size, the Left contributed a large share of the leadership of the Knights, and even the AFL. Moreover, the Left best articulated the sentiments of working class internationalism. Socialist trade unionists — from the Ladies Garment Workers, the Western Federation of Miners, and initially the Brewery Workers — were the most consistent opponents of the AFL's restrictionist immigration policy.

Even within the Left wing itself, however, internationalism was subject to a severe test by the immigration question. The Socialist Party, the strongest and most viable organization ever developed on the American Left, was irreconcilably divided on this question. In large part, the roots of this division lay in the Socialist Right wing's propensity to assume a posture similar to that of the AFL. The Socialist Right, because of its connections with AFL unions on the local level, was subject to similar pressures.

Historically, the roots of the challenge to internationalism within the Left wing, can also be traced to the need for the Left to "Americanize" itself. As is often noted, the idea of socialism was originally a European import. Throughout the history of the working class movement, American workers were rarely enticed by it. Prior to the emergence of the Socialist Party, Left wing organizations were overwhelmingly immigrant in composition — usually German. In 1887, Frederick Engels warned that if socialists were to play an important role in the American working class movement,

> . . . they will have to doff every remnant of their foreign garb. They will have to become out and out American. They cannot expect the Americans to come to them; they, the minority and the immigrants, must go to the Americans, who are the vast majority and the natives.[1]

Engels' statement reflected the need for the American Left to develop an authentic national base in the working class movement. So long as the Left remained immigrant, it would be weak and isolated. From time to time the leadership of the Left — initially, of the American branch of the International, and later on of the Socialist Labor Party — recognized this fact and attempted to draw native-born Americans into their organizations. These attempts met with little success, however, and their organizations remained overwhelmingly immigrant.

Despite early rebuffs, the Left continued in its efforts to Americanize itself. The culmination of this lengthy process came with the Socialist Party, which in terms of membership and electoral support was much more native-born American than the working class. By this time it had become clear that Americanization, taken narrowly, constituted a threat to internationalism: If the Left was to become native-born American in the strict sense, it would have to reflect accurately the interests of its native-born American constituency. During a period in which nativism was strong, such as the period of "new" immigration, this meant that the Left must also tend toward nativism. In fact, a large segment of the Left did become nativist. In their attempt to Americanize, they lost sight of the internationalist goals of the Left wing, and became a caricature of their own projected national base. Americanization presented the Left wing with several critical dilemmas. First, how could it Americanize itself and at the same time retain its internationalist posture? Prior to the rise of the AFL, this did not seem to be a serious problem. As yet, working class nativism had found no major organizational medium for expression, and seemed to be be of little consequence. Once the AFL proposed restrictions, however, the problem was manifest, and socialists began to question their own internationalism. Second, how could the Left wing Americanize and at the same time orient toward the entire working class? If Engels' suggestion were followed strictly, a sizable proportion of the working class would be totally neglected by the Left. Moreover, it would mean that those workers friendliest to a socialist appeal — immigrants — would be neglected. The problem of how to take account of ethnic divisions, and which groups to orient toward, was a permanent one among the Left wing. The American branch of the International consciously chose to orient toward the major immigrant groups. The Socialist Labor Party, under the leadership of Daniel DeLeon, oriented toward native-born American workers but retained their German immigrant base. The Socialist Party oriented toward native-born Americans to the utter neglect of immigrants. With few exceptions, the Left wing made no systematic attempt to resolve these dilemmas, but adopted relatively short-sighted solutions in the context of the immediate situations. As a result, not only was the Left weakened ideologically and organizationally, but the impact of its internationalist spirit on the working class movement as a whole was also weakened.

Chapter 6.

The First International in America:

The Beginnings of an Immigrant Left Wing in the Working Class Movement

1. Introduction

The Left wing made its first significant appearance in the American working class movement as the American branch of the First International. At the time, the United States seemed a promising field for the International. The National Labor Union, headed by the internationally-minded William Sylvis, was attempting to unite all trade unions into *a* national federation. Moreover, the membership of the American working class was itself internationally-minded, having been drawn in large part from a variety of European nations. Yet compared with Europe, the International was a failure in the United States. As an organization, it barely got off the ground.

In retrospect, it is clear that the American working class movement was not yet well enough developed to support an international organization. While British trade unions had attained a high degree of maturity by 1864, the American movement was still decades away from gaining a permanent foothold in industry. The National Labor Union failed in its attempt, and so did the Knights of Labor. It was not until the American Federation of Labor arrived that success proved feasible.

Still, the American movement seemed in many respects intellectually prepared for internationalism, if not materially. The presence of large numbers of immigrants in the working class movement insured this. Yet despite their presence, the International fell short of its intellectual tasks. Although the organization achieved much considering its size, it failed to instill a durable spirit of internationalism among the workers — mainly immigrants — with whom it made contact. In part, this was due to internal factors. For one, the International's General Council in London was confused about the national composition of the American working class. Their mandates to the American branch reflected this, and impeded progress in the United States. For another, the American branch was likewise confused, but in the opposite direction. While the General Council placed too much stress on the need for a native-born American following, the American branch tended to under-emphasize this need.

More important were the external factors contributing to ideological failure. First of all, the masses of immigrant workers were not as susceptible to an internationalist appeal as the organization had hoped. Except for its activities in the National Labor Union, which were shaped to the demands of the General Council, the American branch's appeal was strictly a radical one. But radicalism was an unevenly-distributed quality among groups of immigrant workers, and most would not respond consistently. Secondly, few native-born American workers were even remotely interested in international solidarity. With few exceptions, the only native-born Americans the International was able to attract were middle-class social reformers.

Gradually, the leaders of the American branch came to recognize the inherent weakness of their position, and many retired to more limited, trade union activity. But during its brief existence the International showed in miniature most of the problems that would in future years beset the Left wing of the working class movement. These revolved around the question, how to relate politically to the movement's mainsteam? Native-born American workers were heavily insulated against a socialist appeal devised in Europe. In order to reach them, the Left would have to "Americanize" both its appeal, and eventually itself. At the same time, the Left could not afford to neglect immigrant workers, who because of their backgrounds or the conditions they currently faced, were more susceptible to a socialist appeal. This chapter explores the uncertain beginnings of the Americanization effort — an effort that eventually retarded internationalism among the Left, and contributed to the Left's ultimate downfall.

2. Immigrant Workers and the International in America

For our purposes it is convenient to group immigrants by three distinct, relevant types, active in the working class movement:

> 1. Political exiles, primarily oriented toward events in their homelands, and planning to return.

> 2. Immigrant workers with training in European labor or revolutionary movements, but primarily oriented toward events in the United States, and planning to stay.

3. Immigrant workers without training in European movements, oriented toward the United States and planning to stay.

There were, of course, other types of immigrant workers — "carpet-baggers," for example — but the above types cover those active in the movement. With respect to this typology, the following assumptions can be *made,* taking into account the historical period:

a. Political exiles were for the most part revolutionaries fleeing reactionary regimes. Their radicalism, developed out of European conditions, had little direct relevance to American conditions.

b. Immigrant workers trained in European movements were on the whole to the left of native-born American workers, under similar conditions. Many were radicals by any criteria, but although their radicalism bore a relationship to American conditions, its theoretical roots lay in European movements.

c. Immigrant workers without training in European movements were for the most part politically indistinguishable from native-born American workers, under similar conditions.

d. Proceeding from group 1 to group 3, the degree of ideological insulation from American culture decreases.

There were, of course, numerous exceptions to these assumptions. But prior to the influx of Southern and Eastern European immigrants, the rise of working class nativism, and the crystallization of an aristocracy of labor, these assumptions generally held true.

Throughout the entire period covered by this study, immigrant trade union leaders were drawn from groups 2 and 3, while immigrant socialist leaders came from groups 1 and 2. The American branch of the International followed the socialist pattern.

During its peak years, the American branch was dominated by German immigrants with considerable experience in European movements. Their strategy for instilling an internationalist spirit in the American working class movement, however, was to orient toward immigrants with negligible European experience. These comprised a large segment, perhaps a majority, of the working class. Their assumptions were two. First, they believed that for the time being, it was hopeless to try to arouse native-born American workers. Second, the leaders of the American branch felt they had ready-made access to this type of immigrant. They assumed that these immigrants retained some interest in events in their homeland; where these events were obviously subject to a radical interpretation, the immigrant became susceptible to an internationalist appeal. As it turned out, the American branch's approach to the mass of immigrants met with little success. Just as the General Council failed to develop a sense of international solidarity out of the one-sided issue of immigration, so did the American branch fail to develop the sense out of national questions. The leadership, with their theoretical backgrounds were able to envision connections between, for example, the Irish national movement and the Commune uprising. But making these connections was by no means dependent on the events alone, and to the mass of immigrants they remained discrete, and often contradictory phenomena.

The leadership's only hope for impressive ideological — or organizational — success lay in the radicalization of the working class by material and ideal conditions entirely outside the branch's modest sphere of influence. For a variety of reasons that do not require repetition here, radicalization did not take place. In negative terms, the American branch was incapable of counteracting the effects of dominant American ideology on the masses of immigrants. In time, they recognized this fact.

In the absence of any consistent response from the masses of immigrants, the International sunk its American roots among political exiles and immigrants with European experience. Because of the large exile membership, the American branch to a considerable extent took on the character of an exile organization. It was the scene of countless internal plots and intrigues.

Eventually, the organization also attracted a number of middle-class native-born American reformers.

The German leadership of the American branch soon developed a hostility to both elements, who impeded their efforts to reach the masses of immigrant workers. The leadership also fought a running battle against the General Council, who tended to view all immigrants as either political exiles or carpet-baggers. In the end, this fight was resolved by the General Council's capitulation under the dictates of political expediency.

3. Origins and Early Successes of the American Branch

The first American affiliate to the International was the Communist Club, which joined in July, 1867. Founded in New York ten years earlier, the club rejected "all revealed religion and every [doctrine] not founded upon the perception of concrete objects. It advocates the destruction of individual property, the equality of all persons, and its members bind each other to carry these maxims into practice."[1] Despite the distinctly un-Marxist character of their original program, members of the Communist Club were eventually counted among Marx's staunchest allies. Their chief spokesman was Friedrich Sorge, like most charter members a former German revolutionary.

In the fall of 1868, the Communist Club joined with the General German Workingmen's Union of New York, to organize a short-lived experiment in electoral politics, the Social Party. The Union had been formed in 1865 by Lassalleans, but by the time of its joint action with the Communist Club, the differences with the International had either been smoothed out or had disappeared. Following the dissolution of the Social Party, the Union absorbed the Communist Club and, in December 1869, became Section 1 of the International, its mainstay in the United States.[2]

Although small and exclusively immigrant, Section 1 soon transcended its limitations to become a major voice in the American trade union movement. It kept in close touch with other German-American trade unions, and was instrumental in organizing the furniture workers union.

Moreover, Section 1 developed strong ties with the miners of Pennsylvania, and with unions of shoe-makers, machinists, bricklayers and carpenters. It provided much of the early strength of the Cigar Makers' union, and became the major training ground for the founders of the American Federation of Labor. Section 1 sent delegates to every trade union conference of importance, and through its affiliation with the National Labor Union, became the International's closest link to American labor.[3]

4. Political Exiles in the American Branch

In August 1870, Section 2 of the International was formed by the merger of two New York branches of the *Union Républicain*, a French-language organization.[4] In contrast to the Germans, the French were still predominately oriented toward events in Europe. Their presence lent an exile character to the International, which had not been so noticable when Section 1 alone comprised the organization. Section 2 first gained prominence by joining with German-American trade unions in condemning Louis Napoleon's indictment of French Internationalists. Shortly after, in November 1870, the two sections issued a joint address condemning the Franco–Prussian war, and called for a mass, anti-war rally in Cooper Union. The rally, addressed by Sorge in English, German and French, was a tremendous success, publicized throughout the United States and Europe.[5] The International rapidly gained prestige among American trade unions and reform groups. In the meantime, its American leaders were already moving toward the establishment of their own central committee.

Despite the initial successes of its American affiliates, the General Council resisted the idea of a central committee. Its attitude was first expressed during a dispute which arose in the summer of 1870. The dispute concerned the powers of Robert Hume, who had been designated as the Council's propagandist among native-born Americans. Hume had clashed with General Cluseret, a highly ambitious Frenchman and some-time spokesman for the International, residing in the United States. Hume charged that Cluseret treated his colleagues intolerably, and had represented himself to American workers as the legitimate French ambassador to the United States. He demanded that the General Council appoint special French agents to propagandize among French-Americans, and to do the same for other immigrant nationalities.[6]

The General Council, led by Marx, was opposed to this plan. Eccarius replied for the Council, stating that "the International Association recognizes no special national interests among the working men who may happen to have been born in different countries."[7] Eccarius continued with a sympathetic explanation for Cluseret's behavior — a peculiar apology in view of the fact that Cluseret was in trouble with Paris Internationalists[8] — and explained that he did not represent French-American workers, but workers in France. Eccarius concluded, "We cannot admit that either French or Germans have an opposite or special interest from any other workmen, and we always urge them to take an active part in, and identify themselves with, the movement of the working men of the country, in which they reside, particularly in America."[9]

Shortly after, the General Council received another letter from Hume, this time charging that Cluseret had "proclaimed himself as a representative of the Association and established sections."[10]

The General Council responded by limiting Cluseret to the post of correspondent for the New York French section, and granting Hume credentials to establish an American section.   One member of the Council had misgivings since in applying for credentials, Hume had requested, and been given, the power to hand-pick men to organize their own sections. "No one," he warned, "could foresee what that might lead to." Eccarius suggested that such fears were groundless. Marx seconded this notion, stating that "he could only proceed according to the rules; we wanted such a man."[11]

As it turned out, Hume, probably through ignorance, did not proceed according to the rules. He printed membership cards listing himself as agent of the International for the United States, and Benjamin Lucraft of the General Council as President. Section 1 was greatly incensed and Sorge asked Marx to set matters straight. Marx replied that "Hume was empowered to carry on propaganda among Yankees, but has exceeded his powers." He promised to "submit the matter to the General Council ... with an exhibition of his cards".[12]

The incident of the membership cards highlights the precarious situation of the International in America. An association of political exiles and immigrants, it was plagued by petty jealousies and rivalries. The actual damage done by Hume was nil. In his own account of his activities, written before Sorge's charges reached the General Council, Hume stated "that he had been almost prostrate by the heat, that he was an old man and had made only two members as yet."[13] Marx brought the case to the General Council but urged no more than a gentle admonition of Hume.[14]

5. Immigrants Gain Control

While the question of who led the International in America — Cluseret, Hume, or even Osborne Ward, a native-born American reformer — was being debated, Section 1 moved to take the leadership into its own hands. Friedrich Bolte, a cigar-maker, wrote to Marx in December 1870, of their intention to form a central committee.[15] The committee was to be elected by the German, French, and newly-organized Czech sections. Marx disapproved, having been led by Siegfried Meyer, a German-American friend, to distrust the motives of Section 1. Moreover, he feared that the establishment of a central committee would only serve to increase the frequency and intensity of disputes. He urged instead that a federal council be set up, elected by convention and purporting to represent "foreign residents" only. Engels countered that he "did not think that the [General] Council had any right to prescribe forms."[16]

In the meantime, Section 1 went ahead to organize the "Central Committee of the North American Federation" of the International, and immediately began to issue statements under that title. In March 1871, the committee, through Sorge, once again applied for full recognition by the General Council.[17] By then, five new sections had been added, four of them German and one Irish, set up, according to Sorge, to "gain influence in the new combination of Irish Revolutionary Societies in the United States."[18] Despite Sorge's optimism, Marx once again was reluctant. He argued that "the question to decide was whether they were to be made a United States Central Committee or only the Central Committee of the foreign sections," and pointed out that "if we represented the German Club, the Swiss Club and perhaps a French Club here, we could not call ourselves a Central Committee for the English, the Irish and the Scotch."[19] The rest of the General Council, including Engels, by now agreed with Marx, and Sorge was instructed to call his central committee the "Federal Council or Federal Committee." This distinguished it from the Central Committees in other nations. It was to function as the "central point" for similar councils, to be set up in other areas of the United States.[20]

6. Perspectives of Immigrant-based Organizations

The attitude of the General Council toward Sorge and his cohorts followed both from a keen sensitivity to the problems of exile organizations, and a misperception of the American working class movement. The General Council understood fully well that an exile organization was a hothouse for countless plots and schemes. Located in London, they themselves were continuously snared by the intrigues of exile groups gathered from all over Europe. Moreover, the General Council recognized that the International must develop, as in England, a base among the indigenous working class before it could claim any success. As noted above, their mistake lay in confusing political exiles still oriented toward the homeland, with European immigrants oriented toward America. Political exiles could serve as the basis of a cosmopolitan organization only. But to the American branch's leadership, European immigrants, whose numbers predominated in the American working class, could serve as the starting point of an internationally-minded labor movement. Marx seemed to agree with this when he wrote to German-American Internationalists, prior to the formation of the central committee, of the importance of the General Council's agitation on the Irish question. At that time, urged,

> In America you have a broader field for work along the same lines. A coalition of the German workers with the Irish (as well as with those English and American workers who are ready to do so) is the most important job you could start on at the present time. This must be done in the name of the International. The social significance of the Irish problem must be made clear.[21]

By the time of the debate over the central committee, however, Marx seems to have restricted his view to emphasizing the importance of involving native-born American workers. It should be noted at this point that for several years the General Council had been in contact with the National Labor Union and hoped that it, rather than a collection of immigrant groups, would form the basis for an American section. The General Council did not realize that the National Labor Union itself was predominantly composed of German, Irish and English immigrants.

When the General Council refused to grant full recognition to the central committee, Sorge replied angrily, spelling out in detail the perspective of his own group. He wrote,

> We shall act according to the instructions . . . but cannot omit to make some remarks regarding the attitude of the General Council towards our organization. . . . Your communication contains the following passage: 'Still less seemed such a claim admissible in a case, where, as in the U.S., no branches of U.S. workmen do yet at all exist, but only branches formed by Foreigners residing in the U.S.' The term 'foreigner' is here undoubtedly misplaced and adopted simply by judging our situation in America (i.e., U.S.) to be similar to the situation of foreign workingmen in European countries. But this is not the case for many reasons, amongst which: (a) Workingmen from other countries arriving here do not come with the intention of residing but temporarily here; (b) They are in nowise regarded as foreigners or simple residents, but as citizens, the only distinction being made by calling them sometimes adopted citizens; (c) They not only claim to be but are *de facto et de jure* citizens of this country in full and unabridged political right; (d) They form an important and considerable part of this country's Trades Unions and Labor Societies, being well represented in every one, whilst some of the most powerful and best trades organizations in the U.S. consist almost exclusively of so-called "Foreigners," viz. the Miners'

and Laborers' Benevolent Association, the Cigar-makers' International Union, the Cabinetmakers' Societies, the Crispins, etc. The term 'foreigner' therefore does not apply to us at all.[22]

For good reason, Sorge's reply completely ignored the General Council's statement that the International had to attract native-born American workers before it could gain firm footing in the United States. Sorge realized — as did later observers — that its inability to do so was the most obvious sign of organizational failure. In Europe, the International operated from established national bases. In the United States, during Sorge's time, this was an impossible task. Not only was the trade union movement feeble, but from the International's point of view native-born American workers remained politically conservative and bereft of radical leadership. The greatest American labor leader of the period, William Sylvis, had died unexpectedly in 1869. In his absence, the American trade union movement was without a major leader in close agreement with the International's social program. As to the conservatism of native-born American workers, Engels could write two decades later, "It is remarkable, but quite natural, how firmly rooted are bourgeois prejudices even in the working class in such a young country, which has never known feudalism and has grown up on a bourgeois basis from the beginning."[23] Sorge knew this well, in 1871.

In the absence of any clear possibilities for success among native-born American workers, Sorge continued to orient toward immigrants. In the main he was unsuccessful, with the exception of immigrant workers who had gained experience in European labor and socialist movements. By Sorge's own account, the bulk of immigrant workers were nearly as insulated from the International as native-born Americans. In August, 1871, he wrote,

> The great majority of workingmen in the Northern States are immigrants from Ireland, Germany, England, etc. (in California coolies, imported under contract) having left their native countries for the purpose of seeking here that wealth they could not obtain at home. This delusion transforms itself into a sort of

> creed, and employers and capitalists, parvenus having gained
> their wealth in a former period, take great care in preserving
> this self-deception among their employees, and so the German,
> the Irish and every other laborer works on in the belief of finally
> arriving at the desired goal. ... This visionary idea has been the
> cornerstone in founding the trades-unions — in this country at
> least — whilst now it is the stumbling block over which they
> fall and perish.[24]

Sorge added that this delusion was strengthened by the existence of numerous reform parties of the ruling class, which by then were supported by the labor leadership.[25]

7. Americanization

In May 1871, the central committee in New York made its first appeal to American trade unions. The appeal contained a condensed version of the principles of the International, outlined the strength of the association "over the entire civilized world," and listed its American sections. The listing showed that Sorge had been at least somewhat affected by the General Council's criticisms; the word "German" had been dropped from four of the five German language sections.[26]

Also in May, the first native-born American section, Section 9 of New York, joined the International.[27] The General Council was delighted, but it soon became clear that Section 9's membership was far-removed from the trade union movement. This proved to be the case for every native-born American section to affiliate. Section 9 was organized by former members of an eccentric state socialist reform group called the *New Democracy.* In late 1869, the New Democracy had urged the General Council sever its ties with the National Labor Union, which it characterized as backward, and link up instead with the New Democracy. The General Council refused, explaining that:

> Our duty is to endeavor to connect and combine the various
> labor organizations all over the world, independent of any
> particular views, doctrines, or even shortcomings that may

prevail in the advocacy of labor's rights here and there. Our end is the complete political, social and economic emancipation of labor; our conviction is that this must be the work of the working millions themselves. Our main endeavour therefore must be to combine the scattered and isolated local and national movements to present an unbroken front to the enemy . . . . By what particular means the Americans choose to advance is no concern of ours. Practice will ever remain *behind* theory, and the great mass of the population moves but slowly, step by step. Provided it be in the right direction, the goal will be reached.[28]

The position of the General Council was clear: Its primary concern was with the labor movement, regardless of political backwardness. When a choice was open between a middle-class reform group that styled itself advanced, and a working-class organization that had few political pretensions, the Council chose the latter. Ironically, the very person who drafted the General Council's reply, Eccarius, later chose to ally himself with the same middle-class reformers, against Marx.

The native-born American reformers were noted for their wide variety of social panaceas. Osborne Ward, brother of the sociologist Lester Ward, once appeared before the General Council to stress the need for an international, working class cooperative. He chose the following example to make his point:

In Europe, [Ward said,] you grow wines which are an almost indispensable necessity for us in America. We suffer much from indigestion and consumption through the want of such wines. I am an engineer. The life of an engineer in America averages only 35 years of age. In France and Spain they live much longer because of these beverages which assist the digestion of food. We, on the other hand, grow cotton and other things which are necessaries for you and we could exchange without other people making a profit out of them.[29]

Among the most eccentric of American reformers were Victoria Woodhull and Tennessee Claflin, two sisters who ran a Wall Street brokerage and organized a Section 12 of the International in the summer of 1871. The sisters published their own magazine, *Woodhull & Claflin's Weekly*, which advocated a vast range of social reforms, including freedom of sexual relations. Their financial "angel" was Cornelius Vanderbilt, by then an old man. Section 12 gathered either in the sisters' brokerage house or their mansion, with meetings presided over by Stephen Pearl Andrews, expositor of Universology and prophet of the new order, Pantarchy. Another favorite was William West, a founder of the New Democracy, who traveled to the Hague Congress of 1872 to defend Section 12 from attack.[30]

8. Immigrants Versus Native-born Americans

Before long, the newly-established native-born American sections clashed with Section 1. In August 1871, Sorge complained to the General Council that, "Section 12 is rather *diligently* discussing the subject of a universal language and working through the press." Shortly after, he reported, "Section 12 is rather zealous in spreading *its* idea of the I.W.A. abroad through the medium of Woodhull and Clafflin's *Weekly* and trying to create a favorable public opinion in the circles reached by the above *Weekly*."[31] Section 12 in the meantime having developed its own contacts on the General Council, demanded independence from the central committee and even asked that it be placed in authority over the entire American branch.[32] Because Section 12 flaunted its contacts with the General Council, Sorge suspected that his own Section 1 and the central committee had fallen into disfavor. He had reason for such suspicions, first of all, because of the General Council's long-standing coolness toward the American central committee, and secondly, because of a recent adverse decision over the right of the Washington, D.C. native-born American section to operate independently of the committee.[33] Sorge believed strongly that General Council support should be given to Section 1, not 12. Otherwise, it would prove disastrous. In a report to the General Council, he stated that since the Paris Commune, the International was gaining the support of "the more intelligent workingmen" of America. "But," he warned, "if this G.C. [Central Committee] shall not lose all advantages wringing therefrom the G.C. ought to have the undivided, unequivocal, full support of the General Council!" Sorge argued, This G.C. is predominately composed of wages laborers who, working in workshops and being trades unionists, know the condition of the workingmen. . . . as well, if not better, than men who never have been active producers, or men who are not connected with either trades unions nor working-men generally. Nevertheless it appears to us that the General Council paid more attention till now to those scribblers than to the Central Committee."[34]

Marx was "greatly astonished" to discover that Section 1 "suspects the General Council of any preference for bourgeois philanthropists, sectarians, or amateur groups." He assured them that no official correspondence had passed between the General Council and Section 12, but suspected that two English members might have given them support. "Both of them," Marx wrote, " . . . are full of follies and crotchets, such as currency quackery, false emancipation of women, and the like. They are thus by nature allies of Section 12 in New York and its kindred souls."[35] Marx apparently did not suspect that Eccarius, long a staunch ally but by now flirting with Liberalism, also supported Section 12.[36] As the General Council's corresponding secretary for the United States, Eccarius was in a position to lend the reformers a great deal of prestige.

In November 1871, Section 1 brought charges against the reformers. Most concerned violations of the rules of the International. Some, however, were political, including the charge that Section 12 had violated the principles of the International by raising "the old prejudices of nativism (Know Nothingism)." Friedrich Bolte, a cigar-maker and member of Section 1 remarked, "All this talk of theirs is folly, and we don't want their foolish notions credited as the views of this society. This nonsense which they talk of, female suffrage and free love, may do to consider in the future, but the question that interests us as workingmen is that of labor and wages."[37]

Bolte's remarks set the tone for Section l's next move. Faced with the reformers' demand that equal rights for women be given precedence over labor questions, the central committee resolved that no section had a right to a delegate unless two-thirds of its members were wage-earners. The committee would henceforth be concerned with "only the labor question," and those sections that were not "to be excluded, as being strangers to the Labor movement."[38]

At this point the International in America split, on one side Section 1 and its allies, on the other Section 12 and an assortment of sections with their own reasons for splitting. The most serious loss to the central committee was that of Section 2, the first French section. Section 2 had long smarted under criticism from the Germans for their utopianism. The central committee also lost the two native-born American sections besides Section 12.[39]

In December 1871, Section 12 set up a rival central committee or Federal Council, claiming, like the original, to be the sole legitimate representative of the International. Supporters of Section 1 styled their own committee as "the party of Workingmen, demanding to treat exclusively the cause of labor," and the other, "the party of 'reformers,' demanding to treat and to talk on the affairs of the universe." Section 12 responded by branding its opponents "a set of ignorant aliens." Section 1 made a half-hearted attempt to re-unite the organization in January 1872. However, since the conditions for readmission were the same as those that precipitated the split, the attempt failed.[40]

The General Council intervened in the dispute in March 1872. By then, the International in America claimed some forty sections, with perhaps 4,000 members all told. Section 1 could count on the allegiance of only a minority of these, but its disadvantage in numbers was offset by discipline, and the support of Marx.

Marx's attitude toward the disputants followed closely a line of analysis that he had developed as far back as the *Communist Manifesto*.[41] Marx saw the International as an organization that reflected a rapidly developing maturity on the part of the working class. It represented the independent movement of the working class, while its utopian predecessors represented no more than others acting on behalf of the working class. Yet, as part of the dialectic of revolutionary movements, utopianism continually re-emerged within and in opposition to the mature working class movement. Marx saw the history of the International as a struggle of the General Council against utopian sects and "amateur experiments, which sought to assert themselves within the International against the real movement of the working class." They were antiquated forms of struggle which reappeared within the new form, the International:

> The development of socialist sectarianism *and* that of the real labor movement always stand in inverse ratio to each other. So long as sects are justified (historically), the working class is not yet ripe for an independent historical movement. As soon as it has attained this maturity all sects are essentially reactionary.[42]

While serving on the General Council, Marx had waged a long and bitter fight against Proudhonist, Lassallean and, finally, Bakuninist sects. When appraised of the situation in the United States, he assured the followers of Section 1, "Obviously the General Council does not support in America what it combats in Europe."[43]

With Marx's wholehearted support, Section 1 was certain of victory. In a series of resolutions introduced by Marx, the General Council instructed the two central committees to reunite, but under the conditions imposed by the two-thirds rule. Section 12 was suspended until the next general congress of the International, when the matter was to be finally resolved.[44]

Eccarius, along with several British members remained irreconcilably opposed to the General Council's decision. As corresponding secretary for the United States, he had favored Section 12, and concealed damaging evidence from the General Council. Moreover, Eccarius had engaged in a prolonged feud with Sorge, and inflamed passions in the American organization by spreading gossip to Section 12. In April 1871, Marx charged Eccarius with abusing his position as corresponding secretary. There ensued a highly-charged debate that lasted several weeks and ended with Eccarius' resignation as corresponding secretary. Also caught up in the turmoil was John Hales, General Secretary of the International, who had reached an agreement with Eccarius on how to conduct business with the American section.[45]

The revelation of Eccarius' activities was a severe blow to Marx. Having been accused of faithlessness, Eccarius came to believe he had been the victim of a long-standing conspiracy between Marx and Engels to undo him. Marx reminded him of their enduring friendship, and of the numerous times he had defended him from the attacks of the British General Council members. Marx wrote sadly in May 1871, "The day after tomorrow is my birthday, and I should not like to start it conscious that I was deprived of one of my oldest friends and adherents." Eccarius did not respond, and thus ended a friendship of some twenty-five years.[46]

9. Conflict Resolved

The task of finally resolving the dispute in America remained for the Hague Congress of September 1872, the last true Congress of the International, At the Hague, Marx challenged the credentials of William West, representative for Section 12's "American Confederation." His charges against Section 12 were essentially the same as Sorge's.

Marx stated:

> Section 12, founded by V. Woodhull, initially consisted almost exclusively of bourgeoisie; it agitated especially for the women's franchise and released to the English-speaking citizens of the United States the notorious appeal charging them with all sorts of nonsense; this led to the organization of various sections in that country. Among other things in it there was talk of personal liberty, social liberty (free love), dress regulation, women's franchise, universal language, etc.[47]

Marx concluded with the charge that to Section 12 the phrase "the emancipation of the working class by themselves" meant "merely that the emancipation of the working classes could not be consummated against the will of the workers themselves."[48]

Engels moved for suspension of the rules during debate over Section 12, in order to give it adequate time to defend itself. West took the opportunity to deliver a rambling, hour-and-a-half discourse which at times "caused great merriment" among the delegates.[49] He pleaded for the right of Section 12 to say what it wants, then presented his own "development and solution of the social question." West explained,

> First man is a commodity, then he becomes a wage worker, then he becomes a bourgeois — middle class man, etc. — and then man, who has advanced to bourgeois status by means of his higher intelligence, enters into general co-operation . . . [50]

West's oratory was described by an observer as "spasmodic and gesticulatory, his voice rising and falling, now a shout, now a whisper, for all the world reminding one of a veritable Stiggins in the pulpit of an indubitable Bethel."[51]

The delegates eventually grew tired of listening to West, and called on Sorge to reply. Sorge explained that "Section 12 and the free lovers" made it impossible for the International to make contact with the most important segments of the American working class — especially, the Irish. Following the line of analysis he had developed during his clash with the General Council, Sorge said, "The working class in America consists 1) of Irish, 2) of German, 3) of Negroes, and only 4) of Americans." He urged, "Give us free play and a free field, so that we can make something decent out of the International in America!"[52]

By now, leaders of the International were willing to accept Sorge's analysis of American conditions, if only for purposes of expediency. The International was in deep trouble, and so the Hague Congress gave Sorge and German-American colleagues more than they had bargained for. Not only did the Congress refuse to recognize Section 12, but it voted to move the International's headquarters to New York. Thus control of the entire organization was turned over to a surprised and highly reluctant Sorge. Marxists in the General Council were afraid that Commune refugees — Blanquists — in London would take over the fragmented and declining International if it remained there.[53] Marx and Engels planned to resign from the General Council, believing their participation had become a waste of time, but wanted to see it stay in safe hands.[54] Once in the United States, the energies of the International continued to be all but consumed in bitter fighting. Sorge resigned as General Secretary in 1874, following a prolonged fight. "With your resignation," Engels wrote, "the old International is entirely wound up and at an end."[55]

10. Conclusion

The American branch of the First International reflected many of the problems that in the future would plague attempts to develop a viable Left wing within the working class movement. Immigrant based, but failing to make contact with either the masses of immigrant or native-born American workers, the International succummed to the fate of sectarian, exile organizations. Its leaders were frustrated in every attempt to broaden their base.

The German-American leaders of the American branch were uncertain as to how to relate to the working class movement as a whole. Believing native-born American workers to be too conservative, they oriented politically toward immigrants. At the same time, however, they worked within the existing institutions of the working class movement, such as the National Labor Union. Inside the NLU, their political role was negligible.

Under pressure from the London-based leadership of the First International, the American branch took steps to Americanize itself. This was done reluctantly since, as mentioned above, native-born Americans were believed to be too conservative. Moreover, the American branch leadership believed that since immigrants made up the majority of the working class, and were the strongest supporters of trade unionism, they deserved closest attention.

During the International's life-span, there was as yet little opposition to free immigration within the working class movement. The pre-industrial craft unions that formed the backbone of the National Labor Union were concerned only with imported contract labor — a concern shared by the International. Immigration was not yet seen as a threat, nor was the image of the immigrant a hostile one. Consequently, the American branch had little reason to concern itself with the question of immigration, and at the same time felt few qualms about orienting toward immigrants.

For this period, then, Americanization — even when viewed as a necessity — did not have a negative impact on the Left wing's internationalism. Americanization and internationalism became contradictory as pre-industrial unionism faded and the AFL's new craft unionism came into prominence. At that time, the mainstream of the working class movement began to drift rapidly toward a restrictionist position. Then, the Left wing was suddenly confronted with the choice of adapting to an anti-internationalist point of view, thus closing the distance between itself and native-born American workers, or withholding its support, and increasing the distance. Americanization, originally formulated in the offices of the International, had become a dilemma for internationalists.

Chapter 7
Problems on the Left:
Americanization and Division from the Mainstream

1. Split in the Working Class Movement

Several years after the disintegration of the American branch of the International, scattered socialist forces regrouped to form the Workingmen's Party. A year later, in 1877, it became the Socialistic Labor Party, and after that, the Socialist Labor Party.[1] The SLP was the first socialist party of any significance in the United States. It represented the union of diverse groupings of socialists that had sprung up or found renewed life in the economic crisis of the mid-1870s.

In its first fifteen years of existence, the SLP made little impact on the working class movement. Its influence was limited to German-American workers, mainly in the immediate New York City area, and its membership roles fluctuated rapidly. From time to time the SLP experimented with independent electoral campaigns, usually of local labor parties. The organization supported Henry George's single-tax campaign in New York, in 1886, but within a year found itself ousted from George's party.[2]

Internally, the SLP was the scene of considerable turbulence. Continuous fighting occurred between electorally-oriented Lassalleans, and trade unionists. Organizational control swung back and forth between both groups, until the trade unionists finally seized power outright through their domination of the party press.[3]

Prior to the time the trade union faction seized control of the SLP, the party had been on fairly friendly terms with the American Federation of Labor. The AFL had been conceived by socialists and men familiar with socialism, all of them active in the American branch of the International. American socialists as a whole had either kept aloof from trade-union activity — as did orthodox Lassalleans — or joined in it wholeheartedly. There had been occasional instances of socialists' threatening the established trade unions with radical dual unionism, but these came at a time when the entire working class movement was small and unstable. Moreover, they had been limited to a few, ethnically-organized unions.[4]

Now, however, the situation was different. The SLP had taken an interest in trade unionism at precisely that time when the mainstream of the working class movement was coming of age, in the form of the AFL. The AFL was the first nation-wide labor organization to gain a permanent foothold in industry, the first to attract a mass following that outlasted depression. And, its leadership was already becoming conservative.

The architects of the AFL — Gompers, Adolph Strasser, and P.J. McGuire — had, like most Marxists, rejected a Lassallean preoccupation with electoral politics. But unlike Marxists, they had also abandoned the critical and revolutionary content of Marxism. In its place they substituted pragmatic trade unionism with relatively limited immediate goals. The SLP trade unionists, on the other hand, saw the AFL as a potential revolutionary vehicle, and were determined to make it so. It was inevitable that the two tendencies would clash.

The first major confrontation took place in 1890, when a delegate from the SLP-dominated Central Labor Federation of New York was denied credentials for the AFL convention. Gompers and the AFL Executive Committee had ruled that the Central Labor Federation was not a bona-fide labor organization, since it included direct representatives of the SLP. To support his case, he had gathered testimonials from leading European socialists. The convention backed Gompers, and the Central Labor Federation delegate was denied his seat.[5]

The second major confrontation began in 1893. At that time, members of the SLP — acting as delegates for their respective trade unions — introduced a moderately worded but substantively strong socialist resolution on the floor of the AFL convention. Among the resolution's demands was one calling for "the collective ownership by all the people of all the means of production and consumption." Radicalized by a deepening industrial crisis, the delegates passed the resolution overwhelmingly. Sent out on referendum to all AFL affiliates, the entire resolution was upheld by the vast majority of unions. On paper, then, the AFL became committed to a socialist program.[6]

As it turned out, the SLP had won only the first round. Gompers engineered a defeat of the resolution at the 1894 AFL convention, and opened a ceaseless offensive against the socialists. The socialists, in turn, managed to knock Gompers out of the presidency, but only for a year. It was not until 1902, after the birth of the Socialist party, that they were able to return to the AFL in strength.[7]

The 1894 AFL convention marked the opening of a rift between the mainstream and the Left Wing of the American working class movement. Throughout the period that socialism was a force in the movement, this rift never healed. Followers of Daniel DeLeon — the brilliant but domineering SLP leader — had already begun to leave the AFL in 1893. Now their numbers were augmented by a stream of discontented socialists, who found working within the AFL a severe blow to their aspirations for the working class movement. Their exodus was, it has been pointed out, poorly timed, for it came at a point when the AFL rank and file were highly susceptible to socialist ideas. After the socialists left, the AFL's conservative leadership remained unchallenged.

Once outside the AFL, the socialists who followed DeLeon traveled a curious route. First, they attempted to resurrect and capture the, by then, moribund Knights of Labor. After a few apparent successes they were expelled, in late 1895. Immediately, they organized a dual union — the Socialist Trades and Labor Alliance — and began an intensive campaign of villification against Gompers and the AFL. The Alliance gathered support rapidly, most notably from German trade unions in New York, the United Hebrew Trades, and other immigrant elements ignored by or dissatisfied with the AFL.[8]

Gompers' reaction was scathing. He charged that the Alliance was the creation of men who "have always been barnacles on the body of organized labor and at the most critical moments in the movement have either flunked or turned traitor — that is, if they were not traitors and paid hirelings all through."[9] At various times, Gompers accused the Alliance of union wrecking and scabbing.

Membership in the Alliance fell off very rapidly after its first year. The organization had not even enjoyed the unanimous backing of the Socialist Labor Party, and had been denounced by the strongest Left wing union in the country, the Brewery Workers. In 1904 the remnants of the Alliance — still led by DeLeon — joined the Industrial Workers of the World.

2. Americanization and Electoral Action

The Socialist Trades and Labor Alliance was the product of the keen frustration socialists felt, after failing in their efforts to move the AFL leftward.

Despite all intentions, like the American branch of the First International, they ultimately found themselves retreating to the friendlier environment of Left wing immigrant groups.

On the political field, the situation was somewhat different. Paradoxically, just at the time the trade union faction seized control of the SLP, the party began to make electoral gains. Thus the electoral orientation of the Lassalleans was continued by the new leadership, but in this case supplemented by trade union activity.[10]

To the Socialist Labor Party leadership — regardless of faction — electoral activity had always seemed a good means to Americanize the organization. An early indication of this came after the SLP had been ousted from Henry George's United Labor Party, in 1887. The SLP then formed their own opposition group, the Progressive Labor Party, to which George remarked, "It is doubtful if by any other name they will smell more sweet. ... They have also greatly crippled freedom of speech among themselves by determining to conduct their discussions in the English language."[11]

Americanization became a major strategy for the SLP. Morris Hillquit, a former party member wrote shortly after he left the organization,

> The endeavor to 'Americanize' the socialist movement is the keynote to the activity of the Socialist Labor Party throughout its entire career. ... This question was at all times the subject of the most animated discussions and heated controversies within the party, it shaped its policy, determined its actions, and was at the bottom of all its actions.[12]

Daniel DeLeon, who shortly after entering the party had taken over editorship of the SLP's English-language weekly, the People, intensified the Americanization effort. DeLeon became so skilled in editing in an American style, that his archenemy, Victor Berger of the rival Milwaukee Social-Democratic Party, invited him to edit a proposed English-language weekly.[13]

DeLeon used the columns of the *People* to reply to charges that the SLP was an alien organization. At the time of the SLP's first national campaign, in 1892, he pointed with pride to the fact that their Presidential candidate had been an Abolitionist, and their Vice-Presidential candidate was of "pure Anglo Saxon" and "genuine New England American stock."[14] DeLeon's pride — ironic, in view of the fact that he himself was an immigrant — foreshadowed the pride that the Socialist Party would discover in playing out its Americanization effort.[15] On the whole, the SLP's Americanization scheme was a disastrous failure, even in the electoral arena. Although the party gathered more than 80 thousand votes at its peak — shortly before the turn of the century — its membership remained overwhelmingly immigrant.[16] On the trade union front, its following was equally lacking in native-born Americans. DeLeon's dream of an Americanized movement remained a fiction.

3. The Socialist Party

At the turn of the century, the Left wing of the working class movement — small as it was — once again found itself fragmented. The SLP had split over the question of dual unionism. But among the various socialist fragments, there existed one which was at least attracting a relatively substantial native-born American following. That was the Social Democratic Party, which was itself the product of a recent split. The SDP, led by Eugene Debs, was the socialist remnant of the American Railway Union. In March 1900, just two years after its birth, the Social Democratic Party claimed 4500 members. By comparison, the SLP, at its peak after some twenty years of struggle, could not claim more than 6000.[17]

In July 1901, the Social Democratic Party united with a dissident, anti-dual union faction of the Socialist Labor Party. The product of this unity was the Socialist Party — the first American socialist organization not dominated by German or Jewish immigrants.[18]

With respect to the AFL and the mainstream of the working class movement, the new Socialist Party hastened to make its attitude clear. Its first convention proclaimed that the party "will take no sides in any dissensions or strifes within the trade union movement," and would extend the hand of friendship to organized labor without bias. The party envisioned a strategy similar to the German Social Democracy's "twin pillars of socialism." On the economic front, the workers' struggle would be led by the trade unions, without interference from the Socialist Party. On the political front, the struggle would be led by the party, without interference from the trade unions.[19]

As it turned out, the AFL was totally unwilling to become a pillar of socialism. Its leadership, which had often paid lip-service to socialism, moved rapidly to the right. By the time the Socialist Party came on the scene, the AFL leadership had turned against socialism.[20] Gompers not only attacked socialists individually, but he attacked the entire concept of socialism itself. In a famous speech to the 1903 AFL convention, he stated:

> I want to tell you, Socialists, that I have studied your philosophy; read your works upon economics, and not the meanest of them; studied your standard works, both in English and German — have not only read, but studied them. I have heard your orators and watched the work of your movement the world over. I have kept close watch upon your doctrines for thirty years; have been closely associated with many of you, and know how you think and what you propose. I know, too, what you have up your sleeves. And I want to say that I am entirely at variance with your philosophy. I declare it to you. I am not only at variance with your doctrines, but with your philosophy. Economically, you are unsound; socially, you are wrong; industrially, you are an impossibility.[21]

The AFL's leadership's continuing attacks on socialists — despite the Socialist Party's non-interference policy — were demoralizing and often humiliating; but they were not devastating. Despite frequent setbacks, until shortly before World War I Socialists — particularly of the Party's Right wing — were optimistic about their chances for winning over the AFL. They acted as an opposition force to Gompers, although rarely challenging the AFL's craft unionism, or its position as an aristocracy of labor. Their opposition was of a loyal variety. Primarily, it consisted of introducing socialistic resolutions at AFL conventions, and seeing them defeated.[22]

In short time, a Socialist Left wing developed in opposition to the party's neutrality on trade union questions. Perceiving the AFL's craft unionism and rightward drift as irreversible, the Left abandoned the AFL entirely. In 1905, it helped launch the Industrial Workers of the World, the most enthusiastic experiment in revolutionary unionism to date.

At the same time as the Socialist Left abandoned the AFL, the Right wing drew closer to it on the local level. Where the Right was strong — as in Milwaukee, and Reading, Pennsylvania — it relied on a trade union base. The Left, with no definable centers of working class strength, could afford to experiment with revolutionary dual unionism. The Right could not, even had it wanted to. Instead, it pressed forward with its reform program of trade union-based municipal socialism, steadily becoming embroiled in bitter conflict with the Left.

As the conflict between Left and Right in the Socialist Party deepened, the question of Americanization once again became relevant. While the Socialist Labor Party had never been able to break down the walls of isolation between itself and native-born American workers, the Socialist Party was off to a successful start. Yet to the party's left, this direction was improper. While the Right wing oriented toward AFL-organized skilled workers, the Left oriented toward the masses of unorganized, unskilled workers. These were predominately immigrants — more and more, "new immigrants" from Southern and Eastern Europe. Thus, intimately tied in with the Socialist Party's attitude toward the AFL was its attitude toward native-born American and old immigrant workers *versus* new immigrant workers.

In the context of the rise of restrictionist and nativist sentiment in the AFL — described in chapter 5 above — it was inevitable that the question of immigration itself came up within the Socialist Party. The Socialist Labor Party, isolated as it was, and drawing trade union support only from immigrant groups, was neither divided nor greatly concerned with the question of immigration. When it was brought up at AFL conventions, SLP members in attendance opposed restrictions without hesitation. For many Socialist Party members, however, there was a need to hesitate. As the Right wing developed or hoped to develop ties with AFL craft unions, it was beginning to feel a commonality of interests with them. Consequently, for the first time in the history of American socialism, the internationalist tradition on immigration was seriously threatened.

Chapter 8
The Socialist Party and Immigration: The Rise of Socialist Nativism

1. Nativism in the Socialist Party

The Socialist Party evolved its perspective on European immigration in an elusive way. Its traditions of internationalism were stronger than those of the AFL, where no less than a considerable effort had been necessary to overcome them. As with the AFL, the question of restrictions first appeared in a discussion of Chinese exclusion. Unlike the AFL, the entire Socialist debate over immigration was couched in Left wing rhetoric, with anti-internationalist positions shrouded in revolutionary-sounding Marxese. The difference was merely one of symbols, not substance. While the AFL relied on the moderate anti-capitalist language of American trade unionism to favor restrictions, the Socialist Party used the language of European class struggle for the same purpose.

The question of immigration was first raised by the Stuttgart International Socialist Congress of 1907. The Stuttgart Congress passed a resolution condemning restrictions based on race or nationality. The resolution further called for organizing immigrants for political and economic rights. The American delegation — headed by Socialist Party leader Morris Hillquit, a Centrist — were among the only opponents of the resolution.[1] When he returned from Stuttgart, Hillquit explained his position. He stated,

> The majority of American socialists side with the trade unions in their demand for the exclusion of workingmen of such races and nations as have not yet been drawn into the sphere of modern production, and who are incapable of assimilation with the workingmen of the country of their adoption, and of joining the organization and struggles of their class. ...

Hillquit concluded,

> Just what races are to be included in this category is a question that can only be decided from time to time with reference to particular circumstances and conditions of each case.[2]

Some years later, Hillquit revealed how inclusive these criteria could be. He said of the participants in the cloak-makers strike of 1910, "Like most Jewish workers they were long-suffering, meek, and submissive. But every once in a while they would flare up in an outburst of despair and revolt, and go on strike." Prior to 1910, he stated, "they seemed hopelessly unorganizable on a permanent basis."[3]

The Socialist Party's National Executive Committee and later its National Committee agreed with Hillquit that the AFL's position was the tenable one. They rejected the internationalism of the Stuttgart resolution, and instead came out for the exclusion of immigrants from Oriental and other "backward" countries.[4] In 1908, the question for the first time was put before the party convention, in the form of a committee resolution.

The resolution on immigration was reported and defended by John Spargo. In part it said,

> To deny the right of workers to protect themselves against injury to their interests, caused by the competition of imported foreign laborers whose standards of living are materially lower than their own, is to set a bourgeois Utopian ideal above the class struggle.[5]

The resolution went on to specify socialist opposition to "all immigration which is subsidized or stimulated by the capitalist class, and all contract labor immigration." It proposed that the question of exclusion based on race — primarily Asiatics — be left to the next convention, with a committee elected to study it in the meantime.[6]

In the debate that followed, no really clear divisions emerged based on the resolution. Its focus on contract labor was reminiscent of the First International and pre-industrial craft unions. Not relevant in any clear way to current conditions, it could attract both opponents and supporters of restriction or exclusion. One delegate, a staunch opponent of exclusion, began his statement, "I am in favor of the resolution," and ended, "so far as I am concerned, my yellow working wage slaves and comrades, we will stand or fall together."[7] He was followed by Ernest Untermann, a militant racist, who concluded his statement, "I am determined that my race shall be supreme in this country and the world. For this reason I am in favor of the report adopted by the committee."[8] Moreover, the resolution was opposed by both opponents and supporters of restriction or exclusion. Sol Fieldman opposed it because the workers of the world are equal, and Socialists should not believe "that the American workingman needs to make a study of the yellow workingman."[9] Max Hayes, a leader of the Typographers union, opposed it because he wanted "immediate action here and now in favor of the exclusion of the coolies from Japan and China."[10]

But even though the nature of the resolution was elusive, the debate itself began to touch on the fundamental question of nativism and racism *versus* internationalism. Victor Berger, a racist, speaking for exclusion, made the homey suggestion, "Because your neighbor's house is burning, shall you set your own house on fire? No, say I. Defend your own house and then help your neighbor; that is the way."[11] Untermann — a leading translator of Marx and Engels — agreed: "I believe in the international solidarity of the working class. . . . But I do not believe in international solidarity to the point of cutting my own throat."[12] The most eloquent defender of internationalism in the debate, Barney Berlyn, said ". . . if we permit ourselves to go to work and tack amendments to the proposition of 'Workingmen of all countries, unite' — if you tack amendments to that, then tack a clause to the name of the Socialist party, the words, 'A damn lie."[13] (The minutes record "A d__ lie.") The nativists replied that the famous Marxist slogan did not mean that workers should all come to America. It did not mean "workingmen of the world rotate."[14] Max Hayes explained that had he investigated conditions on the Pacific Coast, "Karl Marx would be likely to change his tactics on the question."[15]

The Spargo resolution was adopted by voice vote. The convention elected four exclusionists — Ernest Untermann, Victor Berger, Joseph Wanhope and Guy Miller — and the equivocal John Spargo to the permanent committee on immigration.[16]

At the 1910 party congress, the division between the racists and nativists on the one hand, and the internationalists on the other became more clear. The committee report and the statements supporting it were prime examples of racism and nativism couched in Left-wing rhetoric. Orientals should be excluded, the report stated, because their backwardness makes them "a menace to the progress of the most aggressive, militant and intelligent elements of our working *class* population." Oriental immigration would relegate "the class war to the rear " by weakening labor organizations and increasing race conflict.[17]

The report made no specific mention of European immigration.

John Spargo submitted his own minority report, which quoted the entire Stuttgart resolution and went on to call for breaking down the racial barriers that divide the working class. But once again, he equivocated. Toward the end, the resolution specifically disagreed with the Stuttgart position that exclusion based on race is necessarily "in conflict with the principle of proletarian solidarity." It stated that if a race menace our standard of living, or our democratic institutions," then the Socialist Party "would be compelled, however regretfully, to stand for total exclusion.[18] Spargo felt that current Asiatic immigration was too low to warrant exclusion — but the Chinese Exclusion Act was in effect!

Although the reports and debate focused primarily on Oriental exclusion, there were numerous references to Southern and East European workers. One delegate reminded the congress of the ignorant protests of Italian and Sicialian immigrants, and their divisive influence in the trade unions.[19] A spokesman for the Polish language federation warned, "this talk about America for the Americans is simply proving to the Americans that you are determined to fight the foreign elements of this country and exclude them from the shores of America."[20] Other representatives from foreign language federations feared that restrictions might be extended to people from their homelands.[21] John Spargo explained that "if today you vote Asiatic exclusion, next time you will be voting Italian exclusion or Hebrew exclusion."[22] Several of the militant racists, however, had friendly remarks for the new immigrants. Ernest Untermann contrasted the relative case with which Sicilians, Italians and Greeks were organized with the difficulties encountered with Orientals. But in the same speech — meticulously woven into an anti-imperialist context — he sounded the universal, nativist slogan, "Get out of America and give it back to the Americans."[23] Victor Berger stressed the fact that all European immigrants could be assimilated over time and were welcome. He mentioned the opposition of the German Social Democracy to coolie labor and attacked the notion that "we should have the coolies."[24] But while Berger limited himself to denouncing Asiatic coolies at the 1910 congress, elsewhere he was more inclusive. In June, 1911, before the House of Representatives, he referred to "Slavonians, Italians, Greeks, Russians, and Armenians" as the "modern white coolies" of the steel industry, who have "crowded out the Americans, Germans, Englishmen, and Irishmen."[25]

Early in the debate over the resolutions, Morris Hillquit introduced a substitute. He correctly pointed out that both reports agreed in principle to the exclusion of races as such. "To that," he said, "I am opposed."[26] His resolution was brief. It began:

> The Socialist Party of the United States favors all legislative measures tending to prevent the immigration of strikebreakers and contract laborers, and the mass importation of workers from foreign countries, brought about by the employing classes for the purpose of weakening the organization of American labor, and of lowering the standard of life of American workers.[27]

David Shannon accurately comments that this "might have been written by an AFL convention."[28]

But Hillquit's resolution went on to say,

> The party is opposed to the exclusion of any immigrants on account of their race or nationality, and demands that the United States be at all times maintained as a free asylum for all men and women persecuted by the governments of their countries on account of their politics, religion or race.[29]

Just as in 1908, the resolutions drew confused support. The majority report attracted only racists. But Spargo presented a solidly internationalist defense of his resolution, and it drew support and fire from both sides. The same is true of Hillquit's substitute, which eventually the congress adopted by a narrow margin.

Seen in the context of AFL policy, the Hillquit resolution could have meant no less than restrictions on Southern and East European immigration. As one delegate pointed out, the resolution "will save the face of the majority report in this congress."[30] The first half was strictly AFL. Of the second half, only the phrase pertaining to exclusion based on race or nationality was uniquely internationalist. Yet even the original committee report claimed to advocate "unconditional exclusion" of Asiatic races "not as races per se," but rather because they came from backward places.[31] (It is interesting to note that these backward places included Japan.) The AFL view was that all unskilled immigration was specifically brought about for the purposes of weakening organized labor and lowering the standard of living. It followed that the "new" immigration from Europe must be limited or stopped.

Eugene Debs was outraged by the party's debate over immigration. His views were published in the *International Socialist Review* shortly after the congress — which, typically, he did not attend. Debs felt that the debate betrayed capitulation to the AFL — "civic federation unionism." He called it "utterly unsocialistic, reactionary, and in truth outrageous," and warned:

> If Socialism, international revolutionary Socialism does not stand staunchly, unflinchingly, and uncompromisingly for the working class and for the oppressed masses of all lands, then it stands for none and its claim is a false pretense and its profession a delusion and a snare.[32]

The charge that the opponents of free immigration were simply capitulaters to the AFL was a common one during the congress itself. One delegate saw "some sort of effort to sweeten our program for the A. F. of L."[33] Another claimed, "it is the beginning of catering to the demands of the A. F. of L . . . ."[34] Frank Cassidy said, "We are posing as the champions of the working class. But you are kowtowing to the American Federation of Labor . . . " He asked, "Why must we crawl on our bellies to Sam Gompers?"[35] Ernest Untermann replied to these charges in his summary:

> We are not toadying to the American Federation of Labor.
> We are scientific investigators charged by the Socialist
> Party with the Analysis of a certain problem . . . If Gomp-
> ers or the American Federation of Labor adopts a policy
> which is in the interests of the working class, then the
> Socialist Party will work with them, no matter if we are
> charged with toadying to them.[36]

Untermann went on to say that if the AFL advocated a policy which was in the interest of the capitalist class, the party would "oppose them uncompromisingly."[37]

Whatever the motivations, the lines of division between racists and nativists on the one hand, and internationalists on the other were becoming clear. The division did not follow regional lines, even though frequent reference was made to the Pacific Coast. The Washington state organization instructed its delegates to vote for exclusion, but the Portland local opposed it.[38] Nor was it based on native-born Americans vs. immigrants. Berger and Untermann, for example, were immigrants, although Berger came to this country, he points out, "imbued not only with Socialism but also with the right kind of Americanism."[39] Nor was it based on rural–urban split. Surprisingly, some of the most militant opponents of exclusion came from farm areas. Perhaps the most moving speech for international brotherhood came from a Missouri delegate, W.W. McAllister, who said:

> When I sat down on my plow beam and studied this thing over,
> there was a mental picture that came to me, and the Chinese
> came to me and the Japanese came to me, and the nationalities all
> came around me in that old field on the Ozark Mountains, and I
> said 'We are all of one blood.' I went back home and told the
> folks, and for twenty years I have been preaching the doctrine of
> human solidarity of the laboring class of people all around the
> globe; not here in Chicago, not down in Missouri, not here in
> Illinois, but as far as the sin of capitalism extends, the solidarity of
> every man, woman and child.[40]

Nor was the division based on class. Both sides were supported by "blanket stiffs," trade unionists, editors and lawyers.

The lines of division followed the Left—Right split in the party. The Right wing were municipal socialists, on the whole friendly or at least neutral toward the AFL. Among them were the racists and nativists. The municipal socialists favored an end to free immigration. The Left wing were industrial socialists, generally hostile toward the AFL but friendly toward the I.W.W. and revolutionary industrial unionism. They favored free immigration.

During the debate on immigration, Ernest Untermann charged that "The comrades allied with the I.W.W." led the opposition to the majority report.[41] He was certainly close. At the 1910 congress, the party debated its traditional "no interference" attitude toward the AFL. Frank Cassidy introduced a militant resolution calling for socialist endorsement of industrial unionism.[42] Of those voting, every one of the delegates who had spoken out for restricted immigration voted against Cassidy's resolution. They numbered fifteen in all. Of the ten delegates who had spoken out against restricted immigration, seven voted for the Cassidy resolution. The voting was essentially the same on a milder resolution endorsing industrial unionism.[43] Both were defeated overwhelmingly as the party reasserted its "no interference" attitude.[44]

By 1912, the party position on immigration had crystallized. In full agreement with the AFL, its coverage extended to new immigrants from Europe. The Right wing was in control of the organization, and had used it to their advantage. The 1912 party convention heard a report by the Committee on Immigration which, as Ira Kipnis says, "made the 1910 majority report seem pro-Asiatic in comparison."[45] They also heard a one sentence minority report that simply endorsed the Stuttgart resolution.[46] But there was no debate, and the convention accepted both reports by voice vote.[47] The 1910 Hillquit resolution remained official party policy. Nevertheless, the 1912 Socialist Campaign Book — distributed to party workers throughout the country — gave no hint of this. Edited by municipal socialist theoretician Carl Thompson, the Campaign Book instead filled its section on immigration with relevant exerpts from Robert Hunter's writings on poverty. Hunter was also of the Right wing, and his Campaign Book exerpts advanced the proposal that immigration was a product of two forces: employers seeking cheap labor and steamship companies seeking passengers. Hunter told of agencies established in Europe "for the purpose of making the ignorant peasantry believe fabulous stories of wealth to be had in America." Then he warned that unskilled labor is already too plentiful," and concluded:

> Immigration presents for our serious consideration a formidable array of dangers. It is unnecessary to summarize the facts and the arguments which have been given. These are the two things which, of all that have been stated, seem the most important; the likelihood of race annihilation and that possible degeneration of even the succeeding American type.[48]

The following two sections are relatively detailed explications of municipal and industrial socialism in the Socialist party. An attempt is made to show how these two forms of socialism produce divergent perspectives on immigration. The first focuses on the development of municipal socialist politics in the Wisconsin party, by far the strongest section of the Socialist Party. The second is a more general treatment of the party Left wing.

2. Municipal Socialists and Immigration

No other socialist organization in America could boast of the lasting strength and deep roots of the model for municipal socialism — the Social Democratic Party of Wisconsin, centered in Milwaukee.[49] And outside the Socialist Labor Party, no other socialist organization was shaped so thoroughly by one man — Victor Berger.

Victor Berger was an Austrian immigrant who had studied at the universities of Vienna and Budapest before coming to America as a young man in 1879. He settled in Milwaukee, a city largely German and with a long tradition of mildly-socialist Turn societies. After a brief fling, with the single-taxers, Berger became a socialist and was elected president of the influential South Side Turnverein, which under his leadership became known as the "Red Turn Society." In the late 1880s he became president of the entire Wisconsin district of turners. In 1893, Berger was appointed editor of the socialist tri-weekly *Milwaukee Arbeiter Zeitung* and immediately transformed it into the daily *Vorwärts*, a vigorous but reform-oriented propaganda organ aimed at trade union support.[50] The very first issue of the *Vorwärts* stated:

> ... In formulating our demands, we are obliged to take many things into consideration. To those who regard us as being too moderate, we reply that if you demand too much at one time you are likely to get nothing. ... A daily paper ought not let out of its sight even for a moment the real sentiment of the masses. Nothing more ought to be demanded than is attainable at a given time and under given circumstances.[51]

These words signalled the arrival of Victor Berger, and the narrow sentiment they expressed became the touchstone for municipal socialism. In June 1897, Berger helped found Eugene Debs' Social Democracy of America. In July, Branch One of the Social Democracy was established in Milwaukee, bringing together a number of unaffiliated socialists, many of them trade unionists. Within a month, the Milwaukee Federated Trades Council, comprising most of the city's unions, endorsed the Social Democracy by a unanimous vote.[52] Early in 1898, the Council — along with many independent unions — elected delegates to Branch One's first city convention. Debs' Chicago-based paper, the *Social Democrat* noted,

> The significance of this will be seen when it is remembered that the S.L.P. in its guerilla warfare on organized labor has made the name of socialism odious to a good many working-men. Nevertheless, when labor finds Socialism put forward by a strong, respectful and thoroughly determined American party, it hastens to endorse the movement.[53]

Berger's organization ran its first candidates — all connected with the labor movement — in 1898, but despite union endorsement received only 2400 out of over 44,000 votes. They were undaunted, however, and the *Social Democrat* ran the headline, "The Social Democrats of

Milwaukee Deal the Cohorts of Capitalism a Staggering Blow in the Municipal Election."[54]

Soon after the municipal election, Berger helped split the Social Democracy of America. He led a group of socialists out of their national convention, in protest of the utopian colonization schemes the organization favored — schemes that never had a hearing in Milwaukee. The colonizers fired a parting shot at the dissidents that proved to be ironic in Berger's case. With a strong measure of racism and nativism they said:

> Delegates Winchevsky, Hourwich, Barondess, Levin, Kuhn, Hunger, Moerschell, and Berger were among the bolters. Comment is superfluous. [55]

The dissidents formed themselves into the Social Democratic Party of America, and the Milwaukee Social Democracy — now with ten branches — pledged themselves to the purified movement.[56]

In July 1901, the Social Democratic Party of America combined with the outlawed "kangaroo" faction of the S.L.P. — led by Morris Hillquit — to form the Socialist Party. Victor Berger's Social Democratic Party of Wisconsin joined the Socialists as an autonomous state affiliate, retaining both its traditional name and politics. Debs' weekly newspaper — now called the *Social Democratic Herald* — was shortly thereafter moved to Milwaukee, where it became a mainstay of Victor Berger for a decade. Berger's acquisition of the *Herald* partially fulfilled a longstanding desire: to break down the barriers between European socialists and American society with an English-language newspaper. The *Herald's* politics became identical with Berger's. The second Milwaukee issue said, "Our aim being the Social Democracy, we . . . cannot go any faster than the Demos, the people, will permit."[57]

Between their first municipal election campaign and the acquisition of the *Herald*, Berger and the Social Democrats had made an intense effort to link solidly with the trade unions. In the spring of 1899, the Federated Trades Council elected an executive committee composed entirely of socialists, including Berger, a typographer. They followed a prudent policy, recognizing that some elements in the unions were anti-socialist.

Still, the Social Democratic city convention of February 1900, passed a resolution requiring all its members to join trade unions where possible, and branding "as traitors to the cause of labor all those labor-leaders who . . . sell the working people to the Capitalist parties." The Federated Trades Council appointed a special committee to visit all the local unions to propagandize for Social Democracy. The committee was always well-received, and various unions officially recognized the Social Democratic Party as the Union Labor Party. The Trades Council endorsed the Social Democratic city ticket of 1900 — all trade unionists — even though a split in the labor movement was threatened. The Social Democrats campaigned with such slogans as, "Trades unionism is the class struggle on the economic field. Trade union politics is the class struggle on the political field. Paste this in your hat brother union men." More and more, Social Democratic and trade union politics overlapped. Much of the political program of the Trades Council and also the Wisconsin State Federation of Labor was a direct copy of the Social Democratic program. Finally, when Berger's *Social Democratic Herald* appeared in Milwaukee, the Trades Council endorsed it as its official publication. Without trade union support — money and subscriptions — the paper would have collapsed. In January 1902, Berger claimed that "there is no city in the country where trade unionism and the Social Democracy have become so thoroughly merged." The link between the unions and the Social Democratic Party had been forged; over the years it was strengthened. The unions gave regularly to the party in loans and donations, supported its candidates exclusively and helped finance the Social Democratic Publishing Company. By 1910, the Milwaukee Social Democratic Party — now a mass organization commanding over 20 thousand votes — had become the political arm of the trade union movement.[58]

Victor Berger was reformist, and so was his party. But the Social Democrats never failed to distinguish between the ultimate goal of their reforms, and those of the capitalist parties. In one of his first articles for the *Herald,* Berger explained,

> The Socialist party in this country must be a party which
> will take the cooperative commonwealth as the guiding
> star, and by means of every kind of real, not pretended
> social reforms, gradually work over our present capitalist
> state into the socialistic society.[59]

The Social Democrats consistently refused to participate in voluntary civic reform projects pointing out that the very leaders of reform projects also headed the organizations most in need of it. They even welcomed the prospect of fusion between the major capitalist parties, since that would draw the battle lines more distinctly. In their early municipal campaigns, the Social Democrats did not dwell on personal graft, but pointed out that under capitalism, "public office has become public graft" and, "anyone who wants to abolish corruption entirely must be in favor of the total abolition of the capitalist system."[60]

When the local issue was corruption, Berger at first felt uneasy about increases in the ranks of the party — he did not welcome non-socialists, for the distinctions between Social Democratic and capitalist reforms were, he felt, real.[61] Morris Hillquit describes a 1906 conference, held in Connecticut, of some of the nation's most prominent reformists and muckrakers. Berger attended, and the discussion went on for days. Finally, one night, Hillquit says,

> Victor Berger was holding forth, He spoke loudly and
> emphatically in condemnation of the existing order,
> property rights, and system of law. 'They are your laws,'
> he exclaimed, turning to the group of his listeners. 'We
> abhor them. We obey them because you have the power
> to force them on us. But wait until we have the power.
> Then we shall make our own laws and, by God, we will
> make you obey them!

Hillquit reports,

> An embarrassed silence fell on the gathering. The discussion came to an abrupt end. [62]

Berger had other moments of militancy, too. One that he soon regretted came in July, 1909, when he wrote in the *Herald:*

> And in order to be prepared for all emergencies, Socialists and workingmen should make it their duty to have rifles and the necessary rounds of ammunition at their homes, and be prepared to back up their ballots with bullets if necessary. [63]

The capitalist parties immediately picked this up and flaunted it before the citizenry. The Social Democrats simply refused to reply to their charges. [64]

But although the hearts of the Social Democrats remained fixed on their ultimate goal, the cooperative commonwealth, their vision of what was possible for the present became more and more restricted. Like all municipal socialists, Victor Berger believed that no one would trust workers to rule the nation if they could not first prove they could run cities. [65] But while national workers' rule ushered in the cooperative commonwealth, local workers' rule meant no such thing. Berger correctly repudiated the notion that a socialist society could be built in one city; any administration was severely restricted in what it could accomplish, although a socialist administration would go much farther than a capitalist one. The outside limits, as Berger saw them, were municipal ownership of utilities — *not* manufacturing industry — with union wages for city employees, police protection for strikers, a comprehensive welfare program including free medical clinics and municipal work programs with high wages for the unemployed, and so forth. Yet even these outside limits did not by Berger's own admission approach the cooperative commonwealth, nor did their program for the state. How, then, could successful municipal socialism serve as evidence that the cooperative commonwealth would work? It couldn't, and so the Social

Democratic administration of Milwaukee served for years as merely a model of good, clean government, its program to be imitated by capitalist reform parties throughout the nation. This gradual restriction of vision — which proceeds whether in or out of power — marks the retreat of municipal socialists from a broad, international socialist perspective. From the beginning, the Milwaukee Social Democratic program concentrated on fairly specific reforms, designed for workers. But very early in the party's history, Berger made overtures to small businessmen — without, however, changing the program.[66] Later, dissatisfied with two poor showings at the polls, the Social Democrats began priming for the 1902 elections by catering to some more conservative elements in the population. The *Herald* stated:

> Capitalism will not vanish in one day, in one year or in one decade. Even after the triumph of the proletariat, the commonwealth cannot take upon itself all kinds of production. ... It is not necessary that all industries be immediately taken over by the Socialist government.[67]

The party platform was virtually the same as for previous elections, with one significant exception: a paragraph concerning corrupt municipal government was inserted in the preamble.[68] In 1904, when Berger himself ran for mayor, two more items were added to the preamble. One concerned the operations of the grand jury, and the other explained that a Social Democratic victory would not mean socialism, but only a step in that direction.[69]

In 1904 the Social Democrats got more than 15 thousand votes. They were getting close to victory, and genuine opportunism began to grip them. Berger had the party scrap its major traditional demand — municipal ownership of public utilities — for the 1906 election, and substitute instead one calling for closely-supervised franchise for private corporations. With victory imminent, the Social Democrats evidently felt they they should adjust to the realities of administration by promising only that which was immediately realizable. Furthermore, they were becoming anxious for city power, and wanted to attract enough businessmen and professionals to push them over the hump. They didn't win, but experienced a reversal.[70]

This only caused the Social Democrats to redouble their opportunism. The 1908 city platform concluded that all its measures,

> . . . benefit not only the wage working class but the whole people, and while the working people are the banner bearers in this fight, in the last analysis everybody — the merchant, the professional man and the small shopkeeper — will profit thereby. Therefore, we invite every honest and well meaning voter, without regard to occupation, race or creed to join in our undertaking for the emancipation of mankind.[71]

Thus class consciousness was pushed off the political stage. In 1909, in a special city-wide election for a vacated alderman seat, the Social Democrats for the first time appealed for votes on the basis of the man himself, rather than the party.[72] Their candidate won, marking their initial city-wide victory, and anticipating their vast sweep in 1910.

By this time, even some of the anti-Socialist press was no longer frightened by the Social Democratic Party. Outraged by smear attacks from the capitalist parties, one daily paper defended them by asking:

> Who are these Socialists that so frighten our monopolists and professional politicians? . . . They are workers and home owners, and have a stake in the community.

The editorial continued.

> Instead of being a menace, they are one of the chief sources of its prosperity. In this connection we need not consider Socialism whatever. For it is not within the power of the Socialists of Milwaukee to enact Socialism — the most that they could do, even if given a free hand in municipal affairs, would be to work a program of moderate reforms . . .[73]

The same growth of opportunism was manifested in other municipal socialist campaigns. During the 1906 "Socialism and Hillquit for Congress" campaign in New York, socialism gave way to an emphasis on the integrity of an attorney worth $100,000.[74]

Throughout its early history, the Social Democratic Party was rapidly developing into a mass, working-class movement. Its branches held regular political discussions, and trade unions took up the study of socialist economics. The party saturated working-class districts with socialist literature. By 1908, within 48 hours the party could propagandize throughout the city their position on any political question that came up. They had their own printing plant and bindery, and used a tightly organized, volunteer "Bundle Brigade" to speed literature to every home, in the proper language.[75] Every party member was a party worker. Berger was a master organizer; no socialist in the country could approach his genius in such affairs.

With perfect justification, Victor Berger often bragged to his Socialist Party comrades that his was the only section of the party with a solidly working-class social base. Yet, it stood at the extreme Right of the Socialist Party. This can be partly explained by the nature of their working-class base: the Social Democrats were tied to the established trade unions — mostly AFL — of the organized working class. Therefore, the question of how the working class was to carry out the economic — as opposed to the political — struggle was already settled. The Social Democrats believed the trade unions carried out the economic struggle in their established patterns; there was no issue here. The party program rarely referred to the labor movement, and when it did, it specified the established trade unions. Never was the plight of the unorganized worker as such brought up.

On the national level of the Socialist party, municipal socialists generally favored a policy of non-interference in trade union policies. They were against both a condemnation of craft unionism and an open endorsement of industrial unionism. Inside the AFL, they led fights against the Gompers leadership, but they never challenged the organization's craft-orientation. This refusal to disrupt the AFL flowed naturally from their responsibility to it, by virtue of their participation and leadership in it. And nowhere was this responsibility so great as on the local level, especially in Milwaukee.

The Social Democratic Party was a labor party. But even though there was great overlap between the party and the trade unions — in leadership, rank and file and politics — the party never tried to control the trade unions. It kept trade union questions distinct. Likewise, the party always maintained its independence from the unions. Still, the unions formed its base and made it a mass workers' movement.

But while Victor Berger built this mass workers' movement, he also built an electoral machine. Besides their active working-class base, then, the Social Democrats developed another: their voting base. The two are not always opposed. However, in their anxiety for electoral victory, the Social Democrats chose to expand their voting base by incorporating middle-class elements into it. And they did this, not by trying to educate middle-class elements in Social Democratic politics, but by sacrificing their program bit by bit. By attuning themselves to middle-class consciousness, they could not but fail in their attempt to elevate working-class consciousness along socialist lines. Despite Berger's early intention to reap only genuine Social Democratic votes, the party was swept to victory by spurious ones. Their spurious voting base became more important than their social base. Thus the Social Democrats sacrificed their working-class orientation and with it their basic socialist principles.

Many factors lie behind the hostility displayed toward the new immigrants by municipal socialists in the national party. But the most prominent ones are linked directly to their political history and development.

Municipal socialists throughout the country tried to develop the Social Democrats' close ties to the trade unions. Most could only wish they had them, but even so they began to absorb the limited perspective of trade unionism, at least in anticipation; wherever socialists are linked to trade unions, they must share at least part of the perspective of the unions. For the municipal socialists, this was especially important. Even where they had the opportunity as in Milwaukee, they were unwilling to *broaden* that perspective through aggressive leadership. Instead, they chose to relegate it to the economic dimension of their dichotomy, economic vs. political struggle. Aside from effecting a few reforms, the municipal socialists never did anything extraordinary in the AFL other than challenge its conservative leadership. For the most part they remained officially neutral on the question of how to organize the unskilled, mainly immigrant workers. That was part of the economic struggle.

Similarly, the question of immigration manifested itself in economic terms. The trade unions saw immigration as an economic threat and so, then, did the municipal socialists. When Untermann told the 1910 Socialist Party Congress that the pro-restriction forces were not selling out to Gompers, but their positions merely coincided, he was probably telling the truth. The municipal socialists felt they were expressing the genuine economic interests of trade unionists. They were in profound agreement with those interests and were incapable of viewing immigration in any way distinct from the AFL.

Their preoccupation with the political dimension of the dichotomy meant that the political struggle came to be everything for the party. Thus they organized to get out the vote more than anything else. In New York, municipal socialists chased votes.[76] In Milwaukee, they built a machine, and Victor Berger was its boss. The municipal socialists then looked upon the new immigrant merely as voting booth fodder. Winfield Gaylord — a former Congregationalist minister and one of Berger's right-hand men — told the 1910 Socialist Party Congress this revealing story about the Social Democratic electioneering:

> I went down to the Italian ward and spent the whole of election day there watching to see that those crooked Irishmen did not lead the Italians around by the nose. Victor Berger took an automobile and went from one Polish precinct to another to see to it that those same Irish politicians did not lead the Poles around by the nose.[77]

By 1916, after working with Berger for several years, A.M. Simons could complain that the Socialist party was "today little more than an organized appetite for office — a Socialist Tammany, exploiting the devotion of its members instead of the funds of corporations, for the benefit of a little circle of perfectly honest, but perfectly incompetent and selfish politicians."[78]

The municipal socialists became so caught up with local campaigns and problems that the notion of an international movement began to fade. As their focus narrowed they reflected more and more the sentiments and interest of their local constituencies. Further, they sacrificed principles and diluted their programs, and thereby decreased their independence even more. The municipal socialists continued to look to European parties as models, but rejected their internationalist proposals such as the one on immigration at the Stuttgart Conference. They empha-sized the immediate, sectional interests of people at home before all else, and thus enhanced the growth of working-class nationalism. From where they stood immigration seemed an invasion from foreign soil, and they wanted it stopped.

Not all of the party's municipal socialist elements developed in the same way as Berger's Social Democratic Party. In Reading, Pennsylvania, another major source of municipal socialist strength, the party's reform program retained its working-class flavor. Yet in most instances, the primary ingredient in municipal socialism's opposition to immigration was present: orientation toward the AFL. The only notable exception to municipal socialism's AFL-orientation was Syracuse, New York. There, the party developed along purely middle-class reform lines, without a working-class base. Elsewhere, as James Weinstein has shown, municipal socialists worked closely with AFL locals, and put up election slates of trade unionists.[79]

3. Industrial Socialists and Immigration

It is somewhat difficult to characterize the politics of the party Left wing prior to 1919. The Left wing lacked the extensive press and propaganda machinery of the municipal socialists. It derived its support from very diverse sources — as diverse as the state parties of Oklahoma and Michigan. Until the Moyer–Haywood–Pettibone case of 1906–7, the Left had only one leader of national fame. That was Eugene Debs, and he usually refused to take part in the fights within the party.[80] But the Left can be characterized accurately on one point: An uncompromising hostility toward the AFL, and the belief that revolutionary, industrial unions were an indispensible element of the struggle for socialism.

The industrial socialists were alarmed by the frankly opportunist politics of municipal socialists, whom they called "sewer socialists." They believed that orienting toward middle-class reform votes constituted an outright betrayal of the working class. Their answer to reformist electoral politics was — with some significant exceptions — to concentrate on organizing the working class within revolutionary unions such as the I.W.W. They put relatively less emphasis on electoral action, although they were pleased with the party's municipal victories because socialist city governments, they felt, made their tasks easier. Their fundamental criticism of municipal socialist campaigns was that they ignored the class struggle, and instead tried to patch the rotten cloth of the capitalist order. Frank Bohn said of the 1910 Milwaukee victory:

> Some of our Socialists go into their closets and pray for a system of society the direct opposite of all that capitalism stands for, and then, coming into the open, drag out the de-cayed carcass of our Constitution and law, clothe it in the robes of divine right, and worship the rotten fabrics which a century and a quarter of American capitalism has despised and spit on.[81]

For much of the Left wing — perhaps the majority — political action meant merely arousing workers about socialism. Ultimately, they did not want to seize the state for workers' government, but wanted instead to build up an industrial workers' democracy that would emerge directly from the industrial union and the shop floor. These syndicalists — typified by Bill Haywood and Bohn — were strong believers in spontaneous self-enlightened "mass action" from below, and were part of the backbone of the I.W.W.[82]

It would be a mistake to attribute the syndicalism of the Left wing to purely "foreign" influences. It was a native syndicalism, in its formative years a product of conditions in the western United States, especially the mining communities. The most cursory reading of Bill Haywood's memoirs shows that. Haywood describes the rootlessness of the Western miners — he had been one from the age of 15 — their violent lives, the oppressive and dangerous work conditions, the spontaneous acts of sabotage, the indifference of the AFL, and most important, the nakedness of the conflict between miners and operators, and between workers and capitalists. For many years, class conflict was settled mostly by spontaneous "mass action" by *both* sides — the workers using strikes, boycotts and sabotage, and the capitalists using murderous vigilance committees and the blacklist to suppress these. Somewhat later, when the energies of the syndicalists were focused in the East, the conflict still retained many of the same aspects. Once again, work conditions were oppressive and dangerous, and the AFL was indifferent — this time to unskilled, immigrant workers. There was certainly much more law than in the West, yet the immigrants couldn't make much use of it — they were the day-to-day victims of it. There were citizens' committees — brutal, but not so much as in the West — that made the exclusion of the immigrant workers from capitalist society final.[83] These are the American conditions that nourished syndicalism, and fed the Left wing's distrust of political action.

While some of the more syndicalist elements of the Left began to renounce all political action, a significant minority upheld its efficacy. The leaders of this minority were Debs, Louis Boudin — the Left's astute revolutionary Marxist — and Henry Slobodin. They shared the syndicalists' disdain for the AFL and desire to organize a revolutionary industrial union as the primary task. But they felt that Socialists must also build a political party on the increasing consciousness of in- dustrially-organized workers, because the state as well as factory must be seized. They had in mind a two-pronged attack on the forces of capitalism, each reinforcing the other. Still, the rank and file of the party remained unconvinced, and was more and more purely divided between the municipal socialist and syndicalist industrial socialist positions. Even Debs — who never considered himself more than a rank-and-filer — came to emphasize simply the industrial union aspects of his politics.[84]

Debs felt compelled to do this because of the increasingly opportunist postures of the party's municipal socialists. If there is any *internal* reason for the growth of syndicalism among the party's Left wing, it is this. For while the municipal socialists were catering to middle-class reform votes, the working class was beginning to show signs of renewed militancy. Yet, municipal socialists like Victor Berger were promising less industrial strife to their broadened electorate.

In September 1909, an entire branch of the Denver local — made up of "fifty-five proletarian members" — withdrew from the party. They charged that the leadership had become a

> . . . cockroach element composed of preachers without pulpits, lawyers without clients, doctors without patients, storekeepers without customers, disgruntled political coyotes and other riffraff. . . . In their mad scramble for votes (they continued) these muddleheaded. marauders of the middle class have seen fit to foist upon the Socialist Party, in the name of the working class, such infamies as 'Craft Unionism,' Anti-Immigration,' 'State Autonomy,' and a series of ludicrous and illogical 'Immediate Demands.'[85]

Several other locals followed suit. Eugene Debs was so alarmed by this trend that he entered the fight within the party. In the *International Socialist Review* he wrote,

> . . . The Socialist Party has already CATERED FAR TOO MUCH to the American Federation of Labor and there is no doubt that A HALT WILL HAVE TO BE CALLED. . . . If the trimmers had their way, we should degenerate into bourgeois reform. But THEY WILL NOT HAVE THEIR WAY.[86]

Debs did not issue another statement for six months. Then he made his outraged reply to the 1910 party resolution on immigration. By that time it appeared to him the "trimmers" were having their way. Ernest Untermann replied to Debs' statement on the immigration debate, charging *him* with being "one of the poorest generals and tacticians that our movement has."

Untermann went on to say that Debs "has shown himself utterly unreliable in the meeting of the practical problems of the day."[87]

In an article called *Danger Ahead*, published in January 1911, Debs made a blistering attack on the municipal socialists. He warned that party leaders were sacrificing principles for votes, and said,

> Not for all the vote of the American Federation of Labor and
> its labor-dividing and corruption-breeding craft unions should
> we compromise one jot of our revolutionary principles; and if
> we do we shall be visited with the contempt we deserve by all
> real socialists ...[88]

Actually, the municipal socialists on the whole favored industrial over craft unionism, Still — in line with their policy of non-interference — they were unwilling to fight the AFL leadership on that question. In April 1907, Max Hayes suggested that "it is absurd for Socialists to waste a lot of valuable time in splitting hairs over the question of industrial organization."[89] Hayes was a leading member of both the party and the International Typographer's Union. Early in 1909 the party National Executive Committee adopted Victor Berger's proposal that Socialists, as Socialists, should refuse to participate in organizational and tactical debates within any union. "Our motto," Berger said, "must be under all circumstances, join the union of your craft and the party of your class."[90]

The municipal socialists remained active in the AFL, supremely confident that Socialists would eventually win out. This spirit of optimism was given a tremendous boost by the 1912 AFL convention, which cast nearly one-third of its votes for Max Hayes, Socialist opponent to Gompers.[91] William English Walling reflected this spirit when he wrote in 1912:

> The old conservative trade unionism is not only going, but it is
> going so fast that one or two more years like the last would
> overwhelm it in the national convention of the Federation of
> Labor and revolutionize the policy of the whole movement.[92]

The Socialists never threatened again. Nine Years later, after they had been thoroughly routed, Walling found himself collaborating on a book with none other than Samuel Gompers. It was called, *Out of Their Own Mouths; a Revelation and an Indictment of Sovietism.*

While the municipal socialists were highly critical of the "pure-and-simple" trade unionism of the Gompers leadership, the industrial socialists were far more vitriolic, and completely irreconcilable. Their attacks against the AFL bureaucracy were highly reminiscent of those by Daniel De Leon — the brilliant but domineering leader of the Socialist Labor Party from 1892 until his death in 1914. De Leon contributed more than anyone else to a coherent, revolutionary critique of the AFL and conservative trade unionism. He was a founder of the I.W.W., although he and his followers later split. De Leon was viewed by most Socialist Party members as a deadly enemy. Still his revolutionary critique of the AFL had great currency among the Left wing — who disliked him as much as the Right — and was a profound influence. Shortly after the I.W.W. was founded, Max Hayes warned:

> Already in a score of places dissension has developed in the Socialist Party and we find our own members parroting the phrases coined by De Leon a dozen years ago, writing for his disreputable organ, and attempting to revive his malevolent and repudiated policies.[93]

One of the "parrots" of De Leon was Eugene Debs. As early as 1902, Debs saw the AFL as hopelessly reactionary. In that year, he helped launch the industrial American Labor Union, and came under heavy fire within the party for his efforts.[94] The American Labor Union was unsuccessful, however, and faded rapidly. In 1904, Debs wrote a major pamphlet — *Unionism and Socialism* — in which he described the need for revolutionary unions and a revolutionary party. His pamphlet had little influence on the party leadership; that year, Max Hayes told the AFL convention that Socialists would no longer try to capture the official machinery of the unions, but would merely agitate for socialist votes.[95] Debs was disappointed, for even though he had become hostile toward the AFL, he never lost faith in the rank-and-file and supported

Socialist efforts to "bore from within."[96] Early in 1905, Debs began work to organize the Industrial Workers of the World. Once the I.W.W. was launched, it became the major arena of activity for the party Left wing, and remained so off and on until the war.

The opposition of the I.W.W. to craft unionism and the AFL expressed very cogently the views of the entire party Left wing. The I.W.W. stated that craft unions fight disjointed battles for relief from immediate conditions, "but not for the ultimate overthrow of the whole wage system." Craft unionism they said, fragments the working class, compels union men to scab on each other, fosters hatred of worker for worker, creates trade monopolies and an aristocracy of labor, and fosters political ignorance "by not elevating the struggle above the petty issues of the trade. ... " Craft union leadership, the I.W.W. charged, are often corrupt, have no ultimate goal, don't care about the masses of workers outside their jurisdiction, and "bind and deliver the working class into the hands of its enemies" — most notably, the National Civic Federation. Because the leadership are primarily interested in themselves, "they do not organize the unorganized, they do not amalgamate existing craft unions into industrial bodies, they do not fight the employers energetically. ... "[97]

At the founding convention of the I.W.W., Eugene Debs said of the AFL:

> The trade union movement is today under the control of the capitalist class. It is preaching capitalist economics, it is serving capitalist purposes. ...

He went on:

> There is certainly something wrong with that form of unionism which has its chief support in the press that represents capitalism; something wrong in that form of unionism that forms an alliance with such capitalist combinations as the Civic Federation, whose sole purpose is to chloroform the working-class while the capitalist class goes through their pockets.[98]

Debs then stated his belief in an industrial unionism based on the class struggle, "broad enough to embrace every honest worker, yet narrow enough to exclude every faker."[99] He remained true to these beliefs for the rest of his life. In 1916, long after he had left the I.W.W., he stated that the party "can only maintain its own integrity by standing staunchly and uncompromisingly ... for the industrial organization of the workers (and) against the principles of craft unionism.[100]

The leader of most of the party Left wing, Bill Haywood, always expressed his views on the AFL more succinctly. He told the I.W.W. founding convention:

> It has been said that this convention was to form an organization rival to the A.F. of L. That is a mistake. We are here for the purpose of organizing a labor organization.[101]

One reason the industrial socialists were so hostile toward the AFL is that they wanted to unify the working class. They were determined to erase lines of division and sectional interests within the working class. One such line was craft. Another very important one was nationality. Their appeal had to transcend nationality, and it did. If the immigrant workers couldn't be a part of American society, they could be a part of something much greater: the international working class.

The industrial socialists entered the field with a broad, internationalist perspective. They saw the working class as world-wide, and their brotherly contact with so many different nationalities reinforced this belief. To the industrial socialists there were, as Bill Haywood put it, "no foreigners in the working class." They saw the restrictionist policies of the AFL as an attempt to bolster the privileged position of craft unions, thus strengthening the aristocracy of labor and deepening divisions within the working class. In opposition to the AFL's policies, the I.W.W. stated:

> The A.F. of L. is fighting against Chinese, Japanese, and the Southern European races calling them an 'undesirable' class of immigrants; and is agitating for laws to bar them from America. The I.W.W. extends a fraternal hand to

> every wage-worker, no matter what his religion, fatherland, or trade.[102]

In contrast to municipal socialists, industrial socialists were responsible neither to AFL trade unionists, nor a broad electorate. Thus, they were liberated from the necessity to deal with many of the pressures that municipal socialists confronted. Importantly, they could afford to write off the AFL's restrictionist sentiments, without suffering any negative consequences. The industrial socialists' internationalism, then, remain unchecked.

The absence of pressures against a political perspective is, however, no explanation for its existence. Just as important is the fact that industrial socialists owed more allegiance to a consciously-formulated model of revolutionary class struggle, than to existing realities. This does not imply that they were simply "unrealistic"; it means, rather, that industrial socialists were more interested in shaping existing realities to fit their model than in working within narrow limits seemingly imposed by existing realities.

Concretely, this meant that industrial socialists were restricted to the role of propagandists in times of quiescence. On the other hand, they were at their best when dealing with a situation that approximated their model of class struggle. During the 1912 Lawrence, Massachusetts strike, for example, I.W.W. organizers enthusiastically played a major role. The I.W.W. gained ten thousand new members, nearly all of them previously unorganized immigrant workers. After the strike subsided, however, I.W.W. organizers withdrew from the scene, seeking new areas of turbulence. This pattern of entry and withdrawal was repeated again and again. Outside the context of general revolutionary upheaval, the I.W.W. remained a propaganda organization.[103]

The municipal socialists, such as Berger, owed less allegiance to a model or goal than to existing realities. They were much more inclined toward day-to-day organization building than toward upheaval. They developed a constituency to which they were responsible, while the industrial socialists had none, but were responsible to their model. In this respect, the I.W.W. was remarkably similar — both organizationally and tactically — to the present-day Student Non-violent Coordinating Committee, or SNCC. The

I.W.W. was effectively an organizing committee rather than a mass organization. Its conventions were sparsely attended, even when its membership rolls were high. The I.W.W.'s business was conducted, it may be said, by instinct rather than formal procedure. Major decisions were left to a small national office staff — headed, until the War, by Bill Haywood — which remained essentially the same for periods of years.

The industrial socialists' emphasis on their model of class struggle over building an organization and a stable constituency, continually reinforced their internationalism, which was an integral part of that concept. But the industrial socialists also received strong incentive for their internationalism from the immigrant himself. The labor struggles of immigrant workers — particularly new immigrants — best approximated their model. Immigrant workers showed marked inclinations toward spontaneous, primitive rebellion. Their strikes were dramatic, militant, and occasionally violent. Often, they were led by immigrants trained in European revolutionary movements.

Immigrant workers possessed another quality that made them attractive to industrial socialists: they were notoriously hostile toward the AFL. Ignored or rejected by most AFL unions at the same time as they were severely exploited by capitalists, new immigrant workers provided fertile soil for dual unionism and the I.W.W.[104]

Thus, the industrial socialists' image of the new immigrant worker was a very positive one. It was in terms of this image, bolstered by an unswerving spirit of internationalism, that they forged their opposition to restrictions.

4. The AFL's Anti-Radical Campaign

The Socialist Party moved toward the AFL's restrictionist position at the same time as the AFL redoubled its own efforts out of fear of immigrant radicalism. Ironically, then, the Socialist Party unwittingly aided the AFL's drive against socialism.

The AFL's fear of immigrant radicalism took shape with I.W.W. successes in organizing new immigrants. Previously, however, there had been some indications of this threat. Perhaps most notable was the Socialists' success in organizing new immigrant miners during the 1902 anthracite strike in Pennsylvania. Frank Julian Warne, a scholar personally close to the Mine

Workers' leadership, noted with alarm a substantial increase in Socialist votes. In his book, *Slav Invasion and the Mine Workers,* Warne correlated the increase in Socialist votes with an increase in the new immigrant population. All told, Socialist strength increased from less than 1 to more than 12 percent of the vote, while support for the capitalist parties declined considerably.[105] Mine Workers' president John Mitchell wrote urgently to Mark Hanna that Socialists were holding "immense meetings in every mining town," and warned that "there is great and growing independent political sentiment in the coalfields."[106]

Once the I.W.W. took the field, immigrant radicalism became a major concern of the AFL. William Leiserson, writing for the well-known Carnegie series of Americanization Studies, interviewed numerous AFL leaders who indicated the importance to themselves of the socialist threat among new immigrants. The president of one national union told him:

> ... his union ceased trying to organize immigrants because he found they were only recruiting for the I.W.W. Still another official, when asked to the advisability of issuing foreign language literature explaining trade union principles, replied that this would only give the agitators among the immigrants better opportunities to make the American Federation of Labor ridiculous in the eyes of their countrymen. ... And as soon as the organizers announced their connection they would be suspected by the immigrants. A high executive of the American Federation of Labor complained that the socialists and radicals had poisoned the minds of the foreigners against him, making them believe he was dishonest and reactionary. ... And the representative of the Federation in a large industrial state frankly declared he did not want to organize too many foreigners as there were so many radicals among them.[107]

Leiserson also tells of an interview with leaders of the United Textile Workers. The first said:

On the whole . . . the foreign elements are Socialists and radicals . . . They do not appreciate the value of negotiation.

Another told him:

It was not long after the southern and east European nationalities came into the textile industry . . . before the union realized the futility of organizing them and making permanent unionists out of them. It was *easy* enough to organize them, but generally the I.W.W. reaped the harvest.

He went on:

It seems that even those foreigners who do not come here as radicals are carried away by the flighty ideals.[108]

To a large extent, Gompers shared these same views. Worried by I.W.W. gains and briefly reconsidering industrial unionism, he wrote in 1912:

. . . The large body of unskilled workers . . . are composed of workmen brought here from Europe, who do not speak our language, and who in many instances have had their suspicions and prejudices aroused by so-called radical socialist "intellectuals" — writers and orators — who thus make more difficult the effort to organize our fellow-workers of more recent entrance to our country.[109]

The most remarkable instance of Gompers' fear of immigrant socialism came with a strike at McKee's Rock, Pennsylvania, in 1909. Six thousand unskilled, immigrant workers struck against the Pressed Steel Car Company, and were immediately set upon by state police. I.W.W. organizers arrived, warning police that for "every man you kill of us, we will kill one of you." Strikers adopted the Wobbly tactic of refusing to bargain with the company, but simply staying out until it gave in.[110] The militancy of the immigrant strikers sent a shiver through the national press, which cried for restrictions. Gompers seized the opportunity to lobby for the AFL's restrictionist program. He reported to the 1909 convention with optimism, explaining:

> From recent industrial developments especially the widely discussed strike at the Pressed Steel Car Company at McKees Rock, Pa. ... It is becoming more apparent that members of Congress . . . will insist upon some better regulation of immigrants.[111]

5. Conclusion

As the Socialist Party — through the efforts of its Right wing — moved toward a restrictionist position, two consequences were immediately apparent: First of all, socialists could no longer act as a unified, internationalist force within the mainstream of the working-class movement. Although socialists remained the only opponents of Gompers' restrictionist policies within the AFL. It was no longer true that all socialists opposed restrictions.[112] The thrust toward internationalism that socialists had helped to create with the First International, was almost dead; now, they were doing little to keep it alive. Secondly, the Socialist Party was all but cutting itself off from a major, potential source of support — new immigrant workers. In 1908, when new immigrants made up the majority of the nation's industrial working class, they made up less than 35 percent of Socialist Party membership. Of 40 thousand members, 71 percent were native-born Americans, while 17.5 percent were "old" immigrants, from Northern and Western Europe.[113] All Socialists were, of course, pleased that their party included a large number of native-born Americans. Their presence proved that the socialist movement had finally come of age in America. But the Right wing had special reason to be pleased that the number of new immigrants was small. Not only did it fit in with both their notion of an Americanized movement and their opposition to immigration, but ultimately it meant political protection. Just as new immigrant unionists threatened the AFL's conservative leadership, so did new immigrant socialists threaten the party's Right wing leadership. The following chapter details what happened when the number of immigrants in the party became large.

Chapter 9
"New" Immigrants in the Socialist Party:
The Heritage of Nativism and the Decline of American Socialism

Until its 1910 congress, the Socialist Party failed to take an official position on organizing immigrants for socialist ends. Amazingly, even the immigrant socialist had remained virtually invisible to them despite the emergence of numerous, unaffiliated socialist foreign-language groups and newspapers throughout the nation.

In 1904, several of these groups sent fraternal representatives to the Socialist Party convention. They asked to affiliate, and the convention referred the problem to the National Committee, which in turn passed it on to the National Executive Committee.[1] The NEC suggested a peculiar arrangement which involved a choice between high dues or disbanding, and hence was unacceptable to the immigrant socialist groups.[2] In 1906, the NEC allowed a Finnish group of over two thousand members to affiliate in exchange for dues to the national with no vote. The Finnish locals then affiliated with their respective state socialist parties to gain the vote indirectly, while maintaining their distinctive national organization. Numerous other immigrant groups affiliated their locals with state parties, but only the Lettish with the national party.[3]

This kind of arrangement did not satisfy the immigrant socialists. They felt that the problems they faced were unusual enough to warrant separate organizations within the party, yet they wanted equal rights. These included separate representation at conventions, and the right to elect to party committees. They wanted to be able to work among their own people in the name of the Socialist Party, to recruit them to an organization in which they both felt comfortable and played an active role. Immigrant socialists who made their way to the party individually soon dropped away because they and their comrades could not understand each other. The futility of this sort of encounter was unintentionally dramatized before the 1910 party congress. Party Secretary J. Mahlon Barnes was confronted by two sets of delegates claiming to represent the Hungarian Socialist Society. He was unable to choose between them, and explained to the congress, "I do not understand Hungarian. I wish the chairman or someone who understands the language would inquire into the facts."[4]

The immigrant socialists were offended by the party's refusal to recognize their unusual problems, and to give them a fair chance to resolve them. A Polish representative told the 1910 congress:

> . . . a good many foreign organizations being affiliated with the Socialist Party do not participate in the votes . . . for the simple reason that you send out the referendum of the party in the English language.

He added:

> And even suppose they were participating and were voting for our candidates, don't you know that we are in a hopeless minority so that we can not elect a single member to this body, to represent our interests?[5]

The opponents of separate organizations replied that the immigrant socialists must be integrated into the American movement immediately: "You are in America now; get into the American movement."[6] The immigrants countered that it was impossible for the party to hold them unless foreign-language affiliates were set up. Therefore, they were proposing the only effective way of integrating the immigrants into the American movement.

> They don't want to be separate; they don't want to withdraw from the party; they want to join in the party . . . When you go to one of the Italians or Poles and talk to him in English about the party, he does not understand. This is all the privilege we ask; to conduct our work in our own tongue until we learn the American tongue.[7]

The party congress recognized the tremendous potential for growth the immigrant groups offered, and so passed a constitutional amendment providing for fairly autonomous, foreign-language federations. The terms still included a somewhat heavy dues load for the federations and refused them a vote at the national convention[8] — but they were acceptable to the immigrants.

Between 1910 and 1912, five foreign-language federations — South Slavic, Italian, Scandinavian, Hungarian and Bohemian — affiliated with the party, bringing the total to seven.[9] Altogether, they accounted for 16,000 of the party's 118,000 members.[10] The federations had varying successes: The Finns showed the same rapid rate of growth and remarkable stability they had in previous years. They were by far the biggest of the federations with more than 11,000 members and 223 locals, and also the wealthiest, doing an annual "business" of 200,000 dollars and owning property worth over half a million dollars.[11] The Italian federation showed rapid turnover. From December 1910 to October 1911, twenty-two branches joined, but fourteen disbanded.[12] No reasons are given to their report to the 1912 party convention, but an accurate guess can be made. The Southern and East European socialist groups were proletarian, and therefore highly susceptible to fluctuations in the labor market. The South Slavic section reports eight discontinued locals: one because of merger, two "on account of the neglect of the Secretary," one because the members left town, one "on account of closing of mine," and three "on account of unemployment."[13]

Despite turnover all the federations grew fairly rapidly. Most of their growth came from organizing new locals, but of course much came from recruiting previously-established groups. A number of the old party foreign-language locals did not join the new federations.[14] The foreign-language socialist press grew considerably, but not nearly so rapidly as the English. In 1910 the party reported three English dailies and 33 weeklies, and six foreign-language dailies and 22 weeklies.[15] By 1912, there were five English and eight foreign-language dailies, and 262 English and 36 foreign-language weeklies. That was the year of the party's zenith. By 1916 the English dailies had decreased to two and the foreign-language increased to 13; the English weeklies dropped from 262 to 112, an the foreign-language from 36 to 22.[16]

The 1912 party convention was pleased with the successes of the foreign-language federations. But at the same time, a few — mostly of the Left wing — felt that the federations were not integrating immigrant socialists into the party. The reports of the federations indicate that they spent a significant portion of their energy supporting movements in the old country. The Finnish comrades explained,

> This had not been done for the love of the 'fatherland,' nor for the purpose of keeping our nationality alive or to simply save the so-called state autonomy of Finland. At least a great majority of us have had a deeper interest in the matter — have had the aim of international socialism in mind and have given help to that part of the globe where suppression is more felt and where . . . our cause at present has a considerably strong foothold.[17]

Whatever their motives, it is clear that some of the socialist immigrants were at heart political emigrants trying only to build a base for supporting their European movements. Still, the socialist movement among new immigrants on the whole was a product of American conditions, not a "foreign import."[18] The problem was, the immigrant socialists were not taking advantage of the relevant American theory on conditions in the United States, and were not joining directly with their American comrades to fight these conditions. The 1910 congress provided that foreign-language locals would be linked closely to the state parties, but this turned out not to be the case. Instead, they were linked rather loosely through national federations to the party national office. Thus, the foreign-language locals rarely came in contact with neighboring English-speaking locals, and were ignorant about the party and its propaganda. Furthermore, the erection of foreign-language locals sometimes drew members out of integrated locals, thus increasing the distance between foreign and English-speaking comrades.[19]

Charles Ruthenberg of the Left wing Ohio party told the 1912 convention that foreign-language locals affiliated with the party only through the National Office, "never come near our central organization, are not in touch with the central organization, and take no part whatsoever in the business of the local."[20]

He charged that foreign-language groups:

> . . . are now circulating in this country literature for the separation of church and state. . . . They are circulating literature against feudalistic organizations in society, and all this is due to the fact that we permit them to separate themselves from our own organization.[21]

Another delegate gave the example of a Portland foreign-language local, "affiliated with the national organization, paying dues to the national organization, which was all the time under the impression that they *were* part of the Socialist Labor Party."[22]

The Left wing critics did not want to disband the foreign-language groups, but simply wanted to draw them into the activities of the local and state parties. Most federation delegates agreed with their general criticisms.[23]

The 1912 convention altered the section of the constitution pertaining to the federations, but not seriously.[24] They were required henceforth to pay dues to the state and city parties, but only through the National Office.[25] The federations continued to grow, and seven more affiliated with the party by 1915. In the meantime the party membership declined, so that of the 80,000 members in 1915, about a third were in the federations.[26]

However, the immigrant socialists were never integrated into the party. From the very beginning they stood to the left of the party leadership, and this was undoubtedly a major factor in their isolation. The vast majority joined after the Right wing had taken a firm grip on the controls, and were never able to exert influence in proportion to their numbers. David Shannon suggests that the leadership probably would have brought the federations closer to the party had it not been for the following incident which occurred in 1914. A Michigan copper strike precipitated a growth of syndicalism among Finnish federation locals in the area. The federation expelled the syndicalist locals, but they retained their state and national Socialist party affiliations. The Right wing party leadership decided:

> If autonomous foreign groups are permitted to join the
> party like an English local, it becomes possible to annul
> and wreck the work of the regular foreign-speaking
> federations. Any kind of syndicalist or impossibilist
> propaganda can be carried on, and there can be no local
> control, because the language becomes a barrier.[27]

Therefore, the leadership resolved to give the Federations "full charge
and jurisdiction in the organization of the language locals, and of all
propaganda in the particular language."[28]

2. 1919: The Socialist–Communist Split

As it turned out, the Right wing leadership were willing to grant
autonomy only when it served their own interests. In 1919, they expelled
seven Eastern European federations — Hungarian, Lithuanian, Lettish,
Russian, Polish, South Slav, and Ukranian — with some 30,000 members.
Also expelled or suspended were the entire Socialist Parties of Michigan,
Massachusetts, Ohio and Chicago. All told, the leadership purged
two-thirds of the party's membership — the Left wing — which by then
had reached 109,000.[29] Neither the Socialist Party nor the American
socialist movement ever recovered from this disaster. Most of those
expelled droped out of organized socialism. The rest formed two small
Communist parties, which eventually united. The Socialist Party itself
was quickly reduced to a mere skeleton. The political differences that lay
behind the leadership's precipitous actions were extremely complicated,
and will not be discussed in detail here.[30] Of relevance, however, is the
role that the foreign-language federations played in articulating these
differences, and bringing them to the fore. Prior to 1919, the Left–Right
divisions within the Socialist Party were rarely cause for alarm among
the leadership. Although the divisions were deep-rooted, the Left was
never able to mount a serious opposition to the leadership's policies. The
Left failed because much of it was inept organizationally, and the rest
existed on the party's periphery, in the foreign-language federations. In
1912, the Left was beaten badly in a showdown over the question of

industrial sabotage. At that time Bill Haywood, one of the major figures in the Left, was removed from the party's National Executive Committee.[31]

After 1912, the party experienced serious decline, both in membership and votes. Once the United States entered the war, however, this decline was reversed, 1917 proved to be one of the most successful years ever for the party, in terms of votes. But these votes came from new sources. Severe government repression had destroyed the party's voting base in the Midwest — its traditional area of support. Now, its votes for the first time came from the major industrial centers in the East. They were for the most part immigrant votes.[32]

At the same time as the party's voting base shifted, so did its membership base. During the period of war and immediate post-war reaction, the party could not regain its Midwestern, native-born American membership. Instead, it gained new members — once again, from the East — who were predominately immigrant. Radicalized by revolutionary upheaval in Europe, these immigrants swelled the membership lists of the federations until, by 1919, they came into majority. The new recruits were, as Morris Hillquit put it, "Bolsheviks to the core."[33]

The traditional party disputes were laid aside for the duration of the war. On the question of the war itself, Right and Left wings converged in their forthright opposition to it — the most remarkable chapter in American Socialist history.[34] With the end of the war the divisions re-emerged. Now, in the blazing light of European revolution, the fundamental question of reform *versus* revolution became more sharply defined than ever.

At the same time, the Left for the first time began to organize as a coherent force within the party. The foreign-language federations formed the backbone of this organization. Even in the early months of 1919 — shortly before the split — the Right wing leadership was not unduly alarmed by or in many cases aware of the Left's growth.[35] Then, almost without warning, the Left won a smashing victory. Previously with no more than sparse representation among the national leadership, the Left elected twelve of its own to the fifteen-man National Executive Committee, along with four out of five international delegates. Bloc voting by the federations had insured the victory. Shaken, but ever game, old guard party leader Morris Hillquit wrote:

> Better a hundred times to have two numerically small
> Socialist organizations, each homogeneous and
> harmonious within itself, than to have one big party torn
> by dissensions and squabbles, an impotent colossus on
> feet of play. The time for action is near. Let us clear the
> decks.[36]

The old National Executive Committee then voided the election as a fraud, and proceeded to wipe out the Left wing. First to go was the Michigan party, then the seven foreign-language federations, followed by the parties of Massachusetts, Ohio and Chicago. Party organizations that protested the voiding of elections or the expulsion were themselves expelled. As a clincher, the leadership refused to submit a referendum on its actions to the remaining membership, claiming they were too ill-informed to pass judgement.[37] The Left wing international delegates were denied their seats when the old NEC ruled — after the elections — that candidates must have been in the party three years.[38] Both the official statement of the NEC explaining its actions against the Left wing, and the meeting at which the actions were taken, focused on the foreign-language federations. The NEC stated that thorough plans had been made "to vote whole foreign-language federations for a 'slate,' using the foreign-language papers in a disgusting campaign of slander against the party and its elected officials. The party and its officials were helpless against this cowardly tirade as we could not know what was taking place." The NEC further hinted at attempted "dictatorship in the party by certain foreign-speaking comrades."[39] James Oneal, who led the fight against the Left, charged that:

> In the last year or so, a situation has developed where the
> language federations practically attempt to dictate to the
> party its general policies and its general principles, in
> addition to the propaganda they were supposed to carry
> on in their language federations.[40]

Elsewhere, Oneal explained that the language federations' increase in membership indicated "an attempt to colonize for the purpose of capturing the party by sheer force of numbers and not by intelligent discussion."[41]

Clearly, the Right wing was suffering the consequences of having kept immigrant socialists on the periphery of the organization. Politically, this meant that the immigrants were less in touch with conditions in America as a whole than they should have been. The Right wing charged that the federations were operating more with an eye toward Russia than the United States. To a certain extent this was true — and the leadership was largely responsible for it. Besides political conflict, however, there was intense ethnic conflict. Now in a majority, the immigrants were attempting to move into the heart of the party. The Right wing feared not only their revolutionary politics, but sensed that the long-term process of Americanization had suddenly been reversed. One National Executive Committee member expressed concern that the ascendency of the federations would "destroy the possibility of reaching and organizing the English speaking people of this country." He continued:

> No movement can succeed in any country if its methods and officials in the main are to be decided by people other than those native to the country concerned . . . more and more it has become evident that the English-speaking portion of the party has NOT self-determination of officials and methods most sure to get the ear of the English speaking people of this country.[42]

The NEC's attitude toward immigrant socialists was made decisively clear when they provided for the return of the native-born American Michigan party, but not the federations.

3. Conclusion

The Socialist Party's nativism not only ended the role socialists had played in keeping internationalism alive in the working class movement, but turned inward it helped to isolate the party from the masses of new immigrant workers. Immigrant socialists were the party's transmission belt to the new immigrant workers. Yet the party never set this transmission belt in motion. As a consequence, immigrant socialists and their audience were denied an adequate socialist comprehension of the United States. Likewise, the Socialist Party failed to gain insight into the conditions of life of immigrant workers.

The measurable results of the party's nativist policies were severe. They proved to be a major factor in the party's sudden disintegration and decline into oblivion. By 1925, the Socialist Party was once again predominately English-speaking — but no longer working class, and no longer part of a movement. Still, there was room for one more Americanization campaign, as Morris Hillquit and the old guard ironically discovered in later years. This time, however, Hillquit and his Americanized immigrant allies were cleared off the decks by Norman Thomas and his band of purebred Yankees.

Conclusion:
Internationalism vs. Sectional Interests in the
Working Class Movement

With the disintegration of the Socialist Party in 1919, our story is at an end. A few statements about what followed are in order, however. While the Left split into antagonistic fragments, the AFL emerged from the war healthy, and more conservative than ever. The United States government implemented its first major program of immigration restriction in 1921, and followed it up in 1924 with one that virtually eliminated "new" immigrants as a factor. The AFL, representing the mainstream of the working class movement, gave enthusiastic support to the government's efforts. By now, the Gompers leadership — expressing deep concern for national homogeneity, and profound fear of Bolshevism — had adopted a full-fledged nationalistic perspective.

We have traced the development of the idea of working class internationalism in a key aspect — solidarity with immigrant workers — and have analyzed the obstacles to its fruition. Throughout the career of the idea of internationalism, one set of obstacles appeared relentlessly — the sectional interests of the working class movement. By sectional, we mean those interests, applicable to one segment of the working class, which when pursued, enable that segment to accrue limited gains over its previous position, or temporary advantages over another segment of the working class. Where sectional interests were strong, internationalism was weak, and vice versa.

The contradiction between the two betrayed internationalism's heritage: It was the product of two simultaneous currents in the early working class movement — revolution and reform — which converged for a brief period in the movement's history. Internationalism could take firm root only where the working class movement itself developed broad, long-range aspirations and goals — in short, where the movement was revolutionary, or reformist. Where the movement was neither, where it was conservative and developed a narrow focus on short-range goals, the idea of internationalism found barren soil.

The internationalism of the revolutionaries proved to be more durable than that of the reformists. The reasons were fairly clear. For one, the reformists aspired to significantly lower goals than the revolutionaries. They were more easily satisfied, and more amenable to compromising their principles for short-term gains. They were less likely to maintain a posture of internationalism — even though moderate — when other of their goals appeared in sight. Thus, the resurgence of domestic liberalism in England considerably weakened the International's reformist support. In the same vein, many British trade unions became fixated on immigration, and gradually substituted insulation from imported contract labor for internationalist goals.

The reformists, then, were more closely tied to sectional interests among the working class movement than were the revolutionaries. When a contradiction arose, they were likely to line up accordingly. In England, the decisve test came when the reformists refused to support revolution on the Continent. In this historic context, the prevailing influence of sectional interests proved a marked failure for internationalism.

Another reason for the relative weakness of the reformists' internationalism was that trade union reformism — at least in the United States — corresponded to a limited period in trade union development. The cooperative goals of the National Labor Union and the Knights of Labor, for example, had little applicability to modern industrial capitalism. The pre-industrial craft unionism that these goals grew out of, was primarily a resistance movement to the dehumanizing qualities of modern capitalism. The movement's means did not match its aspirations, and it was doomed to failure. With its decline also died the moderate internationalism of trade union reformism.

1. Sectional Interests and the Mainstream of the Working Class Movement.

By the 1890s, the reformism of pre-industrial craft unionism was no longer of any consequence in the American working class movement. It had been supplanted by the narrow conservatism of the AFL's new craft unions on the one hand, and the broad radicalism of socialist organizations on the other. It was now possible to distinguish a "mainstream" in the movement — the AFL — because trade union activity had become sharply differentiated from reformist, or radical activity. Previously, the distinction had not been so clear. With few exceptions, radicals, reformists and trade unionists in the movement had been able to work together.

Far more than its predecessors, the AFL directly represented the sectional interests of its organized constituency. The AFL contained a large proportion of immigrants. Moreover, it had inherited the moderate, internationalist traditions of its predecessors. But once the sectional interests of the AFL's constituency came into conflict with the idea of internationalism, the idea itself was rapidly abandoned.[1]

What was the nature of these sectional interests? It is difficult to specify their nature precisely, because they contained both material and ideal elements. Sectional interests, we can say, emerged out of the complex interaction of material conditions and ideas. The importance of material conditions for the way a working class movement develops, is rarely overlooked. The importance of ideas is, however, often overlooked. Yet, a working class movement is not simply a reflection of its material environment — a fact, so to speak, of economic history alone. As E.P. Thompson has so brilliantly shown in his *Making of the English Working Class*, a working class movement is as much a fact of political and cultural as economic history.[2]

The material elements of the AFL's sectional interests included the basic needs common to the entire working class — the need for livable wages, adequate housing, regular employment, and so forth. With respect to immigration, the heritage of moderate internationalism was challenged when the massive influx of free immigrant workers threatened to roll back the material gains of the organized working class, or to prevent gains from being made. Whether immigration actually posed as serious a threat as was believed is less important than the fact that it was perceived as such a threat. Thus pressured, the AFL moved toward a restrictionist, anti-internationalist position.

Another material element of the AFL's sectional interests was the lack of exceptional circumstances — such as severe war-time dislocation, or extreme class polarization — that historically have enabled an idea that posits broad, long-range goals to take precedence over immediate material needs. In the United States, if anything "exceptional circumstances" tended in a direction opposite to such phenomena as extreme class polarization. Where polarization did exist, however, as in the coal fields of Pennsylvania, the AFL's conservative ideology led the organization to try to narrow, rather than widen the gap between classes.

Similarly, when large numbers of immigrant workers tended toward radicalism, the AFL intensified its efforts to restrict immigration. The conservative ideology that guided these efforts had been in part generated by the lack of extreme class polarization in American society as a whole. Conservatism was itself, then, partly a reflection of material conditions.

Still another material element of the AFL's sectional interests was the organization's success. Workers organized by the AFL experienced measurable improvement in wages, work conditions and employment. Success led the AFL leadership to reject any attempts to transcend the organization's narrow wage-consciousness. Other modes of organization may or may not work, they reasoned, but this one certainly did.

The ideal elements of the AFL's sectional interests were closely related to these material elements. Out of the AFL's success, for example, came the strategy of organizing mainly skilled craftsmen who held key positions in industry. Out of the lack of class polarization came the AFL's "honeymoon period" with American capitalists.

At the same time, however, material conditions alone do not account for the whole range of AFL theory and tactics. The architects of the AFL, for example, rejected the reformism of their predecessors, even those aspects of reformism that still had some currency. They resisted ventures into the field of independent political action, and eventually drew close to the major capitalists parties. Moreover, when socialism finally became a viable force in American politics, they rejected it. Such decisions were not dictated by material conditions. Their theoretical roots in fact predated the founding of the AFL.[3]

As an evolutionist and materialist, Gompers was fond of calling the AFL a natural and inevitable outgrowth of American conditions. However, when the AFL consolidated as an aristocracy of labor against unskilled immigrant workers, its action was in part due to self-conscious choice. The AFL was not only responding to the material elements that comprised the sectional interests of its constituency, but it was also responding to ideal elements — a vision of who among the working class ought to be organized. This vision was limited to skilled workers, and the aristocracy of labor was the ultimate vehicle for defending their sectional interests.

The leadership thus was not simply responding to self-evident sectional interests, but was determining precisely what the boundaries of these interests were. In their words, through the implementation of a theory of trade unionism — an idea — the sectional interests of the AFL's constituency were articulated and given shape. Had the AFL been flexible enough to organize along industrial lines, we can assume that the sectional interests of the working class would have been broadened. Consequently, although objectively the material conditions would have remained the same, their response to immigration would have been — for a time, at least — more along internationalist lines.

Along with material conditions, ideal elements played a critical role in breaking down the AFL's early internationalism. First, irrational — but ideal — currents of nativism counterposed the "old" immigrants inside the AFL to "new" immigrants outside. Second, the convergence of conservative tendencies on three specific issues — Chinese exclusion, American imperialism, and organizing black workers — weakened internationalism and strengthened racism and jingoism. Third, the AFL's total accommodation of American capitalism counterposed the organization to the Left wing of the working class movement, and ideologically insulated it from Left wing contributions.

Still, these ideal elements probably had more to do with the timing of the AFL's retreat from internationalism, than with the retreat itself. As long as the AFL retained its conservative craft union orientation, it could do little more than serve the narrow sectional interests of its constituency. Seriously threatened by the influx of unskilled immigrants, the aristocracy of labor was inherently antagonistic to internationalism, and provided poor soil for its growth. The task of carrying on the idea therefore fell solely to the Left wing of the working class movement.

2. Sectional Interests and the Left Wing of the Working Class Movement.

Within the Left wing itself, there existed no sectional interests, properly speaking. But one segment of the Left — the reformist wing of the Socialist Party — eventually drew support from, identified with, and to a limited extent became spokesman for groups of AFL-organized workers. Inexorably, they abandoned the internationalism traditionally associated with the Left, and substituted for it a defense of the aristocracy of labor. Only after the reformists broke cleanly with the AFL during World War I, were they able to reassert their internationalism.

In the meantime, another segment of the Left — Industrial socialists identified with the revolutionary wing of the Socialist Party, and the Industrial Workers of the World — remained aloof from sectional interests and maintained their internationalist perspective. For them, it may be said that ideas were paramount over material conditions at all times.

This is not to imply that material conditions were of no importance to the revolutionaries. Rather, they sought to work where material conditions — such as severe exploitation — best fit their ideas of a revolutionary situation. They did not adjust their ideas to fit changes in the material conditions, as did reformist Socialists. While reformist Socialists, for example, recognized and embraced the material gains made by AFL-organized workers, revolutionary Socialists did not.

For the revolutionaries then, the ideas, models and concepts of class struggle served as their supreme guide. This accounts for the enduring strength of their internationalism: They owed allegiance to ideas, not to material conditions or sectional interests that might contradict them. At the same time, their allegiance to ideas accounts for their organizational weakness. In acting out their ideas in the purest way possible, the revolutionaries avoided building organizational vehicles — possible resources of contamination.

Since their choice was to maintain their strictly revolutionary outlook, they abandoned mass strikes once the heat of combat had died down, refusing to engage in the routine, day-to-day struggle for bettering immediate, material conditions. This was, of course, the classic dilemma of revolutionaries. How could they maintain their allegiance to revolutionary ideas, while working within a real world where sheer material and sectional interests predominated? Outside the context of general revolutionary upheaval — which the revolutionaries did not enjoy — there was no answer to this dilemma. They could not be both organizationally effective and politically pure. They were relegated to the roles of propagandists and agitators. In the end, much the same fate befell the idea of working class internationalism. The offspring of revolutionary theory, internationalism gained substance only in revolutionary practice. It stood little chance for survival within a conservative trade union movement, which so directly reflected the sectional interests of its constituency.

Outside the trade unions there were large numbers of immigrant workers who might have supported internationalist currents in the working class movement. But they remained unorganized, and whatever sentiments they might have had remained unexpressed. Revolutionaries alone subscribed to the idea, but the time was not a revolutionary moment. Internationalism could not survive on their ardor alone.

APPENDIX

THE CLASS AND ETHNIC BASES OF NEW YORK CITY SOCIALISM 1904–1915[*]

Labor History, Volume 22, Issue 1, 1981

1901, the year the Socialist Party of America appeared, found radical working class politics in New York City in a moribund state. Fifteen years had passed since the United Labor Party upsurge around the figurehead of Henry George, and several attempts thereafter failed to approach the earlier movement in the extent and solidity of its trade union base. Meanwhile, the Socialist Labor Party had also passed its electoral peak, and its influences in trade union circles had become negligible.[1]

During its first few years the New York City Socialist Party could scarcely be called a movement, or even an important part of one. In January 1904, party rolls listed a modest 922 members in Manhattan and the Bronx, with only rudimentary organization in other boroughs. By 1906 the numbers had only gradually increased to 1200. Socialist voters likewise were few. The New York party in this period remained a vestige of earlier Socialist and radical labor efforts. Two-thirds of its members in 1904 were German-born, a feature it shared with the old Socialist Labor Party. Its members were middle-aged — their median age was 42 — and most came from trades that had once formed the basis of the United Labor Party, and also provided the main trade union support for the Socialist Labor Party. Sixty percent of Socialist Party membership were skilled workers, with nearly half of these in the building trades, and large fractions were also in cigar-making and tailoring. Semi-skilled production and service workers made up another 14 percent of the party's membership, with painters and waiters accounting for the largest single fractions. Few factory operatives were evident in Socialist ranks at this time, and the proportion of unskilled laborers was negligible.[2]

The next years, however, saw the influx of the garment workers, an influx which laid the basis for rapid Socialist growth through New York City, and the party's transformation into the advance guard of a genuine

* The research for this study was supported by a fellowship from the Research Foundation of the State University of New York. The author would like to thank Jean Marie Gath for her valuable help.

movement. By fall 1914, the party counted 6,000 members in 135 branches, with half the members and branches in Brooklyn and Queens

Within the next year and a half the party grew to 8,000; and by the end of 1917, it claimed 12,000 members not including members of foreign-language federations.[3]

These figures do not tell the whole story, however, for the Socialist movement extended well beyond the formal party members. The movement also included radical trade unionists and others, who never formally joined. Membership turnover was considerable: to grow by 1200 members between 1908 and 1914, the Manhattan and Bronx local had to recruit 7,000; to grow by 2,000 during 1916 and 1917, the local recruited 7,700 new members. We may assume for this period, however, that those lost to party rolls remained with the movement. As Rosa Luxemburg noted for Germany, participation in a radical union, voting in elections, attending public meetings and reading the party press were sufficient to make the "Social-Democratically-minded average worker" feel Social Democratically organized.[4]

A rough measure of the overall extent of the New York Socialist movement is indicated in election tallies and press readership. The number of "enrolled Socialists" — those who registered as Socialists at the polls — as a rule ran three to four times as large as party membership. From 1912 to 1916, the number of enrolled Socialists averaged 18,000, and reached nearly 46,000 in 1917. Socialist voters usually numbered two to three times the number enrolled as Socialists. In 1912, Socialist voters numbered 33,000 (giving Eugene Debs 11 per cent of New York City's presidential vote). In the 1917 mayorality election they numbered 145,000 (giving Morris Hillquit 22 per cent of the total vote). Yet even these figures may underestimate the extent of the movement, since they refer only to men, who were citizens and of voting age. In 1918, the first year they were allowed to register, women made up close to half the enrolled Socialists. They also made up one-tenth of the membership recruited by the party between 1908 and 1912. Two-thirds of the Socialist membership recruits were non-citizens, indicating a large pool of Socialists uncounted in election figures. It is of course impossible to estimate the numbers of youth and children in the Socialist movement, but youth clubs abounded, especially among Jews, and the garment workers' movement itself was extremely youthful. Finally, we should note the 300,000 readers of the New York City Socialist press, and overlapping with these the 300,000 members of the city's radical and socialist trade unions.[5]

Such figures are not mere statistics, to be manipulated on a page from a distance of decades. They signify a mass movement of considerable importance. But what of the rank and file of this movement? We know a great deal about its leadership, but few details about the membership that would specify the movement's genesis, development, and decline. By selecting one stratum of the Socialist movement — "enrolled Socialists" — and tracing a sample of them in New York census manuscripts, we may now fill in some important details about the rank and file. This article derives mainly from analysis of a sample of 1219 enrolled Socialists, taken from Board of Election rolls for Manhattan, 1915, and traced in census manuscripts for the same year.[6]

In 1915, and surely during the surrounding period, the New York Socialist movement was largely working class in composition. Seventy percent of the enrolled Socialists were manual workers, compared with sixty percent of Manhattan men over 21. Skill levels are difficult to determine with any close accuracy, however, because of the ongoing process of degradation of skills. Brewers, once highly skilled, were now "nothing more than ordinary factory workmen whose work can be performed by anyone." With the advent of speculative building and ready-tinted and mixed paints, the major part of painting "consisted of simple brush work which any worker of ordinary intelligence could learn in a comparatively short time." In carpentry the demand was "for the specialist whose success depends often on the quantity rather than the quality of work he performs." Work in wood mills, meanwhile, had "reached an extreme degree of subdivision of labor," and "the all-around man, when found, is generally the product of foreign training." Among machinists, the "specialization demanded by modern methods often tends to limit the work of an individual workman within very narrow boundaries, generally to tending a single machine."[7]

Nevertheless, we may make some general estimate of skill levels, corresponding to working class standards of the time. Labor in the garment industry, the largest single source of working class Socialists, was for the most part very highly skilled, somewhat more so in women's garments than in men's, where fashions varied less and subdivision had proceeded farther. The great majority of garment workers, whether hand or machine, had been trained in Europe as hand tailors; many had inherited the trade. The machine operator, wrongly classified in the census as "semi-skilled," was a highly innovative worker who translated a most difficult and painstaking hand trade into a machine trade, without loss in quality. The operator, indeed, was in many instances more highly skilled than the cutter, who commanded the industry's highest pay by virtue of strategic location, small numbers, and separate organization.[8] As for the building trades, we may feel safe in assigning painters to the semi-skilled category, and all other crafts to skilled. Printers, machinists, cigar makers, jewelry workers, and stationary engineers we may designate as skilled tradesmen, along with bakers, most of whom worked in small shops. Most transport workers, brewers, and hotel and restaurant workers, we may call "semi-skilled."

TABLE 1. Percentage of Skilled, Semi-skilled and Unskilled Workers among Enrolled Socialists, 1915, and Male Work Force over 21, Manhattan, 1910. (By Percent)

	Socialists (N-1219)	Male Work Force
I. Skilled	52	29
II. Semi-Skilled	17	19
III. Unskilled	1	13

These constitute the major trades among the Socialist ranks. Surveying these ranks we find that the proportion of skilled workers among Socialists was nearly double that in the population; the proportion of semi-skilled slightly less among Socialists; and that of unskilled workers a great deal less. Table 1 shows this.[9]

We may now consider various groups of trades, and their importance for the Socialist movement. The building trades contributed a large fraction of Socialists, about 15 per cent. A little less than a third of these were painters, whom we may classify as "semi-skilled." The rest were skilled workers, with carpenters and cabinetmakers making up by far the largest percentage, followed by plumbers and steam fitters, sheet metal workers, ornamental iron workers, electricians, and others.

Several of the building trades had a long record of labor radicalism, some of which persisted into the period we are examining. Carpenters had been prominent in every political expression of working class discontent, from the Working Men's Party of 1829 to the United Labor Party of 1886. In 1915 a dozen of the 60 New York locals of the carpenters union supported the Socialist Party fairly regularly, at minimum endorsing Socialist candidates and contributing money to the press. These dozen locals included two of the city's four cabinetmakers locals, two of the four machine woodworkers locals, and one of the two framers locals. Five locals regularly sent contingents to march in Socialist parades. All of these Socialist-inclined locals were German, most based in Yorkville.[10]

Prior to 1914 the German Painters Union of Yorkville served as the Socialist center in the otherwise conservative Brotherhood of Painters. In 1914, however, the Brotherhood absorbed the Russian and Austrian Jewish, 9,000-member Alteration Painters Union, more than doubling its size and vastly increasing its radical element. Alteration painters, who repainted old flats and rooms, had been barred from the Brotherhood, which concentrated solely on "new" construction. The end of the building boom, however, drove numerous Brotherhood painters into alteration work, so that many held cards in both organizations. Moreover, alteration painters had organized so successfully for a strike in 1910, that they virtually forced the declining Brotherhood to take them in. "As a result of the merger," a leader of the alteration painters recalled, "little locals which for years had had a membership of no more than two or three hundred, overnight became large and powerful unions, some numbering as many as 1,500 to 2,000 members."

Some autonomous craft locals, such as the hardwood finishers, which had been in decline for years, suddenly found themselves faced with an enormous influx of semi-skilled painters. About half of the 24 locals of the newly-radicalized union regularly endorsed Socialist candidates and newspapers, marched in Socialist parades and elected Socialist officers. Russian Jewish Local 261, with 2,300 members the largest painters union local in the nation, soon became a major Socialist force in Harlem.[11]

The general trend in the building trades, however, was one of diminishing support for socialism. With several important exceptions — Jewish painters and ornamental iron workers, and probably sheet metal workers — the traditional locations of building trades radicalism were fast disappearing. No important instances of radicalism among Irish-dominated trades or locals had appeared since the demise of the United Labor Party. The German unions' unbroken history of radicalism was coming to a close in old age: the median age of German building trades workers enrolled as Socialists was 55. The building trades unions overall had been on a conservative course for some years, growing out of cooperation between union leaders and large contractors, and marked by considerable graft.[12]

A number of other trades are worthy of mention here as sources of Socialist support, among them machinists, teamsters and other transport workers, brewers, cigar makers, butchers, hotel and restaurant workers, printers, and bakers. Machinists and teamsters each accounted for about 4 per cent of enrolled Socialists, the rest from 2 to 3 percent. Socialism and other forms of radicalism were endemic in the machinists union nationally. The Socialist-inclined locals in New York — those of the International Association of Machinists and a dual union Brotherhood of Machinists — were German. The Brewery Workers, a predominantly German union with Socialist principles and an industrial structure, was a mainstay of New York socialism. German Socialist brewers — and machinists also — were younger by a decade than their fellows in the building trades, with a median age of 45. Cigar makers, long part of the vanguard in the American working class movement, now worked in a degraded trade in a locally declining industry, and were among the city's lowest-paid organized workers. Most Socialist cigar makers were German — followed by Russian-born and Bohemian — and were quite old, median age 60. The printing trades, certainly then the elite trades of working class New York, included a number of pockets supporting Socialists. The German-American compositors local of the Typographical Union, often took part in Socialist campaigns and parades. "Big 6," the 6,800 member Local 6, elected at least one Socialist officer, Edward F. Cassidy, and some of its chapels donated to the Socialist press. The bakers were a trade with an unfailing record of industrial militancy and political radicalism, symbolized in a 1909 strike parade when four thousand bakers marched, singing the *Marseillaise* and the *Internationale,* "dressed in white shirts and white caps with red badges on their chests." Local 100, "pride of the East Side," baked for striking garment workers. At least ten of the thirteen Bakers Union locals were Socialist-inclined, six of them Jewish, and the rest German and Bohemian.[13]

The following trades each contributed about one percent of enrolled Socialists: piano makers, jewelry workers, engineers and firemen, musicians and shoemakers. But it was from the garment trades that the bulk of working class New York Socialists were drawn. The uprising of the garment workers during the years 1909–1913, laid the mass basis for the Socialist movement in New York. As the garment workers' movement grew, so did the Socialist Party: the two overlapped and interlocked at every point. Garment workers organized committees to scour shops and neighborhoods for Socialist votes. They provided the muscle to beat back Tammany thugs at election time. They made up the largest single fraction of enrolled Socialists — one-quarter — and predominated in every district where Socialists neared or achieved electoral victory: the Lower East Side, Harlem, Brownsville, and parts of the Bronx.[14]

What are some of the characteristics of these workers? Russian-born made up the majority of male Socialist garment workers, some 60 percent, followed by Austrians and other Eastern Europeans with 31 percent. Germans, Italians, and American-born each made up about 3 percent. Individual trades are difficult to distinguish. As noted earlier, the great majority of garment workers had been trained as hand tailors, and many referred to themselves as tailors whether they worked by machine or hand. About 40 percent of Socialist garment workers called themselves tailors and nearly 25 percent, operators. Within these categories were the first significant numbers of factory operatives to enter the New York Socialist movement. Cutters made up a large fraction of Socialist garment workers, about 10 percent, and pressers another five. Fur workers and cap and hat makers each made up another five percent, followed by an assortment of trades such as designer. The median age of all was 31.

The Socialist ranks included a significant number of white collar and middle class Socialists, although proportionately fewer than in the city as a whole. Thirty percent of New York Socialists came from white collar, professional, and entrepreneurial classes as is shown by Table 2.[15]

TABLE 2. Class distribution of Enrolled Socialists, 1915, and Male Work Force over 21, Manhattan, 1910. (By Percent)

	Socialists (N-1219)	Male Work Force
Manual Workers (I, II and III)	70	61
White Collar Workers (IV)	11	15
Professionals (V)	8	6
Entrepreneurs (VI)	11	18

The proportion of white collar workers among enrolled Socialists was somewhat less than among male New Yorkers, about 11 percent compared with 15 percent. While we might have expected higher white collar specialties such as accounting to be under represented here, because of their identification with the owning classes, it is more difficult to account for the under-representation of the lower ranks of clerks and salesmen who worked long hours for little pay.

The answer, I suggest, lies in the unsettled nature of the white collar class. The white collar class was entering a period of enormous expansion, drawing into its ranks the young, English-speaking offspring of both immigrant and native-born generations, both working and small propertied classes. In the ages of its members it was a young class, much more youthful than the working class. We encounter here a class whose members have broken culturally from their ancestors, but which lacks any coherence, culture, or structure of its own. Its situation is fluid; its traditions and possibilities for organization, none. We may reasonably conclude that there were fewer Socialist white collar workers than we might have expected, because they lacked the organization that carried skilled workers into the movement. Although unions did exist, they organized less than one percent of white collar workers.[16]

The median age of Socialist white collar workers was 29. About 40 percent were born in Eastern Europe. Another 40 percent were American-born, but half with Eastern European parents. Many white collar Socialists with Eastern European ties were brothers or children of garment workers. It seems likely that these and some others made their way into the movement through working class and ethnic community channels.

Professionals appeared in Socialist ranks in greater proportion than among the work force, nearly 8 percent as compared with five. As with many white collar workers, however, their attachment to the movement seems best explained by factors outside usual professional work cultures. Three-quarters of Socialist higher professionals (doctors, dentists, lawyers) were European immigrants. The great majority of them lived and practiced in Harlem and the Lower East Side. They were people's doctors, and labor lawyers who went to night school. Meanwhile most lower professionals (e.g., artists, social workers, teachers, reporters) were American-born, with artists making up the greatest single number. In the first instance we are dealing with professionals enmeshed in ethnic working class communities, and sharing their values and traditions. Among the lower professionals we have some of the same, plus the additional element of free-floating artists who developed a sharp social conscience in this period of upheaval, and are attracted to socialism not only because of its political orientation, but also because of its strength among the working class and its linkages to working class communities and cultures.[17]

The median age of lower professionals was 33, of higher, 38. New York was a city with a vast entrepreneurial class, the great bulk of them dealing in petty capital. The 1910 census lists 59,000 retail dealers living in Manhattan, along with 10,000 real estate and insurance agents, 18,000 manufacturers and officials, 5,000 building contractors, plus others. All told, entrepreneurs accounted for some 18 percent of employed men. They made up considerably less of the Socialist ranks, about 11 percent.[18]

Socialist businessmen were mostly of the small sort. Ten percent were pushcart peddlers, fruit stand operators, and news vendors. Small shopkeepers were somewhat higher on the scale of capital: owners of sweet shops, delicatessens, cigar stores, junk and rag shops, tiny movie houses, laundries and groceries. They made up 50 percent, and insurance agents and the like, another fifteen. Representatives of substantial middle class capital made up about a quarter of Socialist entrepreneurs, or three percent of all Socialists. They ranged from clothing manufacturers at the top, to a furniture store owner, and included the Socialist children of some well-off families. An indication of the small average size of the capital of Socialist entrepreneurs, is in the number of servants the census lists for them. New York was a city with 140 thousand servants in 1910, sufficient for any well-propertied middle class family to include one or two in the household.[19] Eleven of 129 Socialist entrepreneurial families, or nine percent, listed servants. Fourteen of 94 professional families, or 15 percent, listed servants, indicating their generally higher status. Russian and East European Jews accounted for 70 percent of Socialist entrepreneurs. Most Socialists of these types lived in Harlem and on the Lower East Side, and many came from mixed entrepreneurial and working class families, ones that also included manual workers, usually in the garment trades. Although the discontents of small business may have driven some toward socialism, it is more likely that the general push came from the working class community, rather than their own class. The median age for Socialist entrepreneurs was 38.

The roots of the socialist movement lay in the organized working class, for the impetus toward socialism derived specifically from labor struggle and class conflict. Yet, there was no automatic connection between labor struggle and working class political action. Instead, labor struggle was mediated by the organizations that initially grew out of and came to encompass it: the trade unions. Thus an important key to Socialist growth (not only in New York but in other American cities) was located in the trade union movement.

We can suggest here a few features of unionism that affected Socialist prospects. First, while periods of intensive strike activity were also key periods for the spread of socialism, certain kinds of strikes seemed most conducive to Socialist growth. The organizational strike, which directly raised the question of workers' power, was one. A general strike in an industry, which pitted class against class, and which was common in New York because of its great number of small enterprises, was another. Strikes of workers who were concentrated in the same neighborhoods tended to become social outpourings, characterized by mass demonstrations and shows of community solidarity, which provided fertile ground for connecting militancy to political action. It is much more difficult to specify what kinds of strikes were unconducive to socialism, since in a period of heightened labor struggle, even the most circumscribed strike threatens to become much broader. As a rule, however, strikes against single employers, strikes isolated from the community, and jurisdictional disputes appear to have been unproductive of socialism. Finally, while one can come to no firm conclusion without a detailed investigation over a longer period of time, it would seem that unions with a more industrial than craft structure, or if craft which at least sought to organize all workers in a trade, were more conducive to socialism than were unions which were aristocratic and exclusive in practice.

TABLE 3. Country of Birth of Enrolled Socialists (N-1219)

Country	Percent
German	20
Northern European	4
Italy	1
Russia	35
Austria	13
Other East European	8
United States	19

**TABLE 4. Estimated ethnic distribution of Socialist Party
Membership Recruits, Manhattan and the Bronx
1908–1912 (N-6054)**

Country	*Percent*
German	23
Finnish	13
Italian*	3
Eastern European Non-Jewish)	14
Eastern European (Jewish)	39
Anglo/American	8
Other	1

* Italian recruits are 5 percent of total for 1908–1910, the only period for which they are recorded.

What of the Socialists' ethnic base? Eighty percent of New York's enrolled Socialists were immigrants. Table 3 provides a breakdown. Russian-born accounted for one-third of enrolled Socialists, and the addition of Austrian, Rumanian and Hungarian immigrants brings the Eastern European total to more than half. German- and American-born each made up one-fifth.

We must now consider various ethic and national groups in relation to the Socialist movement. I will introduce here some conclusions about the Socialist Party membership (i.e., those actually formally joining the party) based upon examination of a list of some six thousand party recruits who joined between 1908 and 1912. These recruits proved impossible to trace in state census manuscripts; however, party records listed recruits' names, addresses, and the branches they joined including foreign language branches. Thus these records provide some basis for reaching reasonably accurate conclusions about the membership, some of which are indicated in Table 4.[20]

In 1915 one-fifth of enrolled Socialists were German-born, a substantial proportion but considerably less than in the earlier days when German immigrants dominated a smaller party. The German-born members were concentrated in the areas of heaviest German settlement, along Manhattan's East Side and in adjacent parts of Brooklyn, Queens, and the Bronx. Yorkville in Manhattan contained the largest number of German Socialists, and also quartered most German-based unions, including the Brewery Workers and many building trades locals. German unionists and Socialists shared the same halls for public meetings and other affairs. The German Socialist daily the New Yorker *Volkszeitung,* founded in 1878, claimed a circulation of 15,000. One-quarter of all German Socialists were building trades workers and another 10 percent brewery workers, closely followed by metal trades workers and cigar makers. Butchers, teamsters, bakers, waiters, cooks and bartenders, and piano makers also made up significant numbers.

With the decline of labor radicalism after the 1880s and the increasing isolation of the Socialist Labor Party from the mainstream labor movement, German-American support for socialism had diminished steadily, until the garment strikes recharged the movement. Infused with new energy, socialism once again drew many Germans into its ranks. Indeed, even though few had any direct connection to the garment trades, Germans made up nearly a quarter of Socialist Party membership recruits during the period of upheaval.

There can be little doubt, however, that the revival of socialism among Germans was more of a recalling to the ranks of old Socialists, than the creation of new ones. The great majority of German Socialists were working class, 85 percent, and most came from skilled trades with long histories of radicalism. In 1915 the median age of German Socialists was 51, and their median stay in this country 28 years, which meant that nearly half had come prior to the United Labor upsurge of 1886. In 1904 the median age of German Socialists had been 46, and their median year of arrival 1881. Despite the passage of eleven years, we are dealing with much the same cohort.

Friedrich Engels' complaint that German members of the Socialist Labor Party "learn no English on principle," retained considerable validity for German Socialists 30 years later. Seventy percent of the German recruits joined foreign-language branches rather than English-speaking ones, and the number of such foreign language branches multiplied despite complaints from other Socialists. By contrast

80 percent of Russian Jews joined English-language branches. We should note, however, that German-based unions were consistent and generous supporters of other workers' struggles, and that German Socialists were as broadly internationalist as any group. Despite their aging base, German workers remained an important source of Socialist support, second only to East European Jewish workers.[21]

Although Finnish-born Socialists made up less than one percent of enrolled Socialists, they constituted 13 percent of party recruits during 1908–1912. Virtually nothing is known about them at this time, and we can only note that most who joined the party lived in East Harlem; that they appear to have been young; and that, in contrast to the practice among all other national and ethnic groups, women joined in roughly equal numbers to men, rather than fewer. No Finnish newspaper existed in New York. That there were so few Finnish Socialist voters indicates that few must have been citizens at that time. Moreover, Finns made up a tiny fraction of New York's foreign-born in 1910, 0.4 percent.[22]

Between one and two percent of the enrolled Socialists were born in Italy. The proportion of Italians among Socialist recruits was larger, however, about five percent.[23] The difference between the two figures may be explained by the fact that relatively few Italian immigrants became American citizens or voted, and many returned to Italy. Even the five percent figure is rather low, however, compared with the representation of Italians in the working class. Most Italian immigrants derived from the landless peasantry. They were concentrated in unskilled heavy labor, and lacked modern organization at work and in their communities, all factors unconducive to the development of socialism.[24] Italian stonemasons and garment workers were well organized, however, and excavators partly so. Some Socialist development was also evident in the proportion of Socialist recruits, and even enrolled Socialists. Although the numbers available are too limited to allow any firm conclusions, the sample indicates that garment workers made up the largest single group of Italian-American Socialists. Italians organized Socialist branches in Greenwich Village, the Lower East Side, Harlem, and Brooklyn. An examination of the names of Italian recruits suggests that most originated from Southern Italy and Sicily, rather than the industrial North.

Nearly one-fifth of the enrolled Socialists were American-born, about 90 percent of these of immigrant parents. Slightly over half of American-born Socialists were working class, and a large proportion, one-quarter, were white collar workers. The American-born were young, median age 29. The parents of 40 percent of them came from Eastern Europe; another 25 percent, from Germany.

The few black workers whom we encountered in our sample — a negligible fraction — came originally from the West Indies, not the American South, an experience the Communist Party would repeat in its day. A. Philip Randolph estimated that in 1917, 25 percent of black voters in Harlem, voted Socialist. If this was true, it could only have been because the proportion of blacks registering was very small. Like Italians, most black workers of Southern origins were former peasants, or their American equivalent. In New York they were concentrated in unskilled work, many in services. One hundred black men joined the Socialist Party in 1917: all were professionals and small businessmen, an indication of the weakness and lack of organization of the black working class.[25] About 3 percent of enrolled Socialists came from Northern and Western European countries not mentioned so far: Sweden, Norway, Denmark, Switzerland, France, Holland, England and Scotland, with the largest fraction from Sweden. In addition, there were a few from Canada, Greece, Egypt, and Turkey.

The Irish were the missing factor in the New York Socialist movement. They made up fewer than one percent of enrolled Socialists in 1915, of party recruits between 1908 and 1912, and of party members in 1904. We have space here only to sketch out some suggestions why so few were involved. To begin with, except for printers and stationary engineers, the best-organized Irish-American workers were in the building trades, and unions in these trades were generally conservative and closely tied to Tammany Hall. Irish held or shared power in the carpenters, plasterers, electrical workers, plumbers, and pavers unions, and — with Italians — in the bricklayers and laborers unions. Other Irish-based unions, among them teamsters, transit workers and longshoremen, met with a series of defeats in this period, leaving these workers only sporadically organized. These defeats, accompanied by firings and blacklistings, drove many into the ranks of casual labor and the sub-proletariat. The story of one Martin Crooks, for fifteen years "a regular driver at Cronin's establishment," is illustrative: "After the teamsters' strike in 1908, Crooks found himself out of a job and it was three years before he got anything 'regular' again." With defeats inflicted upon some of their unions and favors dispensed to the rest, the Irish working class was highly susceptible to the appeals of machine politics, with its primitive welfare state apparatus and buildings contracts. Moreover, the typical "cadre" developed in Irish tradition, the political lawyer, proved adaptable to and readily absorbed by the machine.[26] There were exceptions to the general picture, which indicate some potential Irish support for socialism under circumstances more favorable to it. A 1916 transit strike brought a sizable number of Irish workers into the ranks of enrolled Socialists for the first time, and Irish support increased during America's participation in World War I.[27]

We cannot take up here the matter of the Church's influence in Irish indifference or hostility toward socialism, except to say: Irish-American Socialists felt the Church to be strongly influential;[28] and second, it would be difficult for us to measure the Church's impact, since the nature of Irish working class organization and disorganization meant that socialism could scarcely gain purchase among them, whatever the other problems. With evident material reasons for socialism's weakness among Irish workers, we have no need to invoke ideological ones.

Immigrants from Eastern Europe constituted the bulk of Socialist supporters — 57 percent of enrolled Socialists and roughly the same proportion of party recruits — for here lay the radical core of New York's working class, the Jewish garment workers. The Socialist press mirrored the Eastern Europeans' importance (see Table 5). The *Call* and *Volkszeiting,* the city's English and German Socialist dailies, each had a circulation of 15,000. The circulation of the Yiddish daily, *Vorwærts* was 200,000. A Hungarian daily, *Elore,* reached 10,000, and the Russian *Novy Mir* (New World), 18,000. Bohemian Socialists also published a daily newspaper, *Hlas Lidu* (Voice of the People), and a weekly, *Obrana* (Defense). Other Socialist weeklies included *Robotnik Polski* (Polish Worker) and a Lithuanian paper, *Laisve.*[29]

TABLE 5. New York City Socialist Newspapers, 1915.

Name	Language	Founded	Approximate Circulation
Dailies			
New York Call	English	1909	15000
New Yorker Volkzeitung (Peoples' Paper)	German	1879	15000
Vorwærts (Forward)	Yiddish	1897	200000
Elöre (Forward)	Hungarian	1900	10000
Hlas Lidu (Voice of the People)	Bohemian	1886	?
Novy Mir (New World)	Russian	1911	15000
Weeklies			
Obrana (The Defense)	Bohemian	1910	?
Laisve (Liberty)	Lithuanian	1911	?
Robotnik Polski (Polish Worker)	Polish	1895	?

Sources: See Footnote 29

It is important to note some distinctions among Eastern European Socialists. Not all were Jewish: among party recruits about a quarter were not, including most of those who joined Bohemian, Slovak, Polish and Lettish branches, and a large minority of those joining Hungarian branches. Among enrolled Socialists, however, all Eastern Europeans except for Bohemians and a minority of Hungarians appear to lave been Jewish. Practically no Slavic names appear on Socialist voting rolls. As with Finns and Italians, it seems likely that relative to Jewish Socialists, few non-Jewish East Europeans were becoming citizens, perhaps because of a higher rate of return to their home-lands.

The transformation of New York socialism was accomplished above all others by Jewish workers, whose stormy upheavals fixed the standards for militancy and radicalism.[30] Jewish garment workers alone constituted one-fourth of enrolled Socialists, and the proportion of Jews overall surely approached 60 percent. Yet it would be wrong to conclude that New York socialism was in some narrow sense "Jewish," for it was characteristic of Jewish workers that they pressed relentlessly across ethnic barriers to forge bonds of solidarity with all other working class groups. In 1913, when Italian, Jewish and German silk workers struck in Paterson, New Jersey, their New York City support came overwhelmingly from Jewish workers. When Irish transit workers struck in 1916, Jewish mobs in Harlem in support of the strikers besieged the trolleys and turned out scab conductors. And although other Irish-based unions promised a general strike in sympathy, the garment and other Jewish-dominated trades provided the only unions that saw the promise through.[31]

Certainly few such acts were ever fully reciprocated. But they were not "tactics" designed to gain special favors or rewards. Rather, they were an expression of class feeling that Jewish workers articulated as a kind of vanguard, informing and inspiring other previously-unorganized "new" immigrant workers, and more militant and class-conscious workers among established craft unions. An Italian seamstress later recalled:

> The Jewish girls, they were much more advanced than the Italians. . . . They fought for us Italians. The chairlady in my shop, she was Jewish. She goes up to the boss and she says, 'Look at this girl! Why are you paying her so little?' She was talking about me! Oh, they were very advanced. . . . Later on we got our own union and we were advanced too.[32]

The desire of Jewish workers to transcend ethnic barriers, and also to "Americanize" their movement, found expression in their work as Socialists.

We noted earlier in contrast to all other immigrant Socialists, including Germans, Finns, Italians, Poles, Slovaks, and Bohemians, few Jewish recruits joined foreign-language branches. Although it is generally assumed that most joined the Yiddish-language Jewish Socialist Federation, this was not the case: only four percent entered the branches that eventually made up the Federation. The Federation's importance lay in the fact that it included a number of Jewish intellectuals, and much of the present and future leadership of the garment unions. However, nearly 80 percent of immigrant Jewish recruits joined English language branches and constituted the bulk of their membership. The remainder joined such foreign language branches as Russian and Hungarian. The English language branches which the Jewish ranks entered were ethnically mixed, if other ethnic groups resided in the district. Harlem and other upper Manhattan branches are examples. Jewish Socialists, like Jewish immigrants in general, were also more likely than members of other "new" immigrant groups to become American citizens, and to vote.[33]

We may also sketch out the following characteristics of Eastern European Jewish Socialists. Seventy percent were working class, the largest number, of course, in the garment trades: 40 percent of all Jewish Socialists. Twelve percent were building trades workers, with painters constituting the largest trade. White collar workers made up another 9 percent, professionals slightly less, and entrepreneurs 14 percent. Jewish Socialists were young, median age 31. Their median year of arrival was 1904.

None of these figures differed much by country of birth. It is striking even for New York, that 80 percent of Socialists were immigrants. No wonder that children of these Socialists thought Elizabeth Gurley Flynn so odd: "You're an American and you believe that too?"[34]

The inability of immigrant Socialists to transmit their political culture to their children was a major failure of socialism. But saying as much scarcely identifies the source of the problem. Shifts in the occupational structure account for much of the break in tradition. Large numbers of the offspring of working class immigrants were drawn into the white collar classes that were growing overtop a base of expanding modern industry. Leaving aside matters of ideology, these new classes were unsettled, unorganized, and consequently unconducive to socialism. Moreover, the decline in the proportion of skilled workers in various industries meant that many of the offspring who remained in the working class entered unorganized semiskilled trades, or defensive and conservatizing skilled trades. The pressures of Americanization, which were rooted in the prospects for individual and family advancement that a dynamic capitalism could deliver, fell most heavily upon the second generation, who neither identified with the old, European-derived cultures, nor were in a position to forge a new collective culture of their own.

Shifts in the occupational structure, although accumulating gradually for society as a whole, sharply divided immigrant and second generations. Table 6, derived from the 1920 census, highlights this division.[35]

TABLE 6. Class distribution of Foreign-born and Native-born of Foreign Parent(s), Male Work Force, New York City, 1920. (By Percent)

	Immigrants	*Second generation*
Manual Workers (I, II, III)	70	51
IV White Collar Workers	10	32
V Professionals	3	5
VI Entrepreneurs		
owners	14	7
managers	3	5

The second generation here does not, of course, consist entirely of offspring of the immigrant generation; nor does the immigrant generation consist entirely of parents of the second. Nevertheless, the table serves well to indicate the general class direction of each group. Several aspects are notable: first, a considerable reduction in the proportion of manual workers from immigrant to second generation, particularly in manufacturing and services; second, a considerable increase in white collar workers; and third, a decrease in owners of capital, with a rise in salaried managers and professionals.

Our sample of enrolled Socialists shows very much the same class differences between generations, as does the census. In this instance, however, we may compare actual fathers and sons. This example includes 143 immigrant Socialists who have sons who work, living with them. The two generations as indicated by Table 7 divide by occupation rather sharply.

TABLE 7. Class distribution of Immigrant Socialists and their Sons.
(By Percent)

	Immigrant Socialists (N-143)	*Sons (N-229)*
Manual Workers (I, II and III)	72	49
IV White Collar Workers)	4	41
V Professionals	3	5
IV Entrepreneurs	20	3

Our sample also enables us to see the movements of the second generation against the background of the first. 103 working class Socialists are among the immigrant generation. Nearly half their sons — 46 percent — leave the working class. This pattern holds for all ethnic and national groups, with children of Russian Jews showing the largest proportion leaving. Whatever the ethnic or national group, the pattern is somewhat more pronounced among children of skilled workers. Moreover, of the skilled workers' children who stayed in the working class, one-third took semi-skilled and unskilled jobs. Age does not seem to be a factor here: in this and other computations, when the offspring are divided into those over 25 years old and those under, the distributions remain similar. Also in the sample are 40 immigrant, white collar and middle class Socialists, with working sons living with them. One-third of their sons are in manual work, two-thirds in white collar and middle class work.

The picture is one of a disintegrating working class, not in its overall features, but in its actual composition. There is practically no inheritance of trade, a traditional source of working class tradition and stability.[36] There is only limited inheritance of class between immigrant and second generations, and thus limited opportunity for the development of continuing and flourishing working class communities. I wish to emphasize that I am not discussing upward mobility here, which is quite another matter. Most men who left the working class entered clerical and sales jobs where hours were far longer and wages considerably lower than those of unionized skilled workers.[37] I see no reason to consider this movement as necessarily "upward," nor any reason to consider it as voluntary (that is, as other than the result of changes in the occupational structure which occur independently of human will).

Socialism was a movement which derived its political aims and its social base from working class organization and struggle. In order for Socialist traditions to pass from immigrant to second generation, there had to be some underlying class continuity between them. There was not, and so the transmission failed. The importance of class continuity is indicated in our sample. We have no way of comparing the political inclinations of Socialist fathers and their sons, since their names are not necessarily paired in voter registration records. However, along with Socialists whose sons live with them and work, our sample also includes 138 Socialists whose fathers live with them and work, and we may compare class continuity in this set, with that in the first.

Suppose we assume that Socialism passes from father to son, with the son's class being of no importance. Since the offspring of Socialists are distributed more widely among white collar and middle class occupations than their fathers, we should expect the same of Socialist sons. Of the Socialists whose fathers live with them and work, 58 percent of their fathers are in manual occupations, 42 percent in white collar and middle class work. We should now expect the sons to be substantially less working class than the fathers as in the first set. But this is not the case: 63 percent of Socialist sons are in working class occupations, nearly three-quarters of these in skilled trades. Eighty of the Socialist sons have working class fathers. If class were unimportant, we would expect nearly half of the sons to have left the working class, as in the first set. Instead,

26 percent have left, while 74 percent remain. All these figures (as detailed in Table 8) indicate that class is important.

Clearly, the shift in occupational structure, with its exaggerated impact on the relationship between immigrant and second generation, reduced the base for the Socialist movement.

TABLE 8. Class distribution of Socialist Sons and their Fathers.
(By Percent)

	Socialist Fathers (N-138)	*Sons (N-138)*
Manual Workers (I, II and III)	58	63
IV White Collar Workers	6	30
V Professionals	5	12
IV Entrepreneurs	31	5

The rise of a mass Socialist movement in New York in the second decade of this century was due mainly to the upheaval of garment workers. But the story is more complicated than that, for in the whole Socialist movement garment workers constituted a minority, although a large one. Coming as they did from a well-organized and extensive movement of their own, garment workers imparted to the Socialist movement a coherence and a structure, as well as some possibilities for success, all factors which attracted other workers actively participating (in struggle) and revived the faded hopes of still others. The movement was working class, but represented organized, predominately skilled sectors of the working class, not unorganized and unskilled. Thus the movement was underlaid by trade unions, making the Socialist Party *de facto* a labor party. Its working class character, however, also proved attractive to members of other social classes, although generally not in the same proportions as they existed in the larger society.

Outside the first generation of Eastern European Jewish workers, the social base of the movement was uncertain and uneven. German-born workers made up a large fraction of Socialists. But they were aging, and their once-independent unions now made up the final preserves of socialism in the conservatizing, skilled building trades. Meanwhile the Irish, who were well-represented in certain areas of the trade union movement, were entirely absent from the Socialist movement except for episodic appearances. Italians were somewhat more evident, but overall lacked modern organization.

The composite picture is of a succession of working class movements that failed to link together at strategically opportune moments because they peaked at different times; and which could establish no continuity from one to another because they involved ever-different ethnic and national groups with different traditions. Thus the Jewish workers' movement arose in the twilight of the German movement, and long after the passing of the Irish.

Ethnic succession meant the continuous remaking of large portions of the working class.[38] Meanwhile, shifts in the occupational structure extended this remaking to virtually the whole working class, as sizable numbers of American-born moved out of the working class, and into white collar classes completely lacking in tradition and organization. Amidst endemic working class instability, socialism could not long find firm rooting.

SOCIALISTS IN THE STREETS:
THE NEW YORK CITY SOCIALIST PARTY IN WORKING CLASS
NEIGHBORHOODS, 1908–1918

Radical America, March–April 1968

DURING THE DECADE PRIOR TO 1918 socialism in New York City became more than the hopeful speculation of a small and isolated party. It became the resounding claim of a movement which gathered scores of thousands of workers, and influenced many thousands more. The period was one of exceptionally sharp class struggle, providing the soil for Socialist growth. Jewish garment workers who had seemed hopelessly unorganizable only a short time earlier, passed through a series of thunderous strikes, an experience that not only firmly established trade unionism among the Jewish working class, but deeply marked their political culture as Socialist. Irish teamsters and public transport workers, among whom socialism ordinarily found extremely difficult purchase, undertook a succession of strikes that brought all organized New York workers to the verge of a general strike, and many Irish workers themselves to the edge of the Socialist movement. "None of our men would have anything to do with Socialism before this," an Irish carman said, "for the reason that it was never brought home to them like the strike has brought it." Socialism also found a base among the predominantly Jewish or German sections of the painters, carpenters, brewery workers, bakers, ornamental iron workers, carriage and wagon makers, piano makers, typographers, machinists and cigar makers unions — many of them involved in struggles of their own making, and all inspired by the garment workers.[1]

The working class unrest which rose to the surface in Bayonne, Paterson, Danbury, Lawrence, Toledo, Chicago, Pittsburgh, Paint Creek, Cripple Creek, Coeur d'Alene, Butte, Los Angeles — and in Europe — rippled into New York and affected the movement there. It was characteristic of the period that when New York workers marched in a 1912 Socialist demonstration, they carried red flags, posters of Eugene Debs, and "transparencies protesting against the farcical trial of Ettor, Giovannitti and Cruso and the imprisonment of Timber Workers in Louisiana...."[2]

The impact of these struggles on the ways in which working people lived, relaxed and enjoyed life — and the influence of these ways of living on the struggles themselves — these are our concerns here. For the Socialist movement drew strength not only from the shops, but from the rich and vibrant working class culture that flourished in the neighborhoods: in the streets, tenements, cafes, taverns, dance halls, theatres, barber shops, church basements, settlement houses and union halls. These too were the arenas of socialism, the meeting places of the self-taught, forums of "music, art and comradeship," where one might encounter "witty criticisms of American life, such as 'Moses comes to Hester Street,' and 'Jesus Comes to Ellis Island' "; or "The Spoken Newspaper," where "A huge audience listened to editorials and special articles read by the authors themselves, and the atmosphere was charged with intense purpose"; or a fiery debate among children, on socialism:

> "You see, gentlemen, it's this way: The millionaires sit round the table eating sponge-cake and the bakers are down in the cellar baking it. But the day will come" — and here the young orator pointed an accusing finger at the universe — "when the bakers will come up from their cellar and say, 'Gentlemen, bake your own sponge-cake.' "[3]

The vital elements of day-to-day working class culture underpinned the socialist movement and provided it with interest and life that went far beyond the narrowly political. Nowhere was the connection between socialism and working class community culture more evident than in the streets.

I. The People's Parade

The unrest that seethed through the garment shops and car barns of New York in this decade found its way into the streets of the working class neighborhoods themselves: on the West Side during the scow trimmers' strike of 1909, it took the form of "Irish rain," a shower of bricks from tenement rooftops, onto the heads of scabs and their police protectors; in Harlem during the 1916 carmen's strike, a crowd of two thousand, besieged trolleys and discharged their scab operators; and in the Lower East Side and neighborhoods adjoining the garment district, legions of striking workers picketed and marched incessantly, and vast crowds surrounded the shops on the lookout for scabs.[4]

Strikes in this period became social outpourings which fused workplace and neighborhood in massive demonstrations of the solidarity of the entire working class, men, women and children: bakers made bread for strikers and their families, and workers paraded to the cheers of thousands of their neighbors. The strike erased the distinction between work areas and living areas — a distinction which had developed historically as the worker was separated from the means of production. Upon entering the shop, men and women passed into another nation — a passage symbolized most tragically in the locking-in of the Triangle workers. The currents of revolt generated in the workplace surged out into the streets and back into the neighborhoods, for here strength could be found in a culture and society of the workers' own making.[5] In an atmosphere charged by the turbulent rejoining of workplace and community, the socialist movement flourished.[5]

The strike as a social outpouring featured parades and marches, both spontaneous and organized. In *an* early strike of children's cloak makers, twelve thousand workers "marched from the shops singing the *Marseillaise.*" The "Great Revolt" of 1910 opened with "a sea of people surging from all side streets toward Fifth Avenue." Abraham Rosenberg writes:

> Every minute the crowds grew larger and all moved in the same direction. By half past two, all the streets, from 38th down and from the East River toward the West, were jammed with thousands of workers. Traffic in most streets came to a standstill. Each worker carried his bundle of tools and all marched in the direction of the strike halls. ... As they passed the headquarters of the union on 10th Street, the strikers cheered. In my mind I could Only picture to myself such a scene taking place when the Jews were led out of Egypt.

German piano makers in a 1912 strike organized parades that wound through the workers' neighborhoods and piano manufacturing districts of the West Side and the Bronx. At the conclusion of the Jewish bakery workers' strike of 1909, four thousand bakers marched, "dressed in white shirts and white caps with red badges on their chests." Their children joined them, one group carrying a long banner saying they were children of "former slave bakers whom they saw very seldom because of long hours of toil."[6]

Strikers' parades were an expression of solidarity on the streets. The parade served many purposes: it gave workers a sense of their combined strength, especially where workplaces were scattered, as in the garment industry and transportation; it was a demonstration of power and determination; it called other workers out from the shops; it enhanced discipline and allegiance among the ranks; it was a combat formation from which pickets could be deployed and police and scabs fought. Furthermore the parade was a demonstration of the strikers' pride in their craft, and in themselves as producers. It was customary for them to march in some sort of uniform of their trade, and under its banner: bakers and butchers paraded in white shirts and caps, with red belts or badges; carmen wore their uniforms; women garment workers wore white blouses with red sashes. On the most mundane level parades broke the monotony of long strikes and bolstered morale. During the Great Revolt of 1910, as over the weeks owners, one by one, signed contracts with the union, each shop returned to work in a group, marching through the streets, carrying American flags. Their vacant places in the halls were filled by other strikers who were also marched in. These little parades were arranged to break the monotony and to bolster the morale of the weak-hearted.[7]

But beyond all this, the parade was a public celebration of the justice of the workers' cause, a cause that found resounding affirmation as the parade made its way through the streets of the neighborhoods. Here husbands, wives, children, friends, neighbors and fellow workers cheered the strikers on and marched with them.

Until their 1916 strike, the street, subway and elevated carmen of New York had never marched in a workers' parade. But in September, 1916, ten thousand uniformed carmen gathered in Yorkville, Manhattan, to march downtown to Union Square.

As they left Yorkville, relatives and friends of the marchers cheered and hurrahed for two hours. Great crowds thronged along Madison and Fourth Avenues, and when the head of the line reached the cloakmaking district below 34th Street, the windows of factories and shops were black with workers. Men ceased work on buildings to cheer as the carmen passed; teamsters parked their wagons on side streets, and stood on the sidewalks, and policemen grinned and openly manifested their pleasure at the parade.[8]

One month later, in October, 1916, 250 of these same carmen made up the "banner division" of a torchlight parade of twelve thousand persons that wound through the streets of Harlem. This, however, was a Socialist parade, with characteristics of its own. Brewery workers, bakers, cloak makers, painters, a division of girls, members of Waist Makers' Union No. 26, paper hangers, iron workers, machinists, carpenters, cigar makers and other trades, marched along with the carmen, "Not only were young and old in the parade, but there were people of all nationalities and races, thousands of Jewish workers and many Finns, Germans, Irish and Italians." In the month between the carmen's and this parade, Socialists had organized three large indoor rallies for the strikers, in Harlem, the Bronx, and the Lower East Side. They had also organized women's brigades of garment workers, and of wives and sisters of carmen, to persuade scabs to quit, and had begun a campaign for municipal ownership of the "traction trust." Many marchers in the Socialist parade wore "Don't Be a Scab" sashes on their hats or shirts, and "As the scab cars passed, the shouts and yells of `scab,' skunk' and 'rat,' endearments intended for the strikebreakers, flew thick and fast."[9]

On its surface this was merely an election parade, called to support Socialist candidates in Harlem. But as with all Socialist parades, underneath it was much more. It took its immediate inspiration not from the fact that elections were being held, but from the actual struggle of the carmen. It overlaid this struggle with the broad theme of class unity. The Harlem parade "fused the clashing races into one kind of working people." After the parade the marchers filled the streets around Harlem's Socialist headquarters. Mothers drew their baby carriages into "one solid line along the stoop line," and for the next two hours the demonstration became a street meeting — not strictly a mass meeting, although Socialist candidates, orators, and trade union leaders addressed as many as could hear — but a shifting constellation of meetings, with carmen gathering here, capmakers there, then dissolving into the larger crowd and again reforming into different groups of meetings, discussing and arguing. Speakers were not only the official leadership of the carmen's union, but rank-and-file agitators. Participants were not only the marchers in the streets, but also the men and women who leaned from the windows of their apartment buildings.[10]

Socialist parades brought the fight for socialism into the neighborhoods. "The people's parade is a revolutionary measure," a New York Socialist organizer explained.

> . . . Music brings the crowds to the windows. It stirs up the entire neighborhood — it catches the kids, the newly-weds and the veteran. Red fire adds to the attraction. Altogether, it catches the mixed multitude through the ear and eye, and also agitates the brain, and is a cause for discussion all along the line, and this discussion is a powerful mental exercise for our own good.
>
> . . . The Socialist party is organizing for the conquest of the world . . . . The great Socialist parades of the future will be the wonder and admiration of the country. They will have an educational value and will stand for harmony, intelligence, discipline, solidarity and power."[11]

In many ways the socialist movement found a natural location in the neighborhoods. Partly this was a matter of sheer convenience. Socialist leaders were election-minded, and elections were held in the neighborhood, not the workplace. Also, there was a political convergence between the problems of working class neighborhoods and Socialist slogans, which included attacks on slum housing and calls for cheap bread and milk.

But to look only at the electoral advantages to be gained from Socialist work in the neighborhoods would be misleading. Such a view sees socialism simply as a movement of party leaders searching for advantages, rather than a movement created by workers, both in the workplace and the neighborhood. Socialist election parades and rallies were demonstrations of working class self-confidence, organization and audacity, not merely appeals for votes. Thus Morris Hillquit's description of a spontaneous Socialist parade during his campaign for mayor in 1917 really describes an episode in a social movement:

> One evening I was to speak at three meetings in the Lower East Side. A gigantic parade was formed spontaneously. The whole East Side seemed to be on its feet, and for three hours countless thousands of men and women surged and swarmed through miles of streets before and behind the car in which I made my laborious progress from one hall to another. They sang and shouted and cheered, and their numbers swelled incessantly .... [12]

Socialist parades traced their recent ancestry and structure to the May Day demonstrations, which began in New York in 1890. Originally called as mass demonstrations for the eight-hour day, May Day parades featured divisions of workers — chiefly Jewish and German — marching in their best dress, under their own union banners and the red flag. Melech Epstein says of the first such demonstration:

> About nine thousand Jewish workers took part. The cloakmakers division numbered around three thousand. Before the start of the demonstration numerous meetings were held to explain the significance of the event. Bands played the *Marseillaise* and other workers' songs. The people were dressed in their best, and red flags fluttered from hundreds of windows. The streets of the East Side took on a new, more cheerful air.'[13]

May Day's eight-hour theme receded in time, but the parades themselves continued as demonstrations of international working class solidarity and power. From year to year particular May Day slogans were voiced — protest against the imprisonment of Moyer, Pettibone and Haywood; opposition to the war; support for the Russian Revolution; endorsement of women's rights. Despite the changes in theme the basic structure — divisions of workers marching under individual union banners. and the red flag — remained.

Whatever their immediate purpose, Socialist parades remained faithful to the May Day spirit and format. In November, 1912, with Eugene Debs running for President, Socialists organized a parade of 40,000 — their largest to that date — watched by another 150,000. Bands played the *Marsellaise* and the *International.* "If your captain don't keep your line in shape," the parade orders read, "RECALL him and elect another to his place." One column of 25,000 started in Yorkville on Manhattan's East Side, but made its way downtown through the Tammany-controlled, heavily Irish West Side, where, according to a reporter, there were "no more sneers" as in years past, but cheers. The "great line of marchers . . . that spoke of discipline and solidarity" finally wound up at Union Square, where another column from the Lower East Side joined it.[14]

In the Yorkville column of the parade there was a great outpouring of labor organizations, "who showed their colors by turning out with red flags and their own bands." Contingents from three locals each of the Machinists, Carpenters and Bakers unions, and two locals of the Painters Union, marched, along with contingents from locals of the Brewers Union, Building Employees Union, Cigar Makers, Ladies' Garment Workers, Fur Workers, Journeymen Tailors, and Pearl Button Workers. Interspersed with these were a dozen branches of the Socialist Party; a dozen more German branches of the party; the Irish Socialist Federation; Polish, Lettish, Russian, Bohemian, Hungarian and Finnish Socialist branches — "The Finnish Socialist women turned out en masse, and some of them carried their babies in their arms . . . "; the Young People's Socialist Federation, Junior Socialist Federation, and the Intercollegiate Socialist Society; and numerous groups from Workmen's Singing Societies, and German and Jewish workmen's benefit societies.[15]

Socialist parades were like May Day parades, and not simply because the Socialist Party organized both. New York City Socialism depended for its growth and strength upon the organization of the working class — garment workers foremost, but also carmen, teamsters, brewery workers, typographers, bakers, painters and carpenters. The "people's parade" — May Day or other Socialist — expressed the organization of the working class into unions, but gave this expression a revolutionary turn: the overall unity of the class in fighting for a new social order.

Not all workers' parades were celebrations: 100,000 marched in grief and anger after the 1911 Triangle fire, which killed 146 workers. Although the parade was a traditional feature of working class culture, not all working class parades were militant protests. Many were religious processions, public funerals, demonstrations for Tammany Hall's political machine, and celebrations of national or ethnic holidays. During religious holidays in New York's Italian neighborhoods, Antonio Mangano observed,

> the greatest and most extravagant celebrations take place. They, as a rule, occur in midsummer, when prodigal decoration, street illuminations — such as one sees so frequently in Italy, fireworks, processions, etc. — are indulged in.... At such a one held three years ago in "Little Italy," in honor of the saints, it was claimed that no less than fifteen thousand men paraded up and down the streets each day, bearing banners on which were pinned offerings of money.

Huge spontaneous torchlight parades and bonfires lit up the Irish and German slum, Hell's Kitchen, for Tammany Hall at election time. And although national or ethnic holidays sometimes included a left-wing demonstration, most were as James Connelly described:

> At all our Saint Patrick's Day or other national celebrations, the highest place of honor is ever given to the grafting politician whose record smells to high heaven with corruption, or to the sleek-tongued lawyer, who uses the choice gift of eloquence to cajole and betray ... [16]

The religious pageantry of Italian neighborhoods evoked pre-working class peasant life, still vital in the minds of recent immigrants. Indeed, it reflected a society still organized along village lines even in the city, with a male working class largely molded by the peasant rhythms of heavy labor, under a paternalistic system.[17] As for Tammany, it based itself not on the organized working class, but on a variety of other strata, including street gangs that frequently evolved into political clubs; cadres of regular city employees such as firemen; the vulnerable petty-bourgeoisie of immigrant communities, including street peddlers, small shop owners and saloon-keepers; the underworld of gamblers, prostitutes and pimps; the unorganized destitute; the corrupt union leadership in industries strategic to Tammany graft, such as construction. Tammany pageantry in districts such as Hell's Kitchen lacked organization of workers, but relied on street gangs instead. Once Jewish workers on the Lower East Side organized themselves industrially, they broke from Tammany and built their own community organizations.[18]

For all that strikers and Socialist parades had in common, there was one crucial difference: the strikers parade was a weapon of combat, the Socialist parade was not. Caught up in the mainstream of trade unionism, antagonistic toward the revolutionism of the Industrial Workers of the World, and limited by their own reformist visions, Socialist leaders never sought to coalesce the fight for socialism with the strike at the point of production, except in spirit. Believing that the party should concern itself with political matters while "economic" questions, including strikes, should be left to the trade unions, Socialist leaders never considered the role of the mass strike in achieving socialism.[19] In the end the strike parade alone, flowing as it did from. the struggle at the point of production, symbolized the ultimate expression of working class power.

II. The Street Corner

Strikes and parades were episodic reflections of the community culture of working class neighborhoods. More usual was the routine street culture of city life, pursuing its day-to-day course: women and men sitting on stoops, watching, talking with neighbors, arguing, buying from peddlers; young men hanging out; children playing.

The Socialist movement grew in these streets. As summer approached and street culture sprang into life, Socialists left their ill-heated halls to begin their outdoor season. Hundreds of home-grown. Socialist orators and spellbinders appeared on the crowded main streets of working class neighborhoods to deliver the message of socialism against a backdrop of clanging streetcars and rumbling, horse-drawn drays, while boys and girls with red bands around their arms passed out leaflets and sold literature. Taught by such pioneer soapboxers as Tom Lewis, who could be heard for blocks, speakers learned to "Breathe deep, use your diaphragm as bellows; don't talk on your vocal chords or you'll get hoarse in no time. Throw your voice out." They adorned their platforms with flags and banners, experimented with taut canvas backdrops to project their voices even farther, gesticulated, paced the platform, and appealed to emotions. The number of rallies was impressive: by 1916, 70–80 per week — and many times more during elections — covering all neighborhoods in all boroughs. Crowds were sizable: Socialist street speakers in Manhattan reported audiences ranging from 35 to 1500, with the majority of rallies attracting 150–300 persons.[20]

In August, 1914, Socialist Party organizers polled street corner speakers on the size of their crowds, their topics, and the problems they encountered. The responses provide good clues concerning the character of the rallies. Some speakers' comments on particular corners in Manhattan were:

> 15th Street & 8th Avenue. "A valuable corner if the early hours of the evening, 7:30–8:30, are utilized. Men get home from work here earlier than those on the lower east side. It is a purely working class neighborhood. The men generally go out on the streets right after their evening meals."

15th & 8th. "Had an exceptionally attentive audience. Many, questions were asked, hostile at first, but melting into genuine frankness and courtesy."

96th & 2nd. "Theoretical and Mandan speeches don't go on this corner."

35th & Broadway. "The nonreligious character of the Socialist Party should be hammered home in this district."

Speakers also reported disturbances, especially on the West Side:

15th & 8th. "We should have some good party members here and get policemen assigned to the corner. There should be no dilly-dallying. If persons are disorderly they should be arrested. A few arrests would quiet the Roman Catholic disturbers."

43rd & 8th. " ... had a dozen (members) been on the job here everything would have been OK. Instead our meeting was constantly interrupted by youthful disturbers."

57th & 8th. "The matter of police protection is becoming an urgent matter. It seems there is a body of young men going around to disrupt meetings."
68th & Amsterdam. "A policeman should be detailed at this corner to preserve order. The *police seem* to be getting *careless* under our reform Mayor."

Serious disturbances were fairly rare: 137 out of 157 reports listed no disturbances at all; and most of the 20 disturbances reported were of a random nature — "throwing of missiles and water from houses and roofs," "rough-house," and "drunkards." Only one rally was actually broken up.[21]

Unquestionably, however, matters were tough in Irish Catholic neighborhoods, where Tammany had strong roots among the street gangs, and where Socialists confronted the usual hostility of Irish Catholics toward socialism. Although a third of the street corner speakers were Irish, only one per cent of the party members were, at least until 1914. Elizabeth Gurley Flynn recalls the special difficulties the Irish Socialist Federation anticipated on street corners:

> The Federation arranged street *meetings* . . . especially in Irish neighborhoods where such meetings had never been held. It had a large green and white banner, announcing who and what it was, with the Gaelic slogan, *Faugh-a-Balach* (Clear the Way) in big letters surrounded by harps and shamrocks. The meetings were stormy but finally accepted at many corners. A German blacksmith comrade built the *Federation* a sturdy platform that could not easily be upset, with iron detachable legs that could be used as "shillelaghs" in an emergency. These helped to establish order at the meetings, and won a wholesome respect for the Federation.
>
> Patrick J. Quinlan, one of the Federation's founders, gave this advice to all Socialist street corner speakers; The meeting should "conclude by 10–10:30 — otherwise it will aggravate the people who live in the neighborhood," and become a rendezvous for "bugs and cranks." Questions Should be invited, not coaxed, and "where a corner is troublesome it may be well to omit questions." Finally, "Religious discussions or wrangles, no matter how well they may be conducted, have no place in a propaganda meeting, nor are they conducive to sound organization.... Kill capitalism. Let the other fellow kill God."[22]

Individual Socialist branches — numbering 135 by late 1914 — organized the great majority of street corner rallies, holding them in the evenings in the neighborhoods near branches headquarters. But Socialists also held noon-hour rallies during strikes, and in the parks and streets where workers gathered during lunch. Brooklyn Socialists appeared regularly along the waterfront, and at entrances to the Naval Yard. In September, 1912, a county judge barred Socialists from speaking near the rope mills of the American Manufacturing Company, or "Cordage Trust," in Brooklyn. For the two previous months, Socialists had drawn crowds of 3000 workers, mainly young Irish-American women, to their rallies, which focused on conditions in the mills. Company bosses had turned fire hoses on the speakers, and had brought in brass bands and hurdy-gurdies to break up the rallies, but to no avail. Seven Socialists were arrested for speaking during the ban, which was finally revoked in a free speech fight carried on by a combination of suffragists, members of the Irish Socialist Federation, and such unaffiliated workers as Patrick Ring, who mounted the platform to say, "I am an ordinary workingman with a loud voice and a strong arm and will always and forever use it in the interests of the downtrodden working class."[23] In the same summer a strike of seamen and some longshoremen brought Socialist speakers to Manhattan piers. A notice in the *Call* stated:

> Speakers are urged to address noon meetings at the waterfront for the striking transport workers. All speakers who have the time to speak at noon meetings are requested to notify the organizer of Local New York and they will be assigned. . . . Comrades, we have an opportunity to reach people who are otherwise removed from the sphere of our activity and at the same time help the strikers . . . .[24]

On Wall Street, where financial workers poured onto the streets at noon, Socialist speakers held crowds "of fully two thousand alongside of Pierpont Morgan's officer.[25]

As elections drew near, Socialists redoubled their efforts in the streets. During the final week of the 1916 elections, they organized 50 rallies a night in the Lower East Side and 15 a night in Harlem and Brownsville — districts where garment workers predominated. In large part Socialists saw election periods as a chance to extend their regular educational work; thus on occasion candidates busy speaking throughout the city had to be reminded to speak in their own districts, since the "possibility of election is good." Many candidates even failed to distinguish themselves as such from their fellow speakers.[26] But Socialists, of course, also saw elections as a means to power and as an opportunity to present both a critique of capitalist politics and an alternative to it. "Old party" candidates, who normally held to their clubs, ventured onto the streets at election time to face Socialist taunts and to suffer crowd-stealing. In Williamsburg, Brooklyn, Nat Rubin "made life miserable for the old party speakers . . . by leaving them without audiences to talk to. At Cook Street and Graham Avenue he won an audience of 800 by outclassing three speakers of the Wilson-Marshall League." A Harlem Socialist, angered by a Tammany speaker's refusal to reply to his questions, mounted his own soapbox and captured the crowd of 500. Shortly, four more Socialist speakers reinforced the one, and Tammany "had to abandon the scene."[27]

What was most important in Socialist street corner speaking was the relationship between speaker and audience, which revealed the essence of socialism as a movement from below. Louis Waldman, a Socialist organizer from the Lower East Side, wrote insightfully of this relationship:

> . . . When I climbed up on my rickety platform for the first time I felt pitifully alone. Timidly, I began to speak. But it seemed as if this were merely pantomime, for I heard no voice. I spoke louder, but still no one in the hurrying crowds slackened his pace to listen to me."Friends and neighbors!" I shouted. But no friends and neighbors paid heed.
>
> Nevertheless I continued speaking, and gradually, almost imperceptibly, I began to find strength and fresh power as I went on. Thought, emotion, and their translation into words became a single instantaneous act. A strolling couple paused to listen to me, a young student with books under his arm stopped and looked up at the platform, a tired housewife laden with bundles also stopped and listened, and in a little while I had a sizable audience. As I continued to speak, and as the audience

> continued to grow, I learned the secret of public
> speaking. I learned that an audience is a thing in itself
> with a life, a logic, and an emotional pattern all of its own.
> . . . Whatever strength I developed came from a realization
> that the relationship between a speaker and his audience is
> an interacting one, that whatever strength is developed by
> the speaker must come from his audience. And now that I
> had grasped this fundamental lesson of public speaking,
> everything that I had learned in my years of struggle on the
> East Side, in its streets and in its factories, returned to me
> and was transmuted into the magic of words.[28]

Many of the best Socialist street corner speakers also developed a strong sense of irony and humor in their speeches. Working class humor also found popular expression in plays and on the vaudeville stage, appealing to a variety of ethnic groups, especially the Jewish, German and Irish. As a movement of the working class, socialism shared the same culture of humor as vaudeville. But the connection was even more direct: many actors, writers and vaudeville performers were themselves Socialists. In 1908, vaudeville performers organized the White Rats, a militant, left-wing union which staged many strike benefits for garment workers. Future impresario Sol Hurok organized extravagant Socialist parades and pageantry in Brooklyn; J.C. Frost, who wrote such working class Irish plays as "The Walking Delegate," was a regular street corner speaker; August Claessens, teacher of street corner oratory and a popular speaker, was a former actor.[29]

Joseph Freeman, who grew up in Brooklyn's Brownsville, vividly recalls one of the funniest and most popular Socialist street corner speakers, Gerald M.P. Fitzgibbon:

> Fitzgibbons, the street-corner soapboxer . . . never used
> mysterious phrases. For one hour he was funny, much
> funnier than any vaudeville in Fox's Folly. When he
> described how the rich lived, the audience nearly died
> laughing. When he described how the poor suffered, they

laughed too, because they loved the way he insulted them. He would start with a workingman getting up at dawn to go to work, his sloppy breakfast, the dingy streetcar, the filthy shop, the fat foreman, the hasty lunch, the rush to the toilet, the weary afternoon, the ride home, the hungry wife and kids, the terrible supper, the noise of the street. The poor sap drops off to sleep, and the next day he goes through the same mechanical motions. Six days of it: work, eat, sleep; work, eat, sleep; work, eat, sleep. And sometimes no eat, and sometimes no work. It was all very ironical, and at the end of every sentence the audience roared with laughter.

We felt it was true. Whatever Marx may have said, Fitzgibbons knew his stuff. That was just the way my friends' fathers lived, like dogs. Then came the seventh day, and that was the funniest because it was the day of rest. The worker went to amuse himself in the filth and noise of Coney Island. We had been to Coney Island and knew Fitzgibbons was right. And when the audience was tired of laughing, he would shout:

"Fools! Jackasses! How long will you stand this slavery?"

And they would laugh some more. Then Fitz pointed at a man in the audience, any man, and said:

"I know why you're laughing. You think I mean those damned fools," indicating the audience. Everybody laughed again, the random man too.

Fitzgibbon went on to explain the "economics of capitalism," how workers produced all the wealth, yet "lived like rats in holes."

The trouble was . . . that the people who worked were robbed by the people who owned the machines and factories. That was what "exploitation" meant. Those who *owned* the means of production lived on the wealth produced by those who *operated* the means of production.

211

> Clear? What was the solution? Abolish this system of
> exploitation. Abolish the private ownership of the mines,
> factories, railways. Turn them over to the People, who will
> run them not for profit but for use.[30]

Whatever their differences in style, Fitzgibbon and Waldman both drew intuitively on what was common to the best of socialist and revolutionary oratory. Socialist speakers knew the contradictions of class society which workers felt: on the one hand, the feeling that they were incapable and unworthy of becoming free; and on the other, the feeling that they must become free, and masters of their situations.[31] In speaking "not *to* people but *for* them," Socialists articulated the most revolutionary and advanced sentiments of their audiences, while simultaneously exposing, criticizing and even ridiculing the conservative impulses the same people felt. "You workingmen have heads," Eugene Debs told a rally at Grand Central Station, "but you fail to make proper use of them."

> You are satisfied to use your hands in the interest of the
> fellows who are shrewd enough to use their heads. Let me
> remind you that you have heads as well as hands. And when
> you use both you will be masters of this earth.[32]

The vibrance and passion in Socialist oratory sprang from the dialectical tensions in working class life — the acceptance of conditions of existence which saw industrial slavery and impoverishment as eternal and deserved, *versus* the desire to abolish those conditions. As part of a movement from below which necessarily summed up contradictions first felt within individuals, Socialist speakers expressed what was revolutionary in those individuals, while revealing what was reactionary. This was what made these orators so dangerous to a capitalist state in time of crisis.[33]

III. Socialism as a Movement from Below

It is simple and convenient to consider the history of socialism as the history of its leadership. Yet the two are not the same, for if we examine socialism as a movement from below, rather than as a set of leaders or political programs and statements, our understanding of it changes. It becomes a living

Socialism in New York was a movement of industrial militancy which transcended the limitations of workplace and ethnicity to proclaim the solidarity of all working people. It was a movement of working class solidarity, manifested not only in the drive to consolidate the struggles of New York workers, but to identify them with workers fighting throughout the nation. It was a movement, too, of internationalism, drawing on many strains, including such different immigrant working class experiences as the struggles of Jews and revolutionaries in Russia, and the fight for Irish freedom. This internationalism may have found its greatest moment in the Socialists' opposition to World War I.

Socialism was also a movement of culture derived from ethnic and class traditions and from the day-to-day experiences of New York working class. life: a movement of drama, humor, sports, musk, song, stories, dance and drawing — on the stage and in the shops, streets, taverns, dubs, cafes and tenements; a movement that in the dancing of Isadora Duncan, the boxing of Benny Leonard and Al McCoy, the poetry of Arturo Giovannitti, the drawing and painting of *The Masses* artists, the concerts of innumerable workingmen's choral groups and "peoples symphonies," and the shop floor singing of Rose Pastor, refuted the bourgeois distinction between high and popular culture.

Benny Leonard, from the Lower East Side, was one of the greatest boxers of all time — American lightweight champion in this period, and soon world champion. Leonard was a member of the Socialist Party, and wrote several dozen columns for the Call. Al McCoy, middleweight champion, was also a Socialist, as were his brothers and sisters. During the 1916 elections, McCoy headed a force of Socialists who deterred Tammany from strong-arm tactics. Boxing and baseball were the most popular sports among New York's working people.[34]

Isadora Duncan and her School offered their services to the Socialist Party during World War I and staged several benefits. In her memoirs, Duncan wrote of an audience for Oedipus, which "consisted mostly of people from the East Side who, by the way, are among the real lovers of Art in America to-day. The appreciation of the East Side so touched me that I went over there with my entire School and an orchestra, and gave a free performance in the Yiddish Theatre, and, if I had had the means, I would have remained there dancing for these people whose very soul is made for music and poetry."[35]

Socialism was a movement, that in its time helped to shape the broadest and most humanistic, the most vibrant and radical impulses in working class life.

State University College, New Paltz, New York

SOCIALIST OPPOSITION TO WORLD WAR I

Radical America, March–April 1968, Vol. II, No. 2

In April, 1917, just one day after the United States declared war on Germany, the Socialist party met in emergency convention in St. Louis. It was the first Socialist convention since 1912. Five years had passed, years of declining membership and vote, of disillusionment with the possibilities for success. In his keynote address to the St. Louis convention, party leader Morris Hillquit charged Socialists with a "growing laxity in our own organization," and said it was a "fatal blunder" not to have held a convention in so long.[1]

But if Socialists had grown lethargic in the past, now they had the opportunity to recoup. The vast majority of Americans, they believed, were opposed to the declaration of war. Yet the Socialists remained the only organized force willing and able to carry on the struggle against the war. Thus, they faced two tasks: First, to maintain their principled opposition to the war, and second, to rally the antiwar elements of the nation behind the Socialist banner. With respect to the first task, the Socialists were eminently successful. With respect to the second, they were also successful, at least on their own terms. As James Weinstein has shown, 1917 proved to be the year of greatest Socialist electoral success — which included, for the first time, heavy Socialist voting in the major Eastern cities.[2]

With renewed vigor, the Socialists at the St. Louis convention adopted an anti war manifesto that remains the most eloquent monument to American socialism. Drafted by Hillquit and Algernon Lee, of the Center, and Charles Ruthenberg, of the Left, it won by a large majority. Sent out on referendum to the party membership, it won by 21,000 to 350 votes over a pro-war statement.[3] The manifesto began,

> The Socialist Party of the United States in the present grave crisis reaffirms its allegiance to the principle of internationalism and working class solidarity the world over, and proclaims its unalterable opposition to the war just declared by the government of the United States. ...

It continued with statements of opposition to class rule and "sham national patriotism," and urged workers to "refuse to support their governments" in war.

After analyzing causes of the war, the manifesto set forth three formulas which more than any other section aroused the government to fury:

> We brand the declaration of war by our government as a crime against the people of the United States and against the nations of the world. In all modern history there has been no war more unjustifiable than the war in which we are about to engage.
> No greater dishonor has ever been forced upon a people than that which the capitalist class is forcing upon this nation against its will.

The manifesto concluded with a call for "an even more vigorous prosecution of the class struggle" during wartime, and pledged Socialists to a seven-point program for action. This program included continuous opposition to the war through all means within their power, unyielding opposition to conscription, and mass action to end the war.[4]

The St. Louis manifesto represented the Socialist party ideal. There did exist backsliding here and there during the war, for a number of reasons. For example, Germany's continued attacks on Russia after the revolution aroused doubts among many Socialists. But despite doubts and equivocation, the party as a whole fought hard against the war and against the most serious repression they ever encountered.

For the Left Wing, this was at least consistent with its internationalist perspective. Questions of war were never prominent in the party until the outbreak in Europe. However, the party had given considerable attention to the question of free vs. restricted immigration, and a prolonged debate on internationalism revolved about it. The Left wing developed a strongly internationalist position, for free vs. restricted immigration. The Right wing, on the other hand, took a nationalist position with very strong overtones of nativism. They favored heavy restrictions on immigration, and this effectively became the public position of the Socialist party. The Center favored some restrictions, but its spokesmen were for the most part free from the nativistic attitudes of the Right.

216

After the outbreak of war in Europe, the reformists, Center and Right, for the most part shed their nationalist perspectives. There still remained vestiges, of course, sometimes important. But the question of immigration was pretty much dropped — no doubt partly because it was a moot point during the war years — and this had a liberating effect on the mentality of the reformists. However inconsistent their newly-developed internationalism was with their past, it did not have to be inconsistent with what they believed for the present.

The Left wing was suspicious of the reformists' entrance into the arena of internationalism, and considered them imposters. Most historians of American socialism feel the same way, and since reformists dominated the party, they ask: How is it possible to account for the strong anti-war position of the Socialist party? It was a reformist party, with reformist leadership, yet did not betray socialist principles like its European counterparts.

HISTORIANS' ERROR

The answers to this question vary. Perhaps the most challenging is the idea that it was really the Left wing that, directly or indirectly, charted the course of the Socialist party during the war. One of the best historians of American socialism, Theodore Draper, suggests this.

To Draper, the Left wing might have stood alone in its opposition to the war if "the government had not flung its legal dragnet so wide. . . ." The reformist leadership adopted a radical posture, he believes, because they were frightened by the possibility that the Left wing would otherwise win control of the party. In order to head off Left wing influence, Hillquit and his allies split the Left wing delegation to St. Louis with a militant resolution. Thus they "made it impossible for the Left Wing to emerge at the convention as a fully developed, independent political force." The fact that reformist Socialists were not to be spared government repression was an accident. Draper writes:

> A head-on collision with the government was not at all what the Hillquit–Berger team had intended. The resolution did call for anti-war demonstrations,

217

"unyielding opposition" to conscription, and other militant measures. But some of those who voted for the resolution were more interested in inner-party maneuvering than in obstructing the war effort. . .

A similar point of view is held by Julius Faulk.[5]

Several objections can be raised to this kind of analysis. Most obvious of all, it is patently unfair to the party's reformists. Take for example, Victor Berger, leading Right wing municipal socialist, head of the Milwaukee Social Democratic Party, and very often used by historians as the model of opportunism. It is probably true that Berger, and some of his fellow reformists, would have preferred a milder anti-war resolution. But what is far more important is how well Berger stood up against government repression, how well he defended the party's anti-war position by his own activities. For someone "more interested in inner-party maneuvering than in obstructing the war effort" he paid heavily. By the end of the war, Berger had been convicted under the Espionage Act of obstructing the draft, and sentenced to twenty years imprisonment. He was freed pending appeal, on a one million dollar bond. The judge who tried the case, Kenesaw Mountain Landis, said after the trial:

> It was my great displeasure to give Berger twenty years at Fort Leavenworth. I regret it exceedingly because I believe that the laws of this country should have enabled me to have Berger lined up against a wall and shot.[6]

Moreover, a multitude of other indictments had been returned against him — for which he still faced conviction — good for fifteen hundred years imprisonment. During the Harding administration, Oscar Ameringer reports, Berger was offered a deal. If he ran for Senator against LaFollette — which he had done once before — the Administration would,

1) see that his twenty year sentence was thrown out by the Supreme Court,

2) quash all pending indictments, and

3) lift the million dollar bond.

Moreover, they would finance his campaign. They wanted to split LaFollette's vote, to enable the Republican candidate to win. Berger refused.[7]

Clearly, the anti-war activity of men such as Berger cannot be explained simply by their fear of the Left wing. It isn't as if, as Draper says, the government cast its net too widely and caught some barely committed reformists by mistake. If that were the case, these reformists could have evaded the net with ease.

Another possible objection to Draper's analysis — perhaps the most important — is that it fails to present an accurate picture of the Socialist Left wing. First of all, Draper focuses almost exclusively upon those elements that were soon to comprise the American communist movement. It is important to realize that once well developed, they differed in many important respects from the traditional Left wing. The traditional Left was a loose aggregate of syndicalistic industrial socialists, orthodox Marxists, and revolutionary populists. Their most representative publication was the *International Socialist Review*, which had a circulation of some 40,000. The English language press of the Bolshevik Left showed much less diversity, and was limited to a very small circulation. Secondly, Draper in some ways treats the embryonic Bolshevik Left as if it were fully developed. If this were the case, then there would have been tremendous differences on the war between them and the reformists — and indeed, the Left wing as a whole. After the Bolshevik Revolution these differences did emerge. But they were not yet Bolsheviks, and on the question of the war remained basically indistinguishable from the traditional Left, of which they were still a part, and even the party's reformists. Quite naturally, they thought their position ought to be different, and spared no opportunity to criticize the reformists. However, their contribution to the party's anti-war position must be measured independently of this criticism, on its own merits. To do this, it is necessary to take a closer look at what the Left wing wrote.

THE RECORD OF THE LEFT WING

War in Europe took the Left wing by surprise. But they soon made up for it, devoting the bulk of space in their magazines and journals to news and analysis of the war. The Left wing was quick to sense the betrayal of international socialism by the European parties — much quicker than the reformists, who adopted a wait-and-see attitude. Since the reformists were long identified with a spirit of nationalism — in particular, in their demands for restricting immigration, and also in their dealings with the International — many Left wingers saw their equivocation as evidence of continuing nationalism. At times they felt certain the reformists would follow the German example, and support the U.S. if it entered the war. Gradually, certain Left wing writers — most prominently, Louis Boudin and Louis Fraina — began to emphasize their internationalism as opposed to the reformists' nationalism. Certainly, there were differences. The Left wing, for example, continued to assert that "The workingman has no nation." The reformists disagreed strongly.

Despite this, however, Left wing attitudes toward the war differed very little from the reformists. Their analyses — which appeared in Left wing publications such as *The New Review, The Masses,* and the *International Socialist Review* — showed great variety and uncertainty. The war was seen variously as a traders' war, a militarists' war, a munitions manufacturers' war, a war between feudalism and capitalism, between democracy and autocracy, and so forth. There were even a few theories of war as an inherent disposition of men (but not women), and war was the nature of mankind. Altogether, there were surprisingly few well thought-out analyses. Prominent among those that were, were articles by European revolutionaries Karl Liebknecht and the ultra-leftist, Anton Pannekoek.

Among the major Left wing writers on the war was Louis Fraina. Fraina was destined to become the leading American Bolshevik during the formative years of the communist movement, but at this time he was something of a syndicalist — a bias shared by perhaps the majority of Left wing Socialists. He was the leading figure on *The New Review*, without question the best revolutionary journal of the period. Fraina's orthodox attitudes toward the war, combined with an uncompromising hostility toward the reformists who shared them, are indicative of the confusion among Left wingers.

Throughout the period that Fraina wrote for the *The New Review* — up to its demise, in June, 1916 — he never believed that the war would result in a socialist revolution. When Italy entered the war he predicted a "new and mightier Capitalism" for its efforts. "Out of the murk and murder and treachery of the war will issue a new Italy — democratic, progressive, powerful." For England, he predicted as "one of the momentous social phenomena of the war," the triumph of "Laborism." He felt, "there is nothing revolutionary about the workers of England." Fraina saw State Socialism as the major outcome of the war; collectivization for the war effort was progressive and irreversible.[8] Strange as it may seem, these were precisely the views held by most reformists, the very Socialists for whom Fraina had nothing but disdain.[9]

Fraina's hostility toward reformists went back a long way. As a youth in 1909, he had joined the Socialist party, but left it, Theodore Draper says, "because it was not radical enough for him."[10] There was further confusion among the Left wing concerning the election of Woodrow Wilson in 1916. Two key writers for *The Masses* — Max Eastman and John Reed — supported him for President.[11] With tortured logic, Eastman criticized the party for nominating a candidate, Allan Benson, especially out-of-touch with the proletariat, then voted for him while endorsing Wilson. Years later he admitted, "I was concealing the fact that I could not make up my mind."[12] Even the *International Socialist Review*, so unswervingly revolutionary, was taken in by Wilson. In August, 1916, the *Review* printed an unsigned editorial attacking the *Milwaukee Leader* — Victor Berger's reformist newspaper — for its criticisms of Wilson. In characteristic straight-from-the-shoulder prose, the editorial charged:

> To howl suspicions of militarism against a president who has kept the working class of America out of war during a hair-trigger period is a species of treachery to the working class that does no good.[13]

Following Wilson's victory, Frank Bohn in *The Masses* lashed out at Socialists who still had the "old-fashioned impossible attitude. . . . of hating every radical because 'he steals our thunder'."[14]

In their concrete proposals for peace, the Left wing Socialists had little positive to offer. In September, 1915, Fraina suggested, "It is our task to *prepare* for peace, not to bring peace," and denounced the current Socialist party program as "apologetic, incompetent and pro-German."[15] In fact, the Socialist peace program was virtually identical to that of the Russian Bolsheviks. It called for no indemnities, national self-determination for countries under foreign rule, no military or naval appropriations, and no exportation of arms. Concerning the last point, Left wing theoretician Louis Boudin went so far as to oppose any stoppage of arms shipments through government action or strikes in munitions factories, because it would affect only the allies.[16]

LEFT VS. RIGHT?

The major positive suggestion of the Left wing for peace was not revolutionary at all. Most, including Boudin, Fraina and Eastman, favored a League of Nations plan, as did the reformists. Boudin was especially enthusiastic about a world democratic federation, as an alternative to nationalism. Such plans were based upon the idea either that war was a remnant of feudalism, or a product of nationalism, based upon capitalist development only up to a certain stage. Thus, capitalist nations could co-exist peacefully in a world federation, especially if compelled by the working class.

On the problem of how to oppose U.S. involvement in the war, the Left wing was for the most part elusive and vague. When Wilson began his preparedness campaign, unlike many of the reformists they refused to give credence to the idea. Beyond this, however, they had little concrete to say. Throughout the Left wing writings there runs the threat of "mass action," but this seemed more rhetorical than real until the Bolshevik Revolution gave it substance. Alexandra Kollontai wrote of turning the war into a civil war, but as a Russian Bolshevik she was referring to European conditions. The idea of the "general strike" was only rarely mentioned.

Louis Waldman tells of a Left wing program for action, introduced at a Socialist meeting in Manhattan, just one month before the St. Louis emergency convention. Leon Trotsky and Louis Fraina appeared there as leaders of the Left wing, and introduced a resolution calling upon Socialists to:

> . . . resist all efforts at recruiting by means of mass meetings, street demonstrations and educational propaganda, and by other means, in accordance with Socialist principles and tactics.

They also called for strikes against industrial conscription.[17]

By the time of the St. Louis convention, however, Left wing members had forgotten what they learned from Trotsky. There, they opposed the Hillquit–Lee–Ruthenberg majority resolution — which contained all the essentials of the Trotsky–Fraina program — and introduced their own. It was drafted by Boudin who, along with Fraina, had also met with Trotsky and others to develop a revolutionary perspective on the war. Yet, from their own perspective, the Left wing resolution was in every way inferior to the one adopted. In contrast to the majority resolution, its prose was unbelievably turgid, it was far milder in tone, and actually devoid of a program for action. The Left wing manifesto began:

> In this grave hour in the history of this country, we, the representatives of the Socialist Party of the United States, in special Convention assembled, deem it our duty to place before the membership of the Socialist Party and the working class of America a succinct statement of our position on the questions involved, and to outline a program of action which we believe to be in the interest of workers of this country to follow.

After going into the causes of the war and warning of a permanent military establishment "all to the great detriment of the democratic institutions of this country and the moral and material interests of its toiling masses," the manifesto concluded:

> All of these reasons lead us to the conclusion that we must oppose this war with all the powers of our command.

That was their program for action.[18]

The convention rejected the Boudin resolution overwhelmingly. Less than half the Left wing delegates voted for it. It could only have been written to distinguish the revolutionaries from the reformists, but on the question of war, at this time, that was impossible. So far, their differences were only superficial.

When the party adopted its St. Louis manifesto, most well-known Socialists defected. Few in absolute numbers, the majority of defecters were simply rejoining the Progressive intellectuals, who had marched en masse into the war camp. There were, however, several important Left wing defectors, who generally get less attention from socialist historians. Already mentioned were William English Walling and Frank Bohn, two of the most prolific Left wing writers on the war, both editors of the *New Review*. Joining them were Henry Slobodin and Robert Rives La Monte. Slobodin, along with Eugene Debs and Louis Boudin, was a leader of the combination industrial-political socialism tendency of the Left wing, and an associate editor of the *International Socialist Review*. La Monte was an editor of *The New Review*. The reformist party leadership had been afraid to send him as an organizer to Lawrence during the famous strike, because he was too radical. During the critical 1917 Hillquit-for-Mayor campaign in New York City — which attracted the attention of the press all across the country — these men joined with Right wing defectors in opposing Hillquit. They issued a public statement to the press, calling Hillquit a "champion of German Kultur" and accusing him of "giving needless aid and comfort to the enemies of democracy the world over. . . ." With respect to Russia and the revolution, they said the Russian people "are not in favor of a German peace. Yet Hillquit takes the position of the anarchist-Socialist Lenin, and opposes the genuine socialism of Kerensky." In a letter to the New York Times, Frank Bohn called

Hillquit supporters "weeping cowards" and "common traitors to civilization."[19]

Of course, these Left wing defecters were exceptions — just as were the Right. The vast majority of Socialists shaped up as soon as the U.S. entered the war, threw their weight behind the St. Louis manifesto, and prepared for the difficult struggle ahead. It is impossible to tabulate all the arrests and convictions of Socialists for obstructing the war effort it went on at all levels. Morris Hillquit, who acted as attorney for many radicals prosecuted by the federal government, writes:

> It is estimated that during the war about two thousand persons were convicted under the Espionage Law and sentenced to terms of imprisonment aggregating twenty-five thousand years. In many if not most of these convictions the St. Louis proclamation played a large and fatal part.[20]

The question remains, if the Left wing alone neither directly nor indirectly motivated the Socialist party to take such a strong anti-war position, how did it come about?

WHY WAS THE SOCIALIST PARTY STRONG?

Daniel Bell, in his essay, claims that there is some truth to the charge that a high proportion of Germans (for Germany) and Jews (against Russia) in the party accounted for much of the opposition.[21] Bell, however, gets his information from Charles Edward Russell, a Right wing defector and the only Socialist to have publicly supported preparedness. Russell is a highly unreliable source. In fact, the party's German language daily, the *Volkszeitung*, was very hostile toward the German SPD and supported Karl Liebknecht. The party's German language federation featured Kollontai and Trotsky as speakers. As far as the Jews' hostility toward Russia is concerned, by the time the St. Louis convention met the Tzar had already been overthrown, and all Socialists supported the new Russia.

More convincing is a point of view shared by most historians of American socialism, including Bell, David Shannon, Nathan Fine, and Julius Faulk.[22] They suggest that had the party been more closely tied to the trade union movement, it would have been more interested in simply protecting the gains and institutions of the workers for the duration of the war. The party probably would have compromised its anti-war principles. This did happen to the AFL, which had been moderately anti-war until shortly before America's entrance, and then pro-war. And of course, it happened to the European socialist parties, which were based on the trade unions. To bolster this viewpoint, several of the historians cite the fact that most important Socialist trade unions left the party after the U.S. declared war, and joined with Gompers in supporting it.

It may be true that many Socialist trade unionists left, although probably as many stayed. More important, however, is the fact that in the only two areas where the party based itself on trade union support, with strong ties developed over the years, it remained anti-war. These areas were Milwaukee, Wisconsin, home of Victor Berger, and Reading, Pennsylvania. The trade unions in these places were heavily German, at least in tradition. But the leader of the Reading Socialists, James Maurer, was also president of the Pennsylvania Federation of Labor. During the war, Maurer — who was famous for his militant anti-war activities — was re-elected president by a three-to-one majority, despite the fact that Gompers sent up a crew to make sure he was defeated.[23]

Another related point socialist historians make is that unlike the European parties, the American Socialist party had few political strongholds, and therefore nothing to conserve. The fact that it had not gained success and responsibility permitted it the luxury of opposing the war without suffering really serious consequences. The problem with this analysis is that it views the American Socialist party purely from the standpoint of the mass European parties. While it is true the Socialist party was small, it did have a lot to conserve. First of all, the party had an extensive press with circulation in the millions, which was almost totally destroyed by government repression. Second, the party was an organization attempting both to maintain itself and to grow. It at least shared these characteristics with the European parties, despite its relatively small membership of some 80 thousand. When the authorities began to raid and plunder national and local headquarters, Socialists were outraged because the party, which they had built over the years, meant a great deal to them. Moreover, they saw their party as a very important force against the war — likely, the only organization which would stand and fight in the face of repression. They even expected to make gains during the war. Thus, from their own standpoint, they had a lot to protect and conserve — but they were unwilling to do it by backing down. Finally, they had their own lives to protect. The dangers they faced — as related by Max Eastman, Oscar Ameringer, James Maurer and others — cannot be exaggerated.

Several historians argue that the geographical distance of American Socialists from the war in Europe enabled them to oppose it. Rather like isolationists, they were not so troubled by an immediate military threat to their nation as were the European socialists. It need only be pointed out, first of all, that the same argument could be used for precisely the opposite point — that distance enabled American Socialists to support the war since they were untouched by its devastation. Secondly, this argument could not account for the opposition of the Russian Bolsheviks, both before and after they took power, or the various minority socialist groups, or conversely, for the support that British socialists gave the war.

Several other points are perhaps more helpful in understanding why the Socialist party was so strongly anti-war.

First of all, as several historians have suggested, American Socialists were helped considerably by the anti-war sentiment in the nation. By the time the U.S. entered, the nature of the war in all its ghoulishness had pretty well been revealed. In this sense it was easier to oppose than at the beginning when, in the midst of popular frenzy and romantic ideas, the European parties had to deal with it.

Second, American Socialists were able to draw from the experience of Karl Liebknecht and the German minority. Distressed by the failure of so many European socialists to oppose the war, Liebknecht appeared as a shining example to them. The entire Socialist press treated him like a hero, and his writings were widely read. He was the model when the real test finally came. Furthermore, American Socialists were uplifted by the resurgence of anti-war sentiment among their European comrades.

Third, the St. Louis manifesto itself was drafted immediately after the U.S. declared war. Morris Hillquit says that war had come so suddenly, the convention delegates "had no time for calm deliberation." They were horrified, and the freshness of their horror is revealed in the manifesto. It should also be noted that at the time of the St. Louis convention, Socialists were accustomed to relatively free speech.[24] It was several months before the government began its campaign of repression. A few historians have suggested that had the Socialists known what was in store for them, they would not have been so militantly anti-war. This is extremely dubious since first of all they anticipated at least some restrictions on civil liberties, and secondly, once they found out what was in store, they still refused to give in.

This list could be extended, but I want to end here with one major point. None of the various reasons that historians suggest for Socialist opposition to the war, are in any sense "causes." Lack of ties to trade unions, for example, did not "cause" Socialists to oppose the war, any more than it caused previously anti-war Progressives to support it. We are dealng here with real socialists, real people — not creatures who are merely pushed and pulled around by conditions and events, but play a large role in making them. Politics are only partly a reflection of material conditions; they are also a creation of intellect. It is this latter dimension of human agency — to paraphrase E.P. Thompson — that must never be forgotten. Whatever the size of the Socialist party, whatever its political strongholds and ties to the trade unions, whatever the conflicts between various political tendencies, the following conclusion should be kept uppermost in our minds: The political position of American Socialists during the war, their forthright opposition to it, was a product most of all of a truly heroic effort of the will, of self-enlightenment against overwhelming odds. It serves as a profound example of the elevation of consciousness through human effort.

Footnotes: Part 1

Introduction.

1. The data for this introduction are taken from the following sources:

   > Maldwyn Allen Jones, *American Immigration* (University of Chicago Press, 1960), 178–79, 208.

   > U.S. Bureau of the Census, *Historical Statistics of the United States, Colonial Times to 1957*, Washington, D.C., 1960, 56–57, 66.

   > William M. Leiserson, *Adjusting Immigrant and Industry* (New York: Harper and Brothers, 1924), 12–13.

2. There were, of course, diverse organizations and tendencies within any given,nationally-based working class movement. By "working class movement" we mean that network of organizations, such as trade unions and socialist parties, that purported to speak for the peculiar class interests — economic and political — of workers. The emphasis is on "movement," as distinct from the working class as a whole.

Chapter 1. The First International and Immigration.

1. Henry Collins and Chimen Abramsky, *Karl Marx and the British Labor Movement* (London: MacMillan and Co., 1965), 3–55.

2. Ibid.

3. The leading body of the International was originally called the Central Council. As other central councils were set up in Europe, it became known as the General Council. The name was made official by the Geneva Congress of 1866.

4. Collins and Abramsky, op. cit., 3–55.

5. Karl Marx, *Inaugural Address of the Working Men's International Association*, Documents of the First International (Moscow: Foreign Languages Publishing House), Vol. I, 277–87; Collins and *Abramsky*, op. cit., 45.

6. *An Appeal from the British Members of the Central Council to their Fellow Working Men of the United Kingdom*, Documents, op. cit., Vol. I, 313–15.

7. *General Council Minutes*, March 27, 1866. The General Council Minutes from October 5, 1864, to October 24, 1871, are published in Volumes I–IV of Documents, op. cit.

8. Quoted in Collins and Abramsky, op. cit., 69.

9. *G.C. Minutes*, April 24, 1866. The wire workers did not join.

10. Collins and Abramsky, op. cit., 70–71; *G.C. Minutes*, October 23, 1866.

11. *G.C. Minutes*, May 1, 1866. For the appeal, see Documents, op. cit., Vol. I, 35–36 (German), and 367–68 (English).

12. Karl Marx, *A Warning*, Documents, op. cit., Vol. I, 367–68. Marx's emphasis.

13. Ibid. Marx's emphasis.

14. *Instructions for the Delegates of the Provisional General Council.* Documents, op. cit., Vol. I, 341. Written by Marx.

15. *G.C. Minutes*, October 30, 1866.

16. The letter is published in Documents, op. cit., Vol. II, 344.

17. *G.C. Minutes*, November 20, 1866.

18. Collins and Abramsky, op. cit., 84; G.C. Minutes, February 26, 1868. The tailors' efforts are also discussed in G.C. Minutes, December 11, 1866, and April 16. April 23, May 14, May 28 and July 9, 1867.

19. Collins and Abramsky, op. cit., 72.

20. *G.C. Minutes*, April 23, 1867.

21. Collins and Abramsky, op. it., 75–78.

22. Ibid.

23. The circular appears in Marx to Kugelmann, March 28, 1870, Karl Marx, Letters to Dr. Kugelmann (New York: International Publishers, 1934).

24. Collins and Abramsky, op. cit., 75–78.

25. Marx to Kugelmann, October 13, 1866, in *Letters*, op. cit,

26. Collins and Abramsky, op. cit., 83; *G.C. Minutes*, March 5, Marsh 12, March 26, April 2 and April 9, 1867.

27. Collins and Abramsky, op. cit., 89; *G.C. Minutes*, April 14, 1868.

28. Collins and Abramsky, op. cit., 92.

29. Ibid., 96.

30. *G.C. Minutes*, August 27, 1867.

31. *Third Annual Report of the International Working Men' Association.* Documents, op. cit., Vol. II, 292–303.

32. *G .C. Minutes*, December 11 1866,

33. See, *The Fourth Annual Report of the General Council of the International Working Men's Association,* Documents, op. cit., Vol. II, 324–29. Written by Marx.

34. Ibid., 328.

35. *Report of the General Council to the Fourth Annual Congress of the International Working Men's Association*, Documents, op. cit, Vol. III, 326–42. Written by Marx.

36. *G.C. Minutes*, July 9, 1867.

37. See, *To the Trade Unionists of Great Britain and Ireland*, Documents, op. cit. Vol. II, 319–23. Written by Hales, Lafargue and Copeland, this was an appeal for trade union delegates to the 1868 Brussels Congress.

38. *G.C. Minutes*, November 16 and 23, 1869.

39. Ibid..

40. *Marx to Kugelmann*, November 29, 1869, in Letters, op. cit.,

41. Ibid..

42. *Marx to Kugelmann*, March 28, 1870, in Letters, op. cit.

43. *G.C. Minutes*, May 31,.1870.

44. *G.C. Minutes*, November 9, 1869. Previously, the cigar-makers had asked the General Council to halt all immigration of foreign cigar-makers. There was no strike, but employment was low. *G.C. Minutes*, April 9, 1867.

45. *G.C. Minutes*, June 20, 1871.

46. *G.C. Minutes*, August 8, 1871.

47. Ibid..

48. See, *The First International, Minutes of the Hague Congress of 1872*, Hans Gerth, Ed. (Madison: University of Wisconsin Press, 1958).

49. Engels to Friedrich Sorge September 12 and 17, 1874, in *Marx and Engels, Letters to Americans* (New York: International Publishers, 1963 ed.).

50. Ibid.

Chapter 2. The National Labor Union.

1. John B. Andrews, *Nationalization* (1860–1877), in John R. Commons, et al., *History of Labor in the United States* (New York: The MacMillan Co., 1918), Vol. II, 85–96.

2. Ibid., 99–100.

3. Ira Steward, *The Power of the Cheaper over the Dearer*, in John R. Commons, et al., *A Documentary History of American Industrial Society* (Cleveland: Arthur H. Clark Co., 1910), Vol. IX, 306–29; 326.

4. Ibid., 315–29.

5. See James C. Sylvis, *The Life, Speeches, Labors and Essays of William H. Sylvis* (Philadelphia: Claxton, Remsen and Haffelfinger, 1872).

6. The pages of the *Workingman's Advocate*, for example, were filled with travel and immigration ads for steamship lines.

7. Charlotte Erickson, *American Industry and the European Immigrant, 1860–1885* (Cambridge: Harvard University Press, 1957) 11.

8. Ibid., 51–52.

9. Ibid.

10. Karl Marx, *Inaugural Address*, op. cit., 282.

11. *G.C. Minutes*, op. cit., Vol. II, 71, 80. Fox was unsuccessful. see *G.C. Minutes*, Vol. II, 307.

12. *National Labor Congress Proceedings*, 1867, in Commons, *Documentary History*, op. cit., Vol. IX, 334.

13. *G.C. Minutes*, Vol. II, 305–06.

14. *G.C. Minutes*, Vol. II, 134, 307.

15. Samuel Bernstein, *The First International in America* (New York: Augustus M. Kelley, 1962), 28–29; *G.C. Minutes*, Vol. II, 154–55.

16. *G.C. Minutes*, Vol. II, 155.

17. *G.C. Minutes*, Vol. II, 165.

18. National Labor *Congress Proceedings,* 1867, in Commons, *Documentary History*, op. cit., 335.

19. Ibid.

20. Ibid., 336.

21. Reprinted in *Documents of the First International*, op. cit., Vol. II, 372.

22. Ibid.; *G.C. Minutes*, Vol. II, 162.

23. *National Labor Congress Proceedings*, 1868, in Commons, *Documentary History*, op. cit., 336–7.

24. Bernstein, op. cit., 31–32.

25. Ibid.

26. Quotes in Richard T. Ely, *The Labor Movement in America* (New York: Thomas Y. Crowell and Co., 1890 ed.), 226–27.

27. Ibid.

28. *G.C. Minutes*, Vol., III, 160.

29. Cameron to the *Workingman's Advocate*, November–December, 1869, in Commons, *Documentary History*, op. cit., 343.

30. Ibid., 343, 346–47.

31. Ibid., 348.

32. Ibid., 350.

33. Ibid., 348–49.

34. Ibid., 349–50.

35. *National Labor Congress Proceedings*, 1870, in Commons, *Documentary History*, op. cit., 338.

36. Ibid., 339.

37. *National Labor Congress Proceedings*, 1869, Workingman's Advocate, September 4, 1869.

38. Ibid.

39. *Workingman's Advocate*, August 6, 1870.

40. Ibid.

41. *National Labor Congress Proceedings, Workingman's Advocate,* August 27, 1870.

42. Ibid.

43. Ibid.

44. Quoted in Commons, *Documentary History*, op. cit., 88.

Chapter 3. The Knights of Labor and Immigration.

1. Except where otherwise noted, the historical material for this introduction is taken from Selig Perlman, *Upheaval and Reorganization*, in John R. Commons, et al., History of Labor in the United States (New York: The MacMillan Co., 1918), Vol 2, 332–55.

2. See Knights of Labor, *General Assembly Proceedings*, 1884, 594.

3. The Knights General Assembly regularly passed anti-Chinese resolutions that were identical in substance to those of the NLU. See for example, K. of L. *General Assembly Proceedings*, 1880, 223; 1885, 160. However, the Chinese question was not given the attention it later enjoyed in the AFL.

4. Perlman, op. cit., 339, 344.

5. Ibid., 344–45.

6. Most of the historical material for the remainder of this chapter is taken from Charlotte Erickson, *American Industry and the European Immigrant,* 1860–1885 (Cambridge: Harvard University Press, 1957).

7. Erickson, op. cit., 107–08.

8. Ibid., 108.

9. Ibid., 109.

10. Ibid., 110.

11. Ibid., 110–11.

12. Ibid., 112–13.

13. Ibid., 109.

14. K of L *General Assembly Proceedings*, 1884, 576–77. The emphasis is Powderly's.The term "Hungarians" probably refers to Southern and Eastern Europeans in general.

15. Erickson, op. cit., 180–82.

16. Ibid., 116–17.

17. K of L *General Assembly Proceedings*, 1884, 576–77.

18. Erickson, op. cit., 141.

19. Ibid., 142.

20. K of L *General Assembly Proceedings*, 1881, 295.

21. Erickson, op. cit., 142–45.

22. Quoted in Ibid., 146–47.

23. Ibid., 140.

24. Ibid., 157.

25. K of L *General Assembly Proceedings Special Session*, 1886, 6–7.

26. In later years, after they were no longer a major force in the working class movement, the Knights strongly favored restrictions. See Gerald N. Grob, *Workers and Utopia* (Evanston: Northwestern University Press, 1961), 58.

Chapter 4. The AFL: New Craft Unionism.

1. Most of the historical material for the first part of this chapter is taken from Perlman, *Upheaval and Reorganization*, op. cit., and Grob, *Workers and Utopia*, op. cit.

2. Perlman, op. cit., 397.

3. Ibid., 427.

4. Letter from McGuire to F.O.T.L.U. Convention, 1882. For report, see Federation of Organized Trades and Labor Unions of the United States and Canada, *Report of the Second Annual Session*, 1882, 19; for complete text see *American Federationist*, October, 1896, 163.

5. F.O.T.L.U., *Report of First Annual Session*, 1881, 20. Ibid., 1884, 16.

6. Ibid., 1884, 16.

7. AFL *Convention Proceedings*, 1889, 24.

8. Ibid., 38.

9. Ibid., 1891, 15.

10. Ibid., 1892, 14.

11. Ibid., 38.

12. Ibid., 1893, 13.

13. Ibid., 73.

14. Ibid., 33–34.

15. Ibid., 1894, 12.

16. Ibid., 47. See McBride's report, ibid., 1895, 1.

17. Ibid., 1894, 45–46.

18. Ibid., 1896, 24.

19. Ibid., 81.

20. Ibid., 82.

21. Ibid., 1897, 88.

22. Ibid. 90.

23. Ibid., 90–91.

24. Ibid.,. 90.

25. For roll-call vote, see ibid., 94.

26. Ibid., 1896, 30–31.

27. Ibid., 1897, 30.

28. Ibid., 1896, 82. The United Mine Workers' delegation voted for restrictions in 1897. Ibid., 1897, 94. The previous year, John McBride of the Mine Workers opposed restrictions. Ibid., 1896, 82.

29. *American Federationist,* December, 1896, 219.

30. Ibid., January, 1911, 18.

31. Ibid., 19–20.

32. Perlman, op. cit., 500.

33. Henry White, *American Federationist,* June, 1897, 69–70.

34. AFL *Convention Proceedings,* 1899, 16.

35. Ibid., 1898, 88.

36. Ibid., 27.

37. Ibid., 1901, 65.

38. Ibid., 1902, 20.

39. Ibid., 145.

40. Ibid., 1903, 26.

41. Ibid., 1905, 30.

42. Ibid., 1903, 205.

43. Philip Taft, *The A.F. of L. in the Time of Gompers* (New York: Harper & Brothers, 1957), 320–24; Marc Karson, *American Labor Unions and Politics,* 1900–1918 (Carbondale: Southern Illinois University Press, 1958), 145–46.

44. AFL *Convention Proceedings,* 1897, 78.

45. Ibid., 1896, 19.

46. Bernard Mandel, *Samuel Gompers* (The Antioch Press, 1963), 234.

47. AFL *Convention Proceedings*, 1900, 23.

48. *American Federationist*, March, 1901, 118–20.

49. Perlman, op. cit., 519–20, 524. Perlman called it a "honeymoon period of capital and labor." See also Mandel, op. cit., 223–24.

50. AFL Convention Proceedings, 1901, 76–83.

51. Ibid., 1902, 21.

52. Ibid., 1903, 26.

53. Ibid., 1907, 39.

54. *American Federationist*, May, 1906, 294.

55. Ibid., January, 1911, 18.

56. Isaac A. Hourwich, *Immigration and Labor* (New York: G. P. Putnam's Sons, 1912), 1–39, 401 ff.

Chapter 5. AFL Industrial Unions and New Immigrants.

1. The historical material for this chapter is taken primarily from the following sources: *The United Mine Workers' Journal*, which provides an overall picture of mining conditions; and *UMW Convention Proceedings*.

2. Virtually every issue of the *United Mine Workers' Journal* reflected this self-image.

3. *UMW Journal*, May 10, 1900; May 22, 1901.

4. See Frank Julian Warne, *The Slav Invasion and the Mine Workers* (Philadelphia, J.B. Lippincott Co., 1904). Warne was very close to the Mine Workers' leadership. A few years after he wrote Slav Invasion, he served on the Immigration Commission.

5. Ibid., 87.

6. *UMW Journal*, June 7, 1900.

7. See the analysis by Isaac A. Hourwich, *Immigration and Labor* (New York: B.W. Huebsch, Inc., 1922), 458–86.

8. *UMW Journal*, July 17, 31, 1902.

9. Reported in William F. Leiserson, *Adjusting Immigrant and Industry* (New York: Harper and Bros., 1924), 187.

10. Charles J. Thain, *UMW Journal*, November 8, 1900.

11. UMW *Convention Proceedings*, 1901, 53.

12. Ibid., 1902, 55.

13. *UMW Journal*, July 12, 1900.

14. Ibid., November 1, 1900.

15. Reprinted in ibid., October 9, 1902.

16. Ibid., January 2, 1902.

17. Ibid., October 30, 1902.

18. UMW. *Convention Proceedings*, 1902, 140.

19. UMW Journal, October 30,.1902..

20. UMW Convention Proceedings, 1901, 30, 90.

21. Ibid., 1904, 161.

22. *Reports of the Immigration Commission* (Washington: Government Printing Office, (1911), Vol. 6, 546–47.

23. Ibid., Vol. 7, 68.

24. Reported in Leiserson, op. cit, 187.

25. *Immigration Commission Reports*, op. cit., Vol. 6, 333.

26. See E.J. Hobsbawm, *Primitive Rebels* (New York: W.W. Norton and Co., 1965 ed.), 1–12.

27. See Mitchell's speech in UMW *Special Convention Proceedings*, 1902, 38 ff.; also his report in UMW *Convention Proceedings*, 1903, 27.

28. *UMW Journal*, September 27, 1900.

29. Ibid.

30. Ibid., October 11, 1900; June 12, 1902.

31. UMW *Convention Proceedings*, 1904, 24.

32. See, for example, Mitchell's statements to the Labor Conference on Immigration, sponsored by the Commissioner-General of Immigration in February, 1909. The transcript appears in *Immigration Commision Reports*, op. cit., Vol. 41, 376–431. For another example see his article, *Protect the Working man*

reprinted in the *American Federationist*, October, 1909, 859–63. Mitchell was prominent in many conferences on immigration, including one sponsored by the National Civic Federation in December, 1906. See National Civic Federation, *Facts about Immigration* (New York: January, 1907), for a transcript of the proceedings.

33. See Hermann Schlüter, *The Brewery Industry and the Brewery Workers' Movement in America* (Cincinnati, Ohio: The International Union of United. Brewery Workmen of America, 1910), and below, Chapter 9.

Footnotes: Part II.

Introduction.

1. Frederick Engels, Preface to the 1887 American edition of *The Conditions of the Working Class in England in 1844*, reprinted in *Letters to Americans*, op. cit., 285–291; 290.

Chapter 6. The First International America.

1. *General Council Minutes*, July 23, 1867. (See Chapter 1 for full reference).

2. Samuel Bernstein, *The First International in America* (New York: Augustus M. Kelley, 1962), 37–39; Perlman, op. cit., 204–09; *G.C. Minutes*, April 14, 1868.

3. Bernstein, op. cit., 37–40.

4. *G.C. Minutes*, August 30, 1870.

5. Bernstein, op. cit., 41–43.

6. *G.C. Minutes*, April 19, 1870.

7. *G.C. Minutes*, May 24, 1870.

8. *G.C. Minutes*, May 31, 1870.

9. *G.C. Minutes*, May 24, 1870.

10. *G.C. Minutes*, May 31, 1870.

11. *G.C. Minutes*, July 5, 1870.

12. Marx to Sorge, September 1, 1870, in Marx and Engels, *Letters to Americans* (New York. International Publishers, 1963 ed.).

13. *G.C. Minutes*, August 23, 1870.

14. *G.C. Minutes*, September 6 and 20, 1870.

15. *G.C. Minutes*, December 20, 1870.

16. *G.C. Minutes*, January 24, 1871.

17. *G.C. Minutes, March* 7, 1871.

18. *To the General Council. Report of the N.A. Central Committee of the I.W.A.* (April 2, 1871). Reprinted in Commons, *Documentary History*, op. cit., Vol. IX, 353–56.

19. *G.C. Minutes,* March 7, 1871.

20. Ibid., Marx to Sorge, November 9, 1871, in *Letters to Americans*, op. cit.

21. Marx to Meyer and Vogt, April 9, 1870, bid.

22. To the General Council (May 21, 1871), in Commons, *Documentary History*, op. cit., Vol. IX, 359–60.

23. Engels to Sorge, December 31, 1892, in *Letters to Americans*, op. cit.

24. The North American Central Committee of the I.W.A., August 20, 1871, in Commons, *Documentary History*, op. cit., Vol. IX, 361–66.

25. Ibid.

26. The North American Central Committee of the International Workingmen's Association. To all Trades Unions and Labor Societies of North America (May 27, 1871), in Commons, *Documentary History*, op. cit., Vol. IX, 356–59.

27. *G.C. Minutes*, May 23, 1871.

28. *G.C. Minutes*, November 9, 1869; *Address of the General Council of the International Working Men's Association to the New Democracy of New York*, in *Documents of the First International*, op. cit., Vol. III, 352–53.

29. *G.C. Minutes*, August 30, 1870.

30. Bernstein, op. cit., 101–02 112–15.

31. Perlman, op. cit., 211.

32. Bernstein, op. cit., 115.

33. *G .C. Minutes*, July 25, 1871; Marx to Sorge, September 12, and November 6, 1871, in Letters to Americans, op. cit.

34. The North American Central Committee of the I.W.A. (August 20, 1871), in *Commons,* Documentary History, op. cit., Vol. IX, 365–66.

35. Marx to Bolte, November 23, 1871, in *Letters to Americans*, op. cit.

36. Bernstein, op. cit., 116.

37. Ibid., 117–19.

38. Ibid., 118; Perlman, op. cit., 212.

39. Bernstein, op. cit., 117.

40. Ibid., 119.

41. See, *Manifesto of the Communist Party, Marx and Engels*, Selected Works (Moscow: Foreign Languages Publishing House, 1962), Vol. I, 61–64.

42. Marx to Bolte, November 23, 1871, in Letters to Americans, op. cit.

43. Ibid. Whether Marx was right in considering Lassaleans a "sect" is not being discussed here.

44. Bernstein, op. cit., 124.

45. Henry Collins and Chimen Abramsky, *Karl Marx and the British Labor Movement* (London: MacMillan and Co., 1965), 250; Bernstein, op. cit., 124–26.

46. Collins and Abramsky, op. cit., 250.

47. *The First International, Minutes of the Hague Congress of 1872*, with related documents, Hans Gerth, ed. (Madison: The University of Wisconsin Press, 1958), 194–95.

48. Ibid.

49. Maltman Barry, *Report of the Fifth Annual General Congress of the International Working Men's Association*, Ibid., 264–65.

50. Ibid., 196.

51. Ibid., 266. Barry Report.

52. Ibid., 197.

53. Franz Mehring, *Karl Marx* (University of Michigan Press, 1962 ed.), 486; G.M. Stekloff, *History of the First International* (New York: International Publishers, 1928), 235; Barry Report, op. cit., 279.

54. Mehring, op. cit., 484–85; F.A. Sorge, *Report to the North American Federation of the International Workingmen's Association*, in Minutes of the Hague Congress, op. cit., 244.

55. Engels to Sorge, September 12 and 17, 1874, in *Letters to Americans*, op. cit.

Chapter 7. Problems on the Left.

1. The historical material for this chapter is taken primarily from the following sources:

Howard H. Quint, the Forging of American Socialism (Columbia: The University of South Carolina Press, 1953), 37–71, 142–74.

Philip S. Foner, History of the Labor Movement in the United States (New York: International Publishers, 1955), Vol. II, 32–46, 279–299, 388–403.

Morris Hillquit, History of Socialism in the United States (New York: Funk and Wagnalls Co., 1903), 213–304.

David J. Saposs, *Left Wing Unionism* (New York: International Publishers, 1926), 9–47.

Gerald N. Grob, *Workers and Utopia* (Northwestern University Press, 1961), 163–186:

2. Quint, op. cit., 47–55.

3. Ibid.

4. Saposs, op. cit., 11–13,

5. Foner, op. cit., Vol. II, 281–86.

6. Ibid.

7. Ibid.

8. Hillquit, op. cit., 286–88.

9. Gompers, *American Federationist*, May, 1896, 52.

10. Quint, op. cit., 59.

11. Quoted in Nathan Fine, *Labor and Farmer Parties in the United States*, 1828–1928 (New York: Rand School of Social Science, 1928, 48.

12. Hillquit, op. cit., 214.

13. Marvin Wachman, History of the Social-Democratic Party of Milwaukee, 1897–1910 (Urbana: University of Illinois Press, 1945), 20–21.

14. Quint, op. cit., 149–50.

15. See Quint, op. cit., 142. Apparently, DeLeon was a Jew, but pretended to be from an aristocratic, Spanish Catholic family.

16. Hillquit, op. cit., 213–14, 284. Hillquit estimates that the Socialist Labor Party membership was never more than 10 percent native-born American.

17. Fine op. cit., 190–95.

18. Ibid., 204.

19. See the excellent chapter in Foner, op. cit., Vol. III, 36, 392, on the Socialist Party and the AFL up to 1905.

20. Ibid., 385.

21. Quoted in ibid., 386.

22. Saposs, op. cit., 35.

Chapter 8. The Socialist Party and Immigration.

1. Ira Kipnis, *The American Socialist Movement, 1897–1912* (New York: Columbia University Press, 1952), 277–78.

2. Morris Hillquit, "Immigration in the United States," *International Socialist Review,* July, 1907, 74–75.

3. Morris Hillquit, *Loose Leaves from a Busy Life* (New York: The MacMillan Co., 1934), 130–31.

4. Kipnis, op. cit., 279.

5. Socialist Party National Convention Proceedings, 1908, 105.

6. Ibid.

7. Arthur M. Lewis, ibid., 110.

8. Ibid., 111.

9. Ibid., 119.

10. Ibid., 121.

11. Ibid., 111.

12. Ibid., 110.

13. Ibid., 114.

14. Ibid., 117.

15. Ibid., 121.

16. Ibid., 312.

17. SP Proceedings, 1910, 76–77.

18. Ibid., 80.

19. Adolph Germer, ibid., 134.

20. I. Kawier, ibid., 153.

21. Nathan Fine, *Labor and Farmer Parties in the United States, 1828–1928* (New York: Rand School of Social Science, 1928), 271.

22. Quoted in ibid., 270.

23. SP Proceedings, 1910, 164–66.

24. Ibid., 118–19.

25. Speech of the Hon. Victor L. Berger, of Wisconsin, in the House of Representatives, June 14, 1911. Congressional Record, 2026–2030. Quoted in Hourwich, op. cit., 394.

26. SP Proceedings, 1910, 98.

27. Ibid., 98.

28. David A. Shannon, *The Socialist Party of America* (New York: The MacMillan Co., 1955), 50.

29. SP Proceedings, 1910, 98.

30. Ibid., 103.

31. Fine, op. cit., 270.

32. Letter from Eugene Debs to George D. Brewer, International Socialist Review, July, 1910, 16–17.

33. Thomas F. Kennedy, SP Proceedings, 1910, 123.

34. Fred H. Merrick, ibid., 104.

35. Ibid., 126.

36. Ibid., 163.

37. Ibid.

38. Mrs. E.D. Cory (Washington), ibid., 122; Tom Lewis (Oregon), ibid., 142.

39. Ibid., 119.

40. Ibid., 106.

41. Ibid., 162.

42. Ibid., 278–79.

43. Based on analysis of voting, ibid., 288–89.

44. Ibid.

45. Kipnis, op. cit., 288. The report is in SP Proceedings, 1912, 209–11.

46. SP Proceedings, 1912, 211.

47. Ibid., 167.

48. Socialist Campaign Book, 1912, 233–34.

49. The historical material for this section on Municipal Socialism is taken primarily from Marvin Wachman, *History of the Social–Democratic Party of Milwaukee, 1897–1910 (*Urbana: University of Illinois Press, 1945).

50. Ibid., 9–12.

51. Quoted in ibid., 11.

52. Ibid., 17–20

53. Quoted in ibid., 21.

54. Ibid., 23–24.

55. Quoted in Fine, op. cit., 194.

56. Wachman, op. cit., 27.

57. Ibid., 32–33.

58 Ibid., 34–41.

59. Quoted in ibid., 73.

60. Ibid., 47–50, 64.

61. Ibid., 51.

62. Hillquit, *Loose Leaves*, op. cit., 58.

63. Wachman, op. cit., 74.

64. Ibid., 75.

65. Victor L. Berger, *Broadsides* (Milwaukee: Social-Democratic Publishing Co., 1912), 173, 179.

66. Wachman, op. cit., 28.

67. Ibid., 41.

68 Ibid., 42.

69. Ibid., 52.

70. Ibid., 58–60.

71. Quoted in ibid., 64.

72. Ibid., 63–67.

73. Quoted in ibid., 68.

74. Kipnis, op. cit., 171.

75. Wachman, op. cit., 62.

76. Shannon, op. cit., 11.

77. SP Proceedings, 1910, 132.

78. Quoted in Shannon, op. cit., 79–80.

79. James Weinstein, *The Decline of Socialism in America, 1912–1925* (New York: Monthly Review Press, 1967), 41–45.

80. Ray Ginger, *Eugene V. Debs: A Biography* (New York: Collier Books, 1962), 361.

81. Quoted in Kipnis, 295. Bohn, a professor, later left the Party because of its opposition to the First World War. A syndicalist in 1910, by 1917 he had become a fanatical supporter of Wilson's war effort, and renounced socialism.

82. Ibid., 313–16.

83. Bill Haywood, *Bill Haywood's Book* (New York: International Publishers, 1958 ed.), 21–173, 239–77.

84. Kipnis, op. cit., 317–18.

85. Quoted in Kipnis, op. cit., 371. See also Ginger, op. cit., 314.

86. Quoted in Ginger, op. cit., 314.

87. Ibid., 315, 328.

88. Debs, *International Socialist Review*, January, 1911, 413–15.

89. Kipnis, op. cit., 237.

90. Ibid..

91. Ibid., 344.

92. William English Walling, *Socialism As It Is* (New York: The MacMillan Co., 1915 ed.), 349. Like Bohn, Walling was a former left-wing Socialist who quit the Party when it opposed the war.

93. Quoted in Fine, op. cit., 282.

94. Ginger, op. cit., 237.

95. Ibid., 252.

96. Ibid., 237.

97. Fine, op. cit., 279.

98. Quoted in Haywood, op. cit., 183.

99. Ibid.

100. Ginger, op. cit., 353.

101. Haywood, op. cit., 184.

102. Philip S. Foner, *History of the Labor Movement in the United States* (New York: International Publishers, 1965), Vol. IV, 82.

103. See the debate on the state of the organization following the 1913 Patterson strike, in Industrial Workers of the World, Stenographic Report of the Eighth Annual Convention, Chicago, September 15–29, 1913, especially, 37–38, 49–57.

104. See David J. Saposs, *Left Wing Unionism* (New York: International Publishers, 1926), 102, 111, 137, 165.

105. Frank Julian Warne, *The Slav Invasion and the Mine Workers* (Philadelphia: J. B. Lippincott Co., 1904), 106–07; see also Foner, op. cit., Vol. III, 96.

106. Quoted in Foner, op. cit., Vol. III, 97.

107. William M. Leiserson, *Adjusting Immigrant and Industry* (New York: Harper & Brothers, 1924), 182.

108. Ibid., 202–03.

109. Gompers, *American Federationist*, May 1906, 294.

110. Marc Karson, *American Labor Unions and Politics, 1900–1918* (Carbondale: Southern Illinois University Press, 1958), 178.

111. AFL Convention Proceedings, 1909, 30.

112. After years of enjoying unanimous support for their immigration policy, the AFL leadership suddenly found themselves challenged by a handful of Socialists at the 1913 convention. J. Mahlon Barnes of the Socialist Party introduced a resolution opposing the literacy test. It lost by a margin of 190 to 5, but three years later these few opponents of restriction were joined by the delegations of the International Ladies' Garment Workers, and the Western Federation of Miners. See AFL Convention Proceedings, 1913, 305, and Proceedings, 1916, 293, 335.

113. Fine, op. cit., 324.

Chapter 9. New Immigrants in the Socialist Party.

1. Recounted by National Secretary J. Mahlon Barnes, in Socialist Party Proceedings, 1910, 267.

2. Kipnis, op. cit., 273.

3. Fine, op. cit., 325.

4. SP Proceedings, 1910, 16.

5. Ibid., 18.

6. Ibid., 261.

7. ibid., 264.

8. Ibid., 260.

9. Fine, op. cit., 325.

10. Ibid., 326.

11. Report of the Finnish Section, SP Proceedings, 1912, 236–39.

12. Report of the Italian Section, SP Proceedings, 1912, 241.

13. SP Proceedings, 1912, 239. The Finnish Section was also proletarian, but its membership was far more stable. One reason may have been that the Finns intended to concentrate in certain areas, and not move around as much.

14. Ibid., 241.

15. Report of the National Secretary, SP Proceedings, 1910, 32–33.

16. Fine, op. cit., 232.

17. SP Proceedings, 1912, 238.

18. See Julius Faulk, *The Origins of the American Communist Movement*, parts I and II (New International, Fall, 1955 and Winter, 1955–56), 152–53, 240–44.

19. SP Proceedings, 1912, 88.

20. Ibid., 86.

21. Ibid.

22. Ibid., 87.

23. Ibid., 89.

24. Compare SP Proceedings, 1910, 259–60, with Proceedings, 1912, 203.

25. SP Proceedings, 1912, 203.

26. Fine, op. cit., 326.

27. Shannon, op. cit., 46.

28. Ibid., 47.

29. Theodore Draper, *The Roots of American Communism* (New York: The Viking Press, 1957), 158.

30. For a detailed discussion, see Draper, op. cit. For a different view see James Weinstein, *The Decline of Socialism in America*, 1912–1925 (New York: Monthly Review Press, 1967), 177-233. See also the exchange between Weinstein and Charles Leinenweber in *International Socialist Journal* (Rome), February, 1968 (Year 5, Number 25), 140–153.

31. See Kipnis, op. cit.

32. See Weinstein, *Decline*, op. cit., 93–118.

33. Morris Hillquit, *Loose Leaves from a Busy Life* (New York: The MacMillian Co., 1934), 291.

34. For detailed discussions of the Socialist Party during the war years, see Weinstein, *Decline*, op. cit., 119–176, and Charles Leinenweber, *Socialist Opposition to World War I*, in Radical America, March-April, 1968 (Vol. II, *No.* 2), 29–49.

35. See statement by Right wing party leaders in National Executive Committee minutes, *Eye Opener*, May, 1919, 7.

36. *New York Call*, May 21, 1919.

37. Statement of the National Executive Committee, *Eye Opener*, May, 1919, 2.

38. NEC minutes, ibid., 6.

39. Statement of the NEC, ibid., 1–2.

40. *NEC* minutes, ibid., 7.

41. Ibid., 8.

42. Ibid.

43. Ibid., 9. The Michigan Party did not return, but after flirting with the Communist Party, became the Proletarian Party.

Conclusion.

1. John Higham, *Strangers in the Land* (New York: Atheneum, 1965 ed.), 305; Maldwyn Allen Jones, American Immigration (University of Chicago Press, 1960), 274.

2. E.P. Thompson, *The Making of the English Working Class* (New York: Vintage Books ed., 1966), 194.

3. See Samuel Gompers, *Seventy Years of Life and Labor* (New York: E.P. Dutton & Co., 1957 ed.), 80.

Appendix

Part I: The Class and Ethnic Bases of New York City Socialism, 1904–1915

1. Irwin Yellowitz, Labor and the Progressive Movement in New York State: 1897–1916 (Ithaca, 1965); John R. Commons, *et al., History of Labor in the United States* (New York, 1966 edition), II, 441–67. © 1981 The Tamiment Institute

2. Numbers calculated from *Socialist Party Membership Book* Local New York January 1, 1904. Tamiment Institute Library (hereafter referred to as Tamiment). 253 members proved traceable in the *New York State Manuscript Returns* for Manhattan and the Bronx, 1905, New York County Clerk's Office. Estimates of class and country of birth based on these.

3. New York *Call*, Sept. 7, 1914, 4; Executive Committee Minutes, Local New York, May 10, 1915, Tamiment; Central Committee Minutes, Local New York, Feb., 1916, Tamiment. By 1915, membership and branches in Brooklyn and Queens equaled those of Local New York (Manhattan and the Bronx). Therefore, to estimate total New York membership after 1915 I have simply doubled the numbers for Local New York, where more comprehensive figures are unavailable. I have no estimates for members of Foreign Language Federations, who were attached directly to the Socialist Party national rather than local office.

4. Recruitment counts based on lists of Socialist Party Recruits, 1908–1912, Tamiment, and regular reports in Executive Committee Minutes, op. cit., 1912–1917. Rosa Luxemburg, *The Mass Strike, the Political Party, and the Trade Unions* (New York, 1971 edition), 83–84.

5. Enrolled Socialists and voters from New York City Board of Elections, Annual Reports, for the years 1912 to 1918. Percent of non-citizens calculated from Executive Committee Minutes, op. cit., July, 1916 to Dec., 1917. 2537 out of 7749 new members were listed as "citizens," the rest as having "first papers" or "no papers." Percent of women recruits estimated from Socialist Party Recruits, op. cit.

6. Our procedure was as follows We drew a sample of every third enrolled Socialists from Manhattan assembly districts, listed in New York City Board of Elections, List of Enrolled Voters, Manhattan and the Bronx, 1915, available at the Board of Elections and several libraries. This yielded 2061 names, 1219 of which proved traceable in the New York State Census Manuscript Returns, Manhattan, op. cit., 1915. The data thus gathered — on occupation, country of birth, age, and so forth — serve as the foundation for this article. Jean Marie Gath worked with me in tracing the sample

7. Hermann Schlüter, *The Brewing Industry and the Brewery Workers' Movement America* (Cincinnati, 1910), 156; Philip Zausner, *Unvarnished, The Autobiography of a Labor Leader* (New York, 1941), 87; New York City Board of Estimate and Apportionment, *The Industrial Education Survey of the City of New York* (New York, 1918), 208, 168, 176, 236. Percent of manual workers among Manhattan men calculated from United States Bureau of Census, Thirteenth Census, 1910 (Washington, 1914), IV, "Occupation Statistics," 575–76.

8. Discussion of skills in garment trades based mainly on interview with Ed Stark, a garment worker of many decades' experience, 1978; also Julie Fippin, 1978. See also Melvyn Dubofsky, *When Workers Organize, New York City in the Progressive Era* (Amherst, MA, 1968), 7.

9. Manhattan figures derived from Thirteenth Census, 1910, op. cit., IV, 575–77. The occupations were reclassified to make them comparable to the Socialists'.

10. For lists of union locals donating to the Socialist press, endorsing candidates, marching in parades, and so forth, see accounts in the Socialist press, for example, New York *Call*, May 30, 1908, 2; July 3, 1909, 4, Nov. 3, 1912, 1–2, Oct. 26, 1916, 1–2; New Yorker *Volkszeitung*, Nov. 3, 1912; *Advance*, Mar. 30, 1917, 3. For a complete directory of New York City union locals, see New York State Department of Labor, New York Labor Bulletin No. 63, July, 1914. For tabulations of numbers of union locals and members, see, for example, New York State Bureau of Labor Statistics, Annual Report, 1910, 98 ff.

11. Zausner, 55; William Haber, *Industrial Relations in the Building Industry* (Cambridge, MA, 1930), 298–99; New York Labor Bulletin No. 74, Sept., 1915, 14; New York *Call*, Sept. 15, 1914, 4, Oct. 26, 1916, 3. See also footnote 10.

12. Haber, 346–69; Zausner, 58–73, 96–129; U.S. Bureau of Labor Statistics, Bulletin No. 124, June, 1913, "Conciliation and Arbitration in the Building Trades of Greater New York"; New York State, Joint Legislative Committee on Housing, Final Report (Albany, 1923), 24–25 (report of Lockwood Committee on, among other matters, corruption in the building industry); John R. Commons, "The New York Building Trades," *Quarterly Journal of Economics*, 18 (1904), 409–36, especially 410–19; Royal E. Montgomery, *Industrial Relations in the Chicago Building Trades* (Chicago, 1927) 209–28.

13. See footnote 10 concerning union locals' support for socialism. See also Mark Perlman, *The Machinists: A New Study in American Trade Unionism* (Cambridge, MA, 1961); John H.M. Laslett, *Labor and the Left: A Study of Socialist and Radical Influences in the American Labor Movement, 1881–1924* (New York, 1970); Herman Schlüter; New York *Call*, July 3, 1909, 3; New York Labor Bulletin No. 63, July, 1914.

14. In 1914, 3000 garment workers canvassed the Lower East Side for Meyer London. New York *Call*, Nov. 2, 1914, 2, Nov. 9, 1914, 2.

15. See footnote 9.

16. New York State Bureau of Labor Statistics, *Annual Report*, 1910, 132, 148; Thirteenth Census, 1910, 571 ff.

17. For the movement's appeal to artists, see for example, Bruce St. John, ed., *John Sloan's New York Scene* (New York, 1965), Isadora Duncan, *My Life* (Garden City, N.Y., 1927), Arthur Young, *Art Young: His Life and Times* (New York, 1939).

18. Thirteenth Census, 1910, 575–76. "Entrepreneurs" includes all employers except professionals, along with all obvious owners of capital, such as shop keepers, and others who, while not necessarily actual owners, are socially identical with them. Real estate agents and stockbrokers are examples.

19. Ibid., 573–74.

20. Socialist Party Recruits, 1908–1912. I wish to thank my colleagues Boris Karash, Richard Varbero, and Gerald Sorin for helping me with the ethnicity estimates for these lists. Some Germans were traced in records of the Workman's Sickness and Death Benefit Society.

21. Engels to Sorge, Nov. 29, 1886, in Karl Marx and Frederick Engels, *Letters to Americans, 1848–1895* (New York, 1953), 163.

22. Ira Rosenwaike, *Population History of New York City* (Syracuse, 1972), 203.

23. The proportion of Italians is 5 percent between Nov. 1908 and June 1910. Beyond that point, records of their joining abruptly cease. About this time the Italian Foreign Language Federation was organized; I assume New York's Italian branches affiliated with it rather than the local, which would explain why no more Italian names. It seems likely that throughout this period of garment strikes, Italians joined in at least as large proportions as before.

24. John J. D'Alesandre, "Occupational Trends of Italians in New York City," in Francesco Cordasco and Eugene Bucchioni, eds., *The Italians* (Clifton, NJ, 1974), 417–31; Antonio Mangano, "The Associated Life of Italians in New York City," ibid., 143–51; Alberto Pecorini, "The Italians in the United States," ibid., 153–65, esp. 154–55; Dubovsky, 7.

25. A. Phillip Randolph, New York *Call*, Oct. 1, 1918, 5; James Weinstein, *The Decline of Socialism in America, 1912–1925* (New York, 1969), 72; New York *Call*, Oct. 29, 1916, 1.

26. Estimates on unions and ethnicity based partly on lists of local union officers in New York Labor Bulletin No. 63, July, 1914. For strikes, see Dubofsky, passim, and Charles G. Barnes, *The Longshoreman* (New York, 1915), 110–28. The quote is from Katharine Anthony, *Mothers Who Must Earn* (New York, 1914). On the Irish, see also William V. Shannon, *The American Irish, a Political and Social Portrait* (New York, 1966), and Tom McConnon, *Angels in Hell's Kitchen* (New York, 1959).

27. New York *Call*, Nov. 8, 1916, 6, Sept. 15, 1916, 1; Melvyn Dubovsky, "Success and Failure of Socialism in New York City, 1900–1918: A Case Study," *Labor History*, 9 (1968), 372–73.

28. James Connelly's paper, *The Harp*, addressed the question of Socialism and Catholicism in virtually every issue. See, for example, *The Harp*, Jan., 1908, 7, Feb., 1908, 3, Sept., 1908, 6. See also letter from Martin M'Mahon, New York *Call*, July 15, 1909, 6. Irish Socialists sought to downplay any anti-religious elements in socialism. See Charles Leinenweber, "Socialists in the Streets: The New York City Socialist Party in Working Class Neighborhoods, 1908–1918," *Science & Society*, 41 (1977), 162–64

29. Nathan Fine, *Labor and Farmer Parties in the United States, 1828–1928* (New York, 1928), 232–35; Weinstein, 99; Robert E. Park, *The Immigrant Press and its Control* (New York, 1922), 275–76.

30. "Jewish Socialists" here refers to those of Eastern European extraction. It is difficult to estimate the proportion of Jews among German Socialists. My guess is that they made up about 5 percent, and certainly no more than 10.

31. New York *Call,* Sept. 1, 1916, 2; Dubovsky, *When Workers Organize,* 126–51.

32. Interview with Gilda Boschetto (Pumonte), Staten Island, 1974.

33. Irving Howe's portrayal of Jewish Socialists as insular, seems quite wrong to me since it does not take into account the extent to which the opposite tendencies were also true. It was the tendencies outlined here that in my opinion made Jewish workers remarkable. See Irving Howe, *World of Our Fathers* (New York, 1976), 287–324.

34. Elizabeth Gurley Flynn, *The Rebel Girl* (New York, 1973 edition), 59.

35. Calculated from Fourteenth Census, 1920 (Washington, 1923), Vol. N, Occupations, 1157–61.

36. William H. Sewell, Jr., "Social Change and the Rise of Working-Class Politics in Nine-teenth-Century Marseille," *Past & Present,* No. 65 (Nov. 1974), 96.

37. Retail clerks and salesmen earned $780 per year in 1910, and worked 59–87 hours per week. Union carpenters earned $970 and worked 44 hours per week. See New York State Bureau of Labor Statistics, Annual Report, 1910, 234–505. See also New York State Factory Investigating Commission, Fourth Report, 1915 (Albany, 1915), Vol. II, Appendix IV, "Wages in Retail Stores.

38. See the analysis by Stanley Aronowitz, *False Promises, The Shaping of American Working Class Consciousness* (New York, 1973), 399 ff.

Part II: Socialists in the Streets

1. Morris Hiliquit, *Loose Leaves from a Busy Life* (New York, 1984), p. 131; MelvynDubofsky, *When Workers Organize: New York City in the Progressive Era* (Amherst, 1968), 126–51. Carman quote from *New York Call,* November 8, 1916, 6.

2. *New York Call,* November 3, 1912, 1–2

3. Elizabeth Curley Flynn, *The Rebel Girl* (New York, 1973) 67–68; Lillian Wald, *The House on Henry Street* (New York, 1915), 265–68.

4. *New York* Call, July 31, 1909, p. 3; September 11, 1916, 2; Melech Epstein, *Jewish Labor in U.S.A.* (New York, 1969) Vol. 1, 383–84.

5. As Drake and Cayton note in *Black Metropolis,* "When work is over, the pressure of the white world is lifted. Within Bronzeville Negroes are at home. They find rest from white folks as well as from labor, and they make the most of it?' St. Clair Drake and Horace Cayton, *Black Metropolis* (New York, 1970), Vol. II, 387.

6. Epstein, op. cit., Vol. I, 383–84; Rosenberg quote in ibid.. 398–99; *New York Call,* September 29, 1912, 2; July 3, 1909, 3. Ron Grele informs me that references to slaves and slavery — such as on the children's banner — constitute a recurring theme in oral history interviews on this period, and suggests that "this rhetoric came from the concept of wage slavery and is an indication of just how deeply the language of socialism penetrated the mind of the working class and formed their consciousness".

7. Epstein, op. cit., Vol. 1, 400.

8. *New York Call,* September 15, 1916, 1.

9. Ibid., October 29, 1916, 1-2; September 15, 1916, 1.

10 Ibid., October 29, 1916, 2.

11. John A. Wall, *ibid.,* November 2, 1912, 6.

12 Hillquit, op. cit. 188.

13. Epstein, op. cit., Vol. 1, 178.

14 *New York Call.* November 3, 1912, 1–2: November 1, 1912, 2.

15. Ibid., November 3, 1912, 1–2; November 1, 1912, 2.

16. Louis Waldman, *Labor Lawyer* (New York, 1944), 34; Antonio Mangano, "The Associated Life of Italians in New York City," (1904), reprinted in Francesco Cordasco and Eugene Bucchioni, eds., *The Italians* (Clifton, N.J., 1974), 143–51; Tom McConnon, *Angels in Hell's Kitchen* (New York, 1959), 100–01; James Connelly, *The Harp,* September, 1908, 2.

17. See Alberto Pecorini, "The Italians in the United States," (1911), reprinted in Cordasco and Bucchioni, op. cit., 153–65, esp. 154–55; Mangano. op. cit., 144; John J. D'Alesandre, "Occupational Trends of Italians in New York City," in Cordasco and Bucchioni, 417–31. On pre-industrial labor rhythms, see E.P. Thompson. *The Making if the English Working Class* (New York, 1966), 432–35.

18. William V. Shannon, *The American Irish, a Political and Social Portrait* (New York, 1966); M.R. Werner, *Tammany* Hall (Garden City, N.Y., 1928); Melvyn Dubofsky. "Success and Failure of Socialism in New York City, 1900–1918," *Labor History,* Vol. 9, No. 3 (Fall, 1968), 365.

19. For a brilliant analysis of the relationship between party and trade union, see Carl L Schorske, German *Social Democracy, 1905-1917* (New York, 1965), 88–145.

20. Waldman, op. cit., 43; Joseph Freeman, An *American Testament* (New York, 1939), 31–32; Flynn, op. cit., 53, 62. 1916 rally count based on *New York Call* daily announcements for August, 1916. Speakers' crowd estimates are in *New York Call,* August 30, 1914, 13. These estimates are in general agreement with those of *Call* reporters in numerous accounts of rallies.

21. The poll results and quota are in *New York Call*, August 30, 1914, 13.

22. The estimate of Irish or Irish American speakers is based on names of speakers listed in the *New York Call*, July and September, 1914 and 1916. The proportion appears to be as high for other years. The estimate of Irish membership is based on a list of names of New York City Socialist Party recruits, 1908–1912, in the Socialist Party collection, Tamiment Institute Library, New York, and on names in the Socialist Party Membership Book., Local New York, 1904, Tamiment Institute Library. For a detailed ethnic count, see my forthcoming article, "The Ethnic Base of New York City Socialism." Flynn quote in Flynn, op. cit., 75; Quinlan quote in *New York Call*, August 30, 1914, 13.

23. *New York Call* September 7, 1914, 4; for "Cordage Trust" rallies, see ibid., October 6, 1912, 1; September 29, 1912, 1. Socialists had fought for free speech outside these mills earlier, during a long strike in 1909–1910. See ibid., July 1, 1910, 1–2.

24. Ibid., July 7, 1912, 5.

25. John Sloan, August 4, 1911, in Bruce St John, ed.. *John Sloan's New York Scene* (New York, 1965), 555.

26. *New York Call*, October 29, 1916, 1–2; Executive Committee Minutes, Local New York, 1916, 148,.152, in Tamiment Institute Library.

27. *New York Call*, October 29, 1916, 2; November 3, 1912.

28. Waldman, op. cit., 43–44.

29. On the White Rats, see *New York Call*, September 14, 1908; *Advance*, March 16, Benny Leonard, from the Lower East Side, was one of the greatest boxers of all time—American lightweight champion in this period, and soon world champion. Leonard was a member of the Socialist Party, and wrote several dozen columns for the Call. See, for example, *New York Call*, November 5, 1916, 4.

30. Freeman, op. cit., 30–31. The correct spelling is Fitzgibbon; Freeman adds an "s".

31. This line of analysis was developed in similar contexts by C.L.R. James, William, Gorman, Martin Glaberman, and others. See, for example, George Rawick. *From Sundown to Sunup: The Making of the Black Community* (Westport. Conn., 1972), 3–13, esp. 3–6.

32. *New York Call*, June 1,1908, 3.

33. When the United States entered World War I, Socialists for the first time found their halls shut by police, their meetings broken up, their speakers beaten and arrested. In October, 1918, after Socialists drew a crowd of two thousand to a Harlem anti-war rally, while the National Security League drew none to a Liberty Bond rally directly across the street, Socialists were banned from the streets. See *New York Call*, October 6, 1918, 1.

34.Benny Leonard, from the Lower East Side, was one of the greatest boxers of all time—American lightweight champion in this period, and soon world champion. Leonard was a member of the Socialist Party, and wrote several dozen columns for the Call. See, for example, *New York Call,* November 5, 1916, 3. Al McCoy, middleweight champion, was also a Socialist, as were his brothers and sisters. During the 1916 elections, McCoy headed a force of Socialists who deterred Tammany from strong-arm tactics. See *New York* Call, November 8, 1916, 5. Boxing and baseball were the most popular sports among New York's working people.

Isadora Duncan and her School offered their services to the Socialist Party during World War I, and staged several benefits. In her memoirs, Duncan wrote of an audience for Oedipus, which "consisted mostly of people from the East Side who, by the way, are among me real lovers of An in America to-day. The appreciation of the East Side so touched me that I went over there with my entire School and an orchestra, and gave a free performance in the Yiddish Theatre, and, if I had had the means, 1 would have remained there dancing for these people whose very soul is made for music and poetry." Isadora Duncan, *My Life* (Garden City, N.Y., 1927), p. 317. For a fine discussion of Socialist writers and artists, see Martha Rose Sonnenberg, *A Contradiction Within* a Contradiction: *The Experience of Radical Writers and Artists in America, 1912 to the 1930s,* unpublished M.A. thesis, University of Wisconsin, 1970.

Part III: Socialist Opposition to World War I

1. *American Socialist,* April 14, 1917.

2. James Weinstein, *The Decline of Socialism in America* (New York: Monthly Review Press, 1967), 119–176, is the best and most comprehensive analysis of Socialist anti-war activity. This article, written prior to the appearance of Weinstein's book, reaches many of the same conclusions but draws from entirely different source materials.

3. David Shannon is mistaken when he says 8,000 voted for the pro-war resolution, giving the anti-war manifesto a three-to-one majority. The majority was sixty-to-one. See James O'Neal and G.A. Werner, *American Communism* (New York: E. Dutton & Co., 1947), 35n for an accounting of the vote.

4. *American Socialist,* April 21, 1917.

5. Theodore Draper, *The Roots of American Communism* (New York: The Viking Press, 1963 ed.), 92–95. Julius Faulk, "The Origins of the American Communist Movement," *New International,* Fall, 1955 , 165–166.

6. Lilian Symes and Travers Clement, *Rebel America* (New York: Harper and Brothers, 1934), 305.

7. Oscar Ameringer, *If You Don't Weaken* (New York: Henry Holt and Co.), 297–298.

8. Louis Fraina, *The New Review,* June, 1915, 80–82; August, 1915, 153–154.

9. Theodore Draper, op. cit., 62.

10. Louis Fraina, *The New Review*, July, 1914, 392n; *The New Review*, January, 1915, 17; March, 1915, 141; June, 1915, 54.

11. Max Eastman, *The Masses*, October, 1914, 5.

12. Max Eastman, *Enjoyment of Living* (New York: Harper & Brothers, 1948), 25.

13. *International Socialist Review*, 1916, 71.

14. Frank Bohn, *The Masses*, January, 1917, 16.

15. Louis Fraina, *The New Review*, September, 1915, 233.

16. Louis Boudin, *The New Review*, May, 1915, 3; July, 1915, 123.

17. Louis Waldman, *Labor Lawyer* (New York: E. P. Dutton and Co., 1944), 67–68.

18. American Socialist, April 21, 1917.

19. *The New York Times*, October 29, 1917, 4; Bohn letter November 3, 1917, 14.

20. Morris Hillquit, *Loose Leaves from a Busy Life* (New York: The MacMillan Co., 1934), 167.

21. Daniel Bell, "Marxian Socialism in the United States," in Donald Drew Egbert and Stow Persons, *Socialism and American Life*, Vol. I (Princeton: Princeton University Press, 1952), 313–314.

22. Daniel Bell, op. cit., 314; David Shannon, *The Socialist Party of America* (New York: The MacMillan Co., 1955), 98; Nathan Fine, *Labor and Farmer Parties in the United States*, 1828–1928 (New York: Rand School of Social Science, 1928), 307–309; Julius Faulk, op. cit., 165–167.

23. James Hudson Maurer, *It Can Be Done* (New York: The Rand School Press, 1938), 228–230.

24. Morris Hillquit, op. cit., 167–168.

BIBLIOGRAPHICAL NOTE

Lack of time has forced me to prepare this bibliography with great haste. I had hoped to compile a more exhaustive list. However, this bibliography should serve as a fairly accurate guide to the literature consulted.

Newspapers and Periodicals.
For Part I of this study, I was able to consult the following: *The Workingman's Advocate*, during the period in which it served as the organ for the National Labor Union; *The American Federationist*, under the editorship of Samuel Gompers; and *The United Mine Workers' Journal*. For Part II, I had access to a number of Socialist publications. The Socialist Party official press included the *American Socialist*, succeeded by the *Eye Opener*. These newspapers contain very tedious feature articles, but they also include minutes and reports of the National Executive Committee, and other Party business. More widely-read of the English language press were the *Milwaukee Leader*, edited by reformist leader Victor Berger, and the *New York Call*.

Of Socialist periodicals, the *International Socialist Review*, published by Charles H. Kerr, best exhibits the variety of viewpoints within the Party. Much more readable, however, is *The New Review*, the first Socialist theoretical journal of its time. Unfortunately, *The New Review* had a short life span — from January, 1913, to June, 1916. Far and away the liveliest and most exciting Socialist magazine of this period was *The Masses*, edited by Max Eastman. *The Masses* represented the synthesis of revolutionary politics and art. *Echoes of Revolt*, a recent anthology edited by William O'Neill, attempts to show how successful *The Masses'* staff were in achieving this synthesis.

Documents and Proceedings.
Both parts of this study relied heavily on published documents and proceedings of the various organizations. These included the following: *Documents of the First International*, in four volumes (Moscow, 1964–1967), which include General Council minutes from October 5, 1864 to October 24, 1871, and all important documents during that period. Later documents and minutes appear in Hans Gerth, ed., *The*

First International, Minutes of the Hague Congress of 1872 (Madison, 1958). Also important were Karl Marx, *Letters to Dr. Kugelmann* (New York, 1934), which covers the period December 28, 1862, to August 10, 1874, and Marx and Engels, *Letters to Americans* (New York, 1963), which covers the period March 17, 1848 to January 16, 1895.

The Convention Proceedings of the National Labor Union were consulted in *The Workingman's Advocate*. The Proceedings of the General Assembly of the Knights of Labor were also consulted, as were those of the Federation of Organized Trades and Labor Unions, and the American Federation of Labor, for the periods studied. Statements by AFL leaders at conferences on immigration appear in Volume 28, *Reports of the Immigration Commission* (Washington, 1910), and the National Civic Federation, *Facts on Immigration* (New York, 1907). I also consulted the Convention Proceedings of the United Mine Workers.

Socialist Party Convention and Congress Proceedings were consulted for the years 1908, 1910 and 1912. The Industrial Workers of the World were covered for their conventions of 1908 and 1913. *Other Socialists Campaign Book*, 1912, and the *Socialist Handbook*, 1916. Mention should also be made of the Lusk Committee report on *Revolutionary Radicalism* (Albany, 1920), in four volumes, which contains many documents pertinent to the Socialist Party during World War I, and the 1919 split.

Biographical Materials.

Autobiographies proved to be indispensable in gauging the spirit of the various elements of the working class movement. Samuel Gompers, *Seventy Years of Life and Labor* (New York, 1957), is both important and readable. Other prominent trade unions' leaders — such as Terrence Powderly of the Knights of Labor — wrote autobiographies, but Socialists were far more prolific. Two of the most informative and best-written Socialist autobiographies are Oscar Ameringer, *If You Don't Weaken* (New York, 1940), and James H. Maurer, *It Can Be Done* (New York, 1938). Ameringer was Party organizer in Oklahoma, and an ally of Victor Berger. Maurer was leader of the highly successful Reading, Pennsylvania, Socialists, a state legislator, and president of the Pennsylvania Federation of Labor. Autobiographies by party leaders include Morris Hillquit, *Loose Leaves from a Busy Life* (New York, 1934), and Charles Edward Russell, *Bare Hands and Stone Walls* (New York, 1934). Hillquit, a centrist, was the major leader within the Party for many years; Russell was a frequent Socialist candidate for various offices, who drifted to the right and finally quit the Party when it opposed America's role in the First World War. His information on the Party during the war is not to be trusted. Louis Waldman, *Labor Lawyer* (New York, 1944), contains interesting information on the 1919 split, from the point of view of the Party Right.

The group of writers, poets and artists around *The Masses* left extensive records of their Socialist activities. Max Eastman, *Enjoyment of Living* (New York, 1948) and *Love and Revolution* (New York, 1948), are the most comprehensive. Eastman was editor of *The Masses*. Cartoonist Art Young wrote *Art Young: His Life and Times* (New York, 1939), which details his path to Socialist politics. Other autobiographies by *The Masses* staff include Floyd Dell, *Homecoming* (New York, 1933), Joseph Freeman, *An American Testament* (New York, 1936), Lincoln Steffens (New York, 1931), and Louis Untermeyer.

Ralph Chaplin, *Wobbly* (Chicago, 1948), is a remarkable autobiography by an I.W.W. member. Also important is Bill Haywood, *Bill Haywood's Book* (New York, 1948). James Cannon, *History of American Trotskyism*, includes important autobiographical materials on the I.W.W. and Socialist Party.

Two other autobiographies relevant to the Socialist movement should be mentioned. These are Ella Reeve Bloor, *We Are Many* (New York, 1940), and William Z. Foster, *From Bryan to Stalin* (New York, 1937). Both are "Stalinist" autobiographies, and extremely wooden. Foster's is not to be trusted at all, but Bloor's contains some interesting reminiscences of Socialist Party activities.

There are numerous biographies of American labor and Socialist leaders. I will only mention two outstanding ones: Bernard Mandel, *Samuel Gompers* (Antioch, 1963); Ray Ginger, *The Bending Cross* (New Brunswick, N.J., 1949).

General Studies.

A complete listing of relevant general studies would be too cumbersome. Instead, I will list only those studies which were most helpful and influential in my own work.

On the question of immigration, I found the following to be indispensable: Isaac A. Hourwich, *Immigration and Labor* (New York, 1922); John Higham, *Strangers in the Land* (New York, 1965).

For the First International, I found Henry Collins and Chimen Abramsky, *Karl Marx and the British Labor Movement* (London, 1965) to be vastly superior to anything else. For the International in the United States, I relied heavily on Samuel Bernstein, *The First International in America* (New York, 1962).

For background in the labor movement, I used the Commons volumes and the recent studies by Phillip Foner. For the attitudes of the National Labor Union and the Knights of Labor toward immigration, Charlotte Erickson, *American Industry and the European Immigrant, 1860–1885* (Cambridge, 1957), proved invaluable. Although somewhat marred by the author's "pure-and-simple" bias, Gerald N. Grob, *Workers and Utopia* (Evanston, 1961), is extremely useful and interesting on the Knights of Labor. Besides the studies already cited, Marc Karson, *American Labor Unions and Politics* (Carbondale, 1958), was valuable for understanding the AFL.

For the Socialist Labor Party, Howard H. Quint, *The Forging of American Socialism* (Columbia, S.C., 1953) was useful, as was Morris Hillquit, *History of Socialism in the United States* (New York, 1910).

The literature on the Socialist Party is much larger. The best general histories are Ira Kipnis, *The American Socialist Movement, 1897–1912* (New York, 1952), and James Weinstein, *The Decline of Socialism in America, 1912–1925* (New York, 1967). Kipnis makes the mistake of assuming that the party declined steadily after 1912. Weinstein is weak on the Socialist split. David A. Shannon, *The Socialist Party of America* (New York, 1955), covers more territory than either of these, but suffers from lack of analysis and a reformist bias. Nathan Fine, *Labor and Farmer Parties in the United States, 1828–1928* (New York,

1928) is still good. There exist several contemporary studies of American Socialism, the most informative being Jessie Wallace Hughan, *The Present Status of Socialism in America*, (New York, 1911). Unfortunately, what is reputed to have been the most detailed survey of American Socialism — George Tweed, *American Socialist Parties and Movements* (Danby, Vermont, 1919) — has been lost. Finally, several special histories of the Socialist movement deserve mention. These are: Marvin Wachman, *History of the Social-Democratic Party of Milwaukee, 1897–1910* (Urbana, 1945); Harry G. Stetler, *The Socialist Movement in Reading, Pennsylvania, 1896–1936* (Storrs, Connecticut., 1943); Henry F. Bedford, *Socialism and the Workers in Massachusetts, 1886–1912* (Amherst, 1966).

What is the *Center for Socialist History* ?

The *Center for Socialist History* is a non-profit corporation founded to promote research and publication in the field of the history of socialism.

We strongly believe that (to paraphrase) socialists who don't know their own history are doomed to repeat all the old mistakes. And the history of socialism shows that they do. The socialist movement is an amnesiac: socialists know little about where they are coming from no wonder they hardly know where they are going. The fact is that little work or publication goes on in the field by socialists; most is by nonsocialists or antisocialists. They too can serve; but socialists concern with their own history is not of an academic character. A living movement has to know the lessons of the past.

There is a big gap that needs closing up, a vacuum that needs filling. We think this can and should be done on an all-inclusive basis across the lines of schools, tendencies, sects and viewpoints. Ideology and program are surely important, but it will not be the task of CSH to work them out or promote organizational forms. We simply think that people who know the socialist past will be better able to solve the problems of the present.

Not to know what happened before one was born is always to remain a child.

CICERO

History is philosophy teaching by examples.

DIONYSIUS OF HALICARNASSUS

An historian is a prophet in retrospect.

A. W. von SCHLEGEL